AN IRISH SOLDIER'S DIARIES

Michael Moriarty

MERCIER PRESS
IRISH PUBLISHER – IRISH STORY

MERCIER PRESS

Cork

www.mercierpress.ie

Trade enquiries to CMD BookSource,
55a Spruce Avenue, Stillorgan Industrial Park,
Blackrock, County Dublin

ISBN: 978 1 85635 668 8

10 9 8 7 6 5 4 3 2 1

A CIP record for this title is available from the British Library

Printed and bound in the EU.

CONTENTS

Dedicated to the memory of all those members of the Defence Forces who have died in the service of Ireland at home and abroad.

On 22 July 1997, the Security Council passed Resolution 1121 to award a special medal to all those who lost their lives in peacekeeping operations under the auspices of the United Nations. It is called the Dag Hammarskjold Medal after the second Secretary General of the United Nations, who died in a plane crash in September 1961.

In September 1998, the Nobel Committee awarded the Peace Prize to the peacekeeping forces of the United Nations. There are many thousands of Nobel Peace Prize winners in Ireland – all those soldiers who have served with the United Nations.

ACKNOWLEDGEMENTS

At the outset, I wish to express my sincere thanks to the many people who helped me with what was a self-imposed task. My own extended family must come first, for their encouragement and support, as well as for their first readings of each chapter. To my son John, who undertook much of the research on the internet, who copied my photographs, who produced the sketch maps and who straightened out my many computer tangles.

To Commandant Victor Laing and the staff of Military Archives in Cathal Brugha Barracks who responded so willingly and so efficiently to my many, often trivial, questions. To the School Commandant, Lieutenant-Colonel Paul Allan and his staff at the Artillery School, to Commandant John Curtin and the many officers of the 2nd and 7th Regiments for their help.

To Major-General John Vize for additional information supplied on the 46th Irish Battalion, and to Colonels E.D. Doyle and Terence O'Neill for their valuable discussions on ONUC. To Brigadier-General O'Boyle, Colonel George Kerton and the editor of The Irish Transmitters Society for permission to incorporate part of their valuable documents. To the editor of *An Cosantóir*, Sergeant David Nagle, and his staff for valuable information and for the use of the cover photograph.

I would like to thank the many officers who have served in UN missions with me for their help, and to the many other good friends who helped me with dates and events from the early years. Finally to those members of my own cadet class, especially Lieutenant-General Noel Bergin, Colonel Seán MacNiocaill, Lieutenant-Colonel Frank O'Donovan, Captain Jerry Healy and Commander Pat O'Mahony, NS.

All the photographs used in this story are my own unless otherwise stated.

I am grateful to Brigadier-General Daniel Opande, Kenya, the Deputy Force Commander of UNTAG, who was kind enough to give me a copy of his video of the parade of PLAN fighters. Many thanks to the members of the Defence Forces Audio-Visual Unit in the Military College for assistance in dealing with these tapes. Finally, I wish to thank the staff of Mercier Press in Cork who have been so unfailingly kind and understanding throughout.

Go raibh míle maith agaibh go léir.

The opinions expressed in my narrative are very much my own and do not in any way reflect official political or military policy or doctrine, either Irish or UN.

Any errors or omissions that might cause offence or disappointment to individuals or groups are very much regretted and were most certainly not intended.

GLOSSARY

2/Lieut	2nd Lieutenant
AEs	Armed Elements
AML 60	A small recce armoured vehicle. It carried a 60mm mortar as its main armament.
AML 90	A similar armoured vehicle equipped with a 90mm cannon.
ANC	Armée Nationale Congolaise
AO	Area of Operations
APC	Armoured Personnel Carrier
ARs	All Ranks
ARP	Air Raid Precautions
ASPC	Army School of Physical Culture
BC	Battery Commander
BQMS	Battalion Quartermaster Sergeant
BS	Battery Sergeant (Artillery)
BSM	Battalion Sergeant Major (Infantry)
CAO	Chief Administrative Officer
Capt.	Captain
CDA	Coast Defence Artillery
CO	Commanding Officer
COO	Chief Operations Officer
Comdt	Commandant
Cpl	Corporal
CQMS	Company Quartermaster Sergeant (Infantry)
CS	Company Sergeant (Infantry)

DFC	Deputy Force Commander
DFF	De Facto Forces, the title given to the South Lebanon Army by the UN
EOKA	Εθνική Οργάνωσις Κυπρίων Αγωνιστών – National Organisation of Cypriot Fighters
FAPLA	Forças Armadas Popular Libertacão da Angola – People's Armed Forces for the Liberation of Angola
FC	Force Commander
FCA	An Fórsa Cosanta Áitiúil
FN	Fabrique National – a Belgian arms manufacturer, maker of the FN rifle
FMR	Force Mobile Reserve – UNIFIL
Gnr	Gunner (Artillery)
HMG	Heavy machine gun
IDF	Israel Defence Forces
JMMC	Joint Military Monitoring Commission – (Namibia)
LCM	Limited Court-Martial
LDF	Local Defence Force
Lieut	Lieutenant
LMG	Light machine gun
Lt-Col	Lieutenant-Colonel
LO	Liaison Officer
MPLA	Moviemento Popular Libertacão da Angola
MPO	Military Personnel Officer
NCO	Non-Commissioned Officer
OC	Officer Commanding
OGL	Observer Group Lebanon
ONUC	Organisation de Nations Unies au Congo
OP	Observation Post
ORs	Other Ranks (all ranks other than commissioned officers)
PB	Patrol Base
PLAN	People's Liberation Army of Namibia
PNCO	Potential Non-Commissioned Course
PR1	Planning and Research 1

Pte	Private (Infantry)
PX	Post Exchange
Rcls rifle	Recoiless rifle
Recce	Reconnaissance
RQMS	Regimental Quartermaster Sergeant (Artillery)
RSM	Regimental Sergeant Major (Artillery)
SADF	South African Defence Forces
SBA	Sovereign Base Area
Sgt	Sergeant
SMG	Submachine gun
SOO	Senior Operations Officer
SOP	Standard Operating Procedure
SRSG	Special Representative of the Secretary-General
SWAPO	South West Africa People's Organisation
TCC	Tiberias Control Centre
Tpr	Trooper (Cavalry)
UNAVEM	United Nations Verification Mission – Angola
UNDOF	United Nations Disengagement Observer Force – the Golan Heights
UNDP	United Nations Development Programme
UNEF	United Nations Emergency Force
UNFICYP	United Nations Force in Cyprus
UNHCR	United Nations High Commissioner for Refugees
UNIFIL	United Nations Interim Force in Lebanon
UNITA	National Union for the Total Liberation of Angola
UN MAC	United Nations Mixed Armistice Commission
UNMO	United Nations Military Observer
UNNY	United Nations New York
UNRWA	United Nations Relief and Works Agency
UNSG	United Nations Secretary-General
UNTAG	United Nations Transition Assistance Group – Namibia
UNTSO	United Nations Truce Supervision Organisation
USGS	Under Secretary-General for Special Affairs

PREFACE

'Halt, who goes there?'
'Friend.'
'Advance friend to be recognised.'
'Pass friend, all is well.'

From the very earliest gatherings of armed men, sentries have stood guard over their comrades while they slept. The above exchange, or a variation thereon, has been heard in a multitude of languages and in all corners of the globe for thousands of years.

Often uttered in the middle of the night, in bad weather and by a bored or nervous sentry, it meant that the person being challenged had to be careful. The sentry – armed with the latest technology of his time, be it throwing spear, bow and arrow, crossbow or rapid fire self-loading rifle with grenade launcher and night vision scope – was likely to use his weapon if he was sufficiently unhappy.

A standing professional force, properly armed and equipped by the State to which it gives its absolute allegiance, is the equivalent of an alert sentry – if it is not there when the need arises, the State will suffer.

In most of the armed forces of the world it is commonplace for senior officers to write their memoirs as soon as possible after retirement. Whatever the motivations of the writer, the result, in one respect at least, is that members of the public are given the chance to read the personal account of the career of a military figure, and to understand and to assess for themselves the importance of the events being recorded. However, to date, no Irish chief-of-staff, divisional commander or officer commanding any of the Commands has written about his experiences. Furthermore, no Irish UN FC – and there have been quite a few by now – has written about what surely must have been a significant event in his own life and that of the world in general. The history of our country and of our armed forces suffers from the lack of such accounts.

In recent times a number of books have appeared dealing in particular with the events of the Irish involvement in the former Belgian Congo and in Lebanon. Although most of them were written by journalists or other non-military individuals, it is nevertheless a welcome development and will surely encourage others to follow.

In doing preparatory reading for this book, I went to Military Archives to read the unit histories of the 34th and the 41st Battalions, the first two UN units in which I had served. I was astonished and disappointed to be told that neither unit had produced a unit history. It seems that in those early days of UN service it had not been mandatory to record a history, as is the case today.

This unfortunate situation provided me with an additional motive for persisting with my book, as I felt that I could provide some useful information, however limited, on the activities of both of those units. I hope that my story may be of value to all those readers who have a general interest in the Defence Forces and who wish to know more.

Having spoken so often about the need for my superiors to write an account of their military lives, and having badgered some of them to do so, I realised that I had painted myself into a corner and had no choice but to follow my own advice. I must stress that this account is not a memoir or even an autobiography and, as I am not an historian, it is most definitely not a history either. It can more correctly be described as a recollection of what was for me a very satisfying career in the uniform of my country. I have decided to relate only the more important episodes in my career, as a blow-by-blow account of my life in the army would be both ponderous and utterly uninteresting.

This is my own story, based not on my memory, but on my habit of keeping a personal diary. I kept diaries, not for every year of my life, but for my later years of service and for all my UN missions. These records enable me to speak with reasonable certainty with regard to dates, places and names, accepting that it is always possible to misinterpret my often hastily written scribbles. It is possible that I may even have recorded a version of an event that is at variance with the official record. I can do nothing about that other than to say that that was how I recorded it.

As well as this, since joining the Cadet School camera club on its formation in 1950, I have remained a dedicated and ardent fan of the photograph and the motion picture. It has been of enormous benefit to me that I have been able to consult my collection of photographs and to view the amateur films I made while serving both at home and abroad. These have proved to be of immense value in jogging my memory.

Fortunately and unexpectedly, this self-imposed task also turned out to be a very enjoyable stroll back in time. I was forced to read my diaries for the first time in many years and I found myself coming across the names of individuals or descriptions of events and locations, the details of which I had completely forgotten. In addition, there was a lot of fascinating detective work involved where I had to match up a photograph with the relevant diary. This process thereby brought back a flood of memories, most, but not all of them, happy ones. However, time is the important factor and to have left any project like this for so long is an invitation to error.

It will quickly become obvious to the reader that in my story there is a great emphasis on UN service. In a small island nation with an under-resourced Defence Forces, the arrival of UN service had an impact far beyond anything we could have imagined when we joined in 1955. My good fortune in experiencing a total of five and a half years of service in different UN missions in Africa and the Middle East is reflected in my account. My UN experiences came as I moved from the rank of lieutenant in Katanga, to captain in Cyprus, to commandant in Israel and in Lebanon, to lieutenant-colonel at HQ UNIFIL and finally to colonel with UNTAG in Angola. In particular when it came to that last appointment, it was the cumulative experiences of my previous missions that enabled me to cope with what proved to be a most unusual and challenging task relating to the liberation of Namibia.

In reading for this project, I also came to realise that my cadet class, the 25th, was very well situated to span the period between the officers of today and the officers of the Old IRA, the National Army and the Army of the Emergency, if I can use those terms. We had the benefit of serving with senior officers and NCOs who proudly wore the 1916 and the War of Independence ribbons, with officers of the very first class of cadets commissioned in 1929, with officers of the Emergency years, and with those who went on into the new era of UN service. We were given the benefit of the experiences of those fine men and I believe that we learned well and carried this knowledge into our own service lives at home and across the world.

How proud and impressed, if not extremely envious, would those early idealists have been if they could have seen the superb military parade in Dublin in 2006. This parade commemorated the 90th anniversary of the insurrection of 1916, and would have been seen by them as the ultimate expression of the expansion of their beloved Defence Forces.

The reputation of our soldiers as a result of their United

Nations activities across the world is of the highest order. Our success in these activities arose in part from the facts of history – we did not have the baggage of being an imperial power, rather Ireland had been a colonised country that fought for and achieved independence from such a power. This meant that our forces were more acceptable to struggling or emergent nations.

Another factor in the success of our soldiers overseas arose out of an important fact that is often overlooked. In the 1960s, most of the armies of the world were composed primarily of national service soldiers, many of whom appeared relatively indifferent to the finer points of military life – they were only interested in serving out their national service commitments. By contrast, Irish soldiers were career soldiers who had volunteered for the military life. This meant that their professional approach to the new and novel UN duties, plus their use of the English language – and in many cases also, the Irish language which permitted them to converse together with a degree of security – enabled them to outshine most of those with whom they were working.

'But what do you do all day long? Are you marching up and down the square or are you just polishing your boots and buttons and waiting for an invasion?' Questions such as these were frequently asked of us, especially in the 1950s, and usually delivered in a sneering or mocking manner. It suggested a deep cynicism in the minds of our so-called friends – that they considered the Defence Forces to be simply a waste of scarce money and resources. It also suggested to me that there was a serious public misconception about the role of the Defence Forces.

Even today, it is surprisingly difficult to answer questions like those above in one or two simple statements. All I can say now is that once the basic recruit training has ended, a soldier will spend little enough time on the barrack square, and thanks to enlightened design and the arrival of DPM (Disruptive Pattern

Material) uniforms, he or she will not have to spend much time polishing buttons or brasses either. I can only hope that the variety and duration of some of my experiences, as detailed in this account, will go a small way towards answering those questions.

My first-born son, John, when he was very small, was asked, 'Is your father a soldier?' He replied with the indignation and conviction that only a four-year-old can muster, 'No, he is not a soldier, he is an opiser [officer]'. The fact is that I was in truth a soldier, but one who had undergone a specialist leader's course which was intended to provide me with additional skills and knowledge to be applied to my duties and responsibilities to the State and to all those under my command. I carried a commission to do so from the president of Ireland, in whom is vested the supreme command of the Defence Forces. In my role as a junior officer, I was expected to lead as much by example as by direction, thus ensuring that, like any young officer, I would find myself at the sharp end of any activity, pleasant, unpleasant or even life-threatening. As an officer's career progresses, the occasions whereby he finds himself at the forefront of any dangerous confrontations usually recede.

I should point out my account is very much that of an officer and cannot adequately deal with the military experiences of the other ranks. It is possible for an individual soldier to travel on a UN mission and, depending on his technical qualifications, spend the entire six-month tour working in the cookhouse, in an administrative office or servicing a Landrover in a workshop. He could be doing pretty much what he would have been doing at home anyway. As such, apart from the normal security duties of his own location, he would be very much out of the general 'line of fire', as it were. But such soldiers are every bit as important to a unit as are their comrades on the check points, on patrols or on the observation posts. Without such administrative staff, any unit would have great difficulty in functioning effectively.

Another curious aspect of my military life is the fact that I spent practically all my service in an all-male society. While women cadets and recruits appeared in the 1980s, after training they were, in the main, confined to appointments in Defence Forces HQ and in command and brigade staffs. It was only when I returned from my final UN mission and served out my remaining years at Command HQ, Eastern Command, that I had what was for me the novel experience of working alongside female officers and soldiers.

Finally I should point out that the list of books in Additional Reading includes a selection of the material currently available on various aspects of the Irish Defence Forces, both at home and with the UN. However, it is obvious to me that there is still a huge amount of detailed Irish military history to be written about our modern Defence Forces. Our servicemen and women deserve a true and accurate account of their activities at home and abroad.

For those civilians who have no concept of the military life, I can only hope that I have given a small flavour of what it meant to me to have worn the uniform of my country. I also hope that this story will give some idea of the remarkable diversity of the Irish soldier's military life in the modern era, both at home and abroad, in a difficult career that one either loves or hates. I am proud and happy to state that I was one of those who drew immense satisfaction from my chosen career.

Michael Moriarty

Chapter 1

ENNIS BATTALION FCA

While a number of preparations were quietly being made by some far-seeing people in Army Headquarters in the late 1930s for a possible war in Europe, it was only after war had broken out that a bill was introduced in Dáil Éireann in 1939 to cover the many essential legal measures to be taken to ensure the integrity of a new and very inexperienced State. The bill was entitled 'The Emergency Powers Act' and made provisions for securing public safety, maintaining public order, and the provision and control of supplies and services in Ireland throughout the Second World War. Unfortunately, the press, the public and even the politicians ensured that the term 'Emergency' became entrenched in the public mind to describe this period, defying all attempts to remove it or to replace it with a more suitable title. It was a completely inadequate term to describe the Second World War of course, and was often used by Allied politicians or journalists to mock or attack Ireland's neutral stance.

The British influence was still very strong in Ireland at the outbreak of the war, as only seventeen years had passed since Irish independence. The population was still exhausted by the events of 1916, the First World War, the Spanish flu that killed an estimated 20,000 people, and the War of Independence. All this was quickly followed by the tragedy and bitterness of the Civil War. Poverty was endemic and later in the 1930s a damaging economic war had broken out with Britain over the question of the land annuities. The morale of the nation had not yet recovered from the shock and novelty of having freedom and the responsibility for decision-making thrust upon it. Now the situation was suddenly and drastically changed. Our politicians were faced with many new realities, one of which was the need to consider the defence of the State from external threats, something that had received inadequate attention since 1922. Fortunately, the negotiations to end the economic war had a very important sideline. Britain agreed to return the ports and the coastal forts to Irish control, which allowed Ireland to maintain its neutrality during the war.

For the duration of the Emergency, my family lived in Listowel, north Kerry. There was great uncertainty about the future, money was in short supply, coal was very scarce and the cutting of turf for domestic fuel became a necessity for most families. It was a time of ration books and severe petrol rationing. My memory of Listowel was that hardly a day passed without my seeing large numbers of soldiers marching past our gate on Church Street. They were usually followed or preceded by armoured vehicles or large convoys of trucks and they passed by at all hours of the day or night. The vehicles were painted in camouflage colours and the cheerful and tanned young soldiers marched in full field kit with their collars open and their forage caps perched jauntily on the sides of their heads. When remaining in the vicinity for some days, they camped on the banks of the Feale under cover of the old woods near the town, with their little brown tents and vehicles scattered about under the trees. As well as this, military aircraft frequently flew low overhead.

With my friends, I would go down after school and hang around, talking to whoever would listen to me, trying to collect lapel badges of the various units or corps. The soldiers always seemed to be hungry or in dire need of cigarettes and we were often asked to go to the local shops to buy bread or packets of cigarettes. The five Woodbines in a paper pack were the most popular then, most probably because they were the only cigarettes the soldiers could afford. I watched in fascination as Army Engineers worked on the bridge over the Feale at Listowel, boring a series of deep holes in the structure to receive the demolition charges, should the need arise to destroy it. I also remember seeing an artillery unit in the wood, and being shown the live ammunition in one of the limbers (a special trailer designed to carry ammunition).

By good fortune on one occasion, I was on the spot when a unit was leaving and I was offered a short ride in the towing vehicle across the field to the exit gate. Some years later when I was describing this event to officers in Columb Barracks, Mullingar, Capt. Thady Brick declared that it was almost certainly his battery. Thady was known to us all as 'The Yank', as he had lived in the United States for a number of years. When the Emergency was declared, the Volunteer Force, part of the Reserve Defence Forces, was called out on active service and Thady Brick, with thousands of others, answered the call.

My family spent each August by the sea in Ballybunion, where we were all entertained by the activities of what seemed to me to be huge gatherings of soldiers, equipment and vehicles. In retrospect it was probably only a battalion-sized unit having a break by the sea. An infantry battalion at that time would be in the region of 1,000 or more ARs (All Ranks), with supporting elements attached such as artillery, medical or military police. I have a vivid memory of watching a swimming parade being assembled on the beach, south of the town towards the mouth of the Cashen river. When a whistle was blown, about 400 naked soldiers charged, yelling and screaming, into the waves.

In 1935 work had begun on the construction of a base for international flying boats at Foynes, with the first flight in 1937.

Located on the south side of the Shannon, during the war it became a vital refuelling stop for flying boats between Southampton, Lisbon, the Azores and the United States. Carrying many high-level Allied civilian and military passengers and important messages across the Atlantic, it was an indicator of our 'practical neutrality' that even then was quite obviously leaning towards the Allied war effort. For young people like myself, it was a romantic destination for our many cycling trips from Listowel to watch the aircraft landing or taking off. The various air crews rested at the Cliff Castle Hotel in Ballybunion and it was the custom of the pilots of the slow, lumbering flying boats to dip low over the village and fire a flare from the cockpit before flying west into the setting sun.

In 1943, along with hundreds of spectators, I was taken up to see the firing practice at the coastal artillery fort at Ardmore Head near Tarbert. I did not know it then, but while we had taken over all the other forts from Britain in 1938, Fort Shannon was the only coastal fort built by our State. It was built presumably to protect the very important deep-water anchorage and the new seaplane base on the estuary of the Shannon river. My best friend at that time was Mick Mulcahy, son of the local Garda Superintendent and I was very disappointed when he was allowed to travel on the target-towing vessel while I had to make do with observing the firing from the hill to the rear of the fort. The target was a wooden structure built on a large raft and towed at a safe distance behind the hired trawler. Mick himself entered the army as a cadet two years before me.

The Emergency was a period of intense patriotism, when all males, old and young, were part of a national 'movement' prepared to defend the country against any invader. Women were not permitted to serve in the armed forces, even though an organisation called the Army Nursing Service existed. However, women were free to serve in the Red Cross and the Air Raid

Precautions organisation. This was a joint military-civilian voluntary organisation with a dedicated training school at Griffith Barracks in Dublin. The Casualty Service, one of six services in the ARP, combined volunteers from the St John's Ambulance Brigade, the Order of Malta and the Red Cross, where women were given plenty of opportunities to wear a uniform and to participate in the national effort.

An under-appreciated aspect of this unexpected coming together to defend the State was the reconciliation between individuals who less than twenty years before had been engaged in bitter fighting during the Civil War. It could not have been easy for individuals to accept, to give orders to, or to serve alongside others for whom they felt such bitterness. To their credit, the circumstances of the time and the tight discipline of the military system played a big part in ensuring that they co-operated very well. As with family quarrels, the Emergency and the threat to the country gave them the opportunity to bury their differences. The Emergency lasted long enough to heal or at least ease the still-raw wounds of the Civil War, something for which the entire nation should be grateful.

Without being aware of it, I had grown up in the lingering shadow of the British military presence in Ireland and was quite knowledgeable about the history and exploits of the British forces in the far-flung countries of the world. I was familiar with British regiments and the history and development of the British Empire, for which so many Irish soldiers had given their lives. On a visit to Crosshaven, County Cork, one summer in the 1930s, I remember hearing the commands and the sounds of British soldiers marching within one of the coastal forts in Cork Harbour (the forts did not revert to Irish control until 1938).

Other influences also had a bearing on me. I was certainly aware of the progress of the war and of listening to the radio, mainly the BBC, as our own national radio was only broadcasting for a few hours each day. In looking back at my years in Listowel from 1939 to 1945, it now seems clear to me that I was being conditioned, without being aware of it, for a career in the uniform of my country.

I had no background or experience of the military life and apart from two uncles, Ned and Tadhg Kavanagh who served in the Dingle Battalion, Local Defence Force (LDF), none of my relatives had served in any army. I was not subjected to any pressure from my parents – it was my career of choice. However, the war ended before I could enlist in the LDF and my father Tomás, a Cigire Scoile (Inspector of National Schools) was transferred to Ennis, County Clare. There I had to wait until I completed my Leaving Certificate before I could fulfil my dream of enlisting in the FCA (An Fórsa Cosanta Áitiúil – literally the Local Defence Force), the new national second line reserve force that replaced the LDF.

On 1 December 1949, I presented myself for enrolment in A Company of the Ennis Battalion, FCA, an infantry unit that had its headquarters in Ennis, County Clare. The battalion was commanded by Capt. George A. Moloney, the principal teacher of the national school in the town. Because the FCA was a local defence force, units were generally named after the principal town in their area. The officer commanding the Clare area FCA was Commandant F.J. Slater, a Coast Defence Artillery officer, who had previously commanded Fort Berehaven, and was by this time living in Kilkee. He had responsibility for all the FCA battalions in the county area.

Ennis Battalion HQ occupied a seriously dilapidated premises in the old workhouse at the junction of Harmony Row and Bindon Street, quite close to my home on Cusack Road. The building no longer exists, as it was demolished to make way for a modern health centre. The present-day 32nd Army Reserve Battalion, the successor to my old unit, is currently located in only slightly more suitable accommodation in the old Garda Síochána barracks in the centre of the town. Ennis Battalion had a small cadre of regular NCOs and soldiers to provide the necessary expertise in administration and in the direction and supervision of training. The administrative officer, a regular officer who doubled as training officer to A Company, was Capt. Tom O'Neill. He supervised and co-ordinated all aspects of training in the battalion. Most of the FCA officers and NCOs had served during the war years and had endured the intensity of training and the experience of operating with and against the regular army for some years.

The spirit of the Emergency years was still present in the FCA when I joined in 1949 and while the numbers had fallen away dramatically in the late 1940s, the officers and the senior NCOs retained both the capability and enthusiasm for their tasks. As was the case across the country, in the late 1940s and early 1950s, there had been a great decline of interest in the military life, as peace of a sort had returned to Europe, and Ireland was no longer under threat of invasion. For this reason the more rural FCA units and sub-units suffered a major decline in numbers. Like all the other FCA units, the Ennis Battalion operated on a shoestring, rarely with a full complement of its regular staff and always with less than adequate equipment, weapons, transport or training support from the regular army. Modern weapons, integral transport or radios were non-existent – we had to do without or borrow from the nearest regular unit, the 12th Infantry Battalion, stationed in Sarsfield Barracks, Limerick. In order to have a reasonable level of military training, one must have an acceptable minimum number of 'bodies' who can meet frequently to ensure continuity of training. The larger towns such as Ennis obviously had a much greater pool of young men from which to draw their new recruits and thus it was possible to maintain a reasonable level of activity in A Company, of which I was now a proud recruit.

I remember very clearly the strange emotions when going into the quartermaster stores at the rear of the building to be handed the various items of my uniform. The sight and the smell of the neatly folded uniforms, the leather boots and other items on the shelves are still with me. It was a source of great wonder to me that I could be handed out expensive items of clothing and footwear simply by signing for them on a complicated-looking army form. In the grim days of 1949 when most of my classmates were actively planning to emigrate to find work, it was unusual to have this largesse.

This experience was to be my first introduction to military terminology. Trousers were (and still are) called slacks and the jacket top was called a tunic. Up to this I thought that only women wore slacks (only the daring women in those years would even wish to be seen in them, and then only on the golf course). The slacks were very long, as they were intended to turn out over the top of the accursed leather gaiters and they came so far up at the waist that one had to wear braces to 'suspend' them. The braces had to be supplied by the wearer as the State presumably assumed that individuals would possess their own.

I was given a sturdy pair of size 9 brown leather boots, equipped with a formidable array of studs, or 'segs', as they were known to us schoolboys, on the soles. The toes carried half-moon-shaped metal tips, while the heels were firmly shod in iron 'horseshoes' – the combination made the boots feel very heavy, but they made a most satisfying sound when marching. Next, I was given a pair of brown leather gaiters, known to all as 'leggings', items that I quickly came to detest. The leggings were worn at the ankles and were intended to keep the trouser legs tucked in neatly. If the wearer had long legs (as I had) it became nearly impossible to prevent the end of the trousers from escaping. All I had to do was to sit down, or even to bend my knees fully, as in a deep squat, and out would pop the trousers from the leggings, to my great annoyance. A soldier with short legs – universally known to us all as a 'short-arse' – rarely had a problem with his leggings.

The tunic was really a blouse or blouson with a fabric belt that folded across the waist, held in place by a metal buckle. It had a row of large metal buttons down the front, was fairly loose at the waist and had a most unpleasant scratchy collar which had to be worn in the buttoned up position at all times. This was my first encounter with what was called 'bull's wool' – so-called because the material was so heavy and so uncomfortable. In common with many others I wore a civilian shirt beneath it to protect my neck in particular from the irritation of the cloth. The material was certainly very hard-wearing and warm, and it was supposed to turn away a lot of water. However, in my experience it seemed to attract rain and became very heavy when sodden; it was also very slow to dry out.

In military parlance an overcoat is called a greatcoat. Mine swept down to halfway between my knees and my ankles and it had two angled rows of metal 'brass' buttons down the front and a completely pointless row of three similar buttons across an equally pointless half-belt at the back. The design was a direct copy from the First World War or even earlier, and when fully dressed one would not have looked out of place on the Russian Steppes or the Western Front in 1914.

Next, I was issued with a beret, an over-sized and inelegant piece of headgear with a wide headband that sported a green double swallowtail ribbon fluttering at the back. I was given a dark coloured metal cap badge bearing the crest of the Defence Forces to be affixed to the front of the beret. The letters 'FF' (Fianna Fáil – Soldiers of Destiny) were set centrally in a stylised leather belt with flames as a background. The crest was designed by Professor Eoin MacNeill when he was chief-of-staff of the Irish Volunteers, and was formally adopted by that organisation in 1914.

Finally, new members were given some minimal instruction on how to wear and adjust the different items of clothing, how to polish the buttons and how to keep our boots clean. We were expected to provide the brasso, polishing cloths and boot polish ourselves.

Thus attired, I took great pride in clunking to and from parades, especially after I had been issued with my Lee-Enfield rifle and associated cleaning kit. The .303in single-shot, bolt-action rifle was of First World War vintage and it carried the scars of much use and abuse collected over the years. We kept the rifles and uniforms in our homes, a carry-over from the Emergency days when immediate access to weapons was essential. However, carrying out a weekly check on the presence of the rifles was a major chore and a source of great anxiety for the commanding officer of every unit. There is a story, the accuracy of which I cannot guarantee, that summed up the hazards of having weapons scattered all over the landscape.

One morning a CO learned to his horror that the unit appeared to be down a rifle. To be unable to account for even one weapon in your unit was one of the most serious military sins, carrying grave consequences for one's future career. So in his wisdom, he employed what would only be described in today's military terminology as PsyOps (Psychological Operations). Having waited until quite late in the afternoon when most of the staff had already gone home, he reported to Command HQ in Collins Barracks, Cork, that they appeared to be missing five rifles. He said that he was pursuing all avenues urgently and hoped to be able to give a better situation report in the morning. He phoned in early the following morning to report that four of the rifles had been located and that they were hopeful of getting the final one soon. This took all the heat out of the situation and avoided the possibility of a large posse of staff officers from Command descending on the unit, always a dreaded prospect.

Heaven knows what other awkward discoveries they might have made if allowed full access to the unit records and stores. The CO and his staff at their leisure eventually discovered the missing rifle in a hay barn, where the 'owner' had innocently managed to get it buried under bales of hay.

The battalion had a Ford Estate vehicle as part of its equipment. It was a very unmilitary vehicle with beautiful wood panels, very soft suspension and a purring V8 engine, but it did Trojan work carrying personnel or equipment for the many activities of A Company. On a day trip in May, I travelled for the first time to the rifle range high in the hills above Killaloe in East Clare, enjoying the comfort of this vehicle.

On the firing range, the group was divided up and about one-third were required to work in the butts and later to change around with those who had completed their firing practice. The butts, or stop butts, was the place where the butt party, safely under cover, hoisted and lowered the targets and gave an indication of where the bullet struck the target to assist the firer. Each round (bullet) made a loud snapping noise as it struck the canvas or the wooden frame of the target and carried on to impact in the soil of the butts. When a practice was completed, the holes created by the rounds had to be patched up, using paper patches, before the next group of firers could be permitted to open fire.

My first FCA training camp was held in the camp at Lahinch, County Clare, in June 1950. The camp included a large modern hall called the Sluagh Hall, together with a number of wooden huts and a toilet block. 'Sluagh' means a large crowd or many people, and this hall was one of the many built across the country during the Emergency to facilitate training by all the voluntary services. Each of the wooden huts was heated by two pot-bellied stoves and a room orderly was appointed from our number each day to clean out the stoves, draw more turf, to prepare the fire for the next night, to brush the floor and to generally 'mind the house'.

It was here that I was introduced to another of the delights brought on by the exigencies of the Emergency – the trestle bed. Each man was provided with three six-foot long boards and two small wooden trestles which, when assembled, made a bed just three inches off the floor. A mattress was placed on the boards, and due to the flexing of these boards, it made a reasonably comfortable bed.

The food and the conditions under which we were expected to eat were simply atrocious. If one was not in for the first sitting, it was necessary to clear a place at table for oneself, as the tables were only tidied once – at the end of the meal. When the potatoes arrived from the cookhouse, they were simply dumped in a heap on the table. Each man was given a half-loaf of bread with some butter attached. It was dreadful, but I never heard anyone complain and indeed I assumed that this was the standard to be expected in all such camps. The ration scale was based on that used during the Emergency and there was barely enough food to sustain a young and active male. Great emphasis was placed on prunes and custard for dessert. It was jokingly said that the prunes were to keep the soldiers 'regular', otherwise they could become 'irregular', a reference to the anti-Treaty side during the Civil War who were known as Irregulars.

At the camp, before firing on the open range, it was the custom to fire a smaller number of rounds on the 25-yard range that backed onto the estuary of the River Shannon near Kildysert. The targets were small cardboard squares marked in the same way as the full-sized targets, ascribed with concentric circles called bulls (the smallest of the circles), inners, magpies and outers. The firer earned a score of four points for striking the bull, three for an inner, two for a magpie and one for an outer. No points were allotted for striking the target outside the outer circle. The targets, pinned to small wooden stakes, were proportionally equal in size to the full target when viewed at 100 yards.

At one stage, I was employed to recover the used targets after each group had fired and to replace them with fresh targets. Myself and a couple of others were busily performing this task, paying no attention, while the next group was being given the order to load and apply safety catches. However, one idiot managed to accidentally fire a shot in our direction, but it passed harmlessly over our group. When it came to my turn to fire, I remember being shocked at the force of the recoil, as well as having a sore shoulder for a few days, of which I was very proud.

In August 1950, I participated in a training camp in Youghal, County Cork. As many as 500 soldiers, drawn from all the units of Southern Command, were gathered there for their two-week annual training camp. We were accommodated in small two-man bivouac tents known to us as 'bivvies' into which we had to cram our equipment, rifles and personal possessions. One particular aspect of this camp was that a bugler provided the full range of calls, from reveille to tattoo, every day. I have a clear recollection of those beautiful calls, especially that one at midnight, the Last Post, when all good soldiers were expected to go to sleep in the security of their quarters.

We had travelled to Youghal by special train, and because it was a special train, carrying as many as 300 wild Claremen and only slightly less wild Limerickmen, it did not stop at stations along the route, apart from Limerick city itself. This was the era of the non-corridor trains and when someone was caught short – as was frequently the case – there was no option but to open a window and let fly. This often meant that much of what should have exited entered again – if not in the same compartment, then further down the train – much to the annoyance of the others.

One did not dare to open the window to look at the scenery. I did, once, and initially thought that it was raining!

Conditions at Youghal were rough, but the food was better than that at Lahinch. The cookhouse had been enlarged to cater for the numbers, but in our section of the camp, the cooks worked in a temporary lean-to extension under a corrugated roof. We had to queue up in the open to collect our meals. If it was raining, we handed in our tin plates through a sheet of rain falling from the galvanised roof and then had to withdraw it swiftly to eat the food before it started to swim off the plate.

By this time I was an acting corporal and was retained at Youghal for a third week as part of the battalion platoon (a platoon consisted of one junior officer, one sergeant, six corporals and twenty-seven privates) to participate in the annual command platoon competitions, involving probably as many as fifteen platoons. This was a very keenly fought competition, featuring arms drill, foot drill, first aid, platoon in defence and grenade throwing, and participants got up to all sorts of tricks to try and gain an advantage. The competition included the very important high-scoring rifle practices in which every soldier had to participate. Each firer was allocated a large printed number – his competition number – attached to the haversack on his back. I must have been a reasonable shot, because when I had fired my rounds and had returned to the platoon, who were gathered in a huddle at the rear of the 600-yard firing point, the number on my back was surreptitiously removed and the number of another member of our platoon was substituted. I was then sent back up to fire again, using a false identity.

I was discharged from the FCA on 20 November 1950, having served for a total of 354 wonderful days with Ennis Battalion. My LA (*Leabhar Airm* – literally Army Book) 89/FCA – the Certificate of Service – states that my service number was S/668845 (the S stood for single) and that I had enlisted for a period of five years. As it transpired, having successfully applied for a cadetship, I was discharged early from the FCA to allow me to enlist in the regular army.

Chapter 2

THE CADET SCHOOL

At the end of the Civil War, much thought and effort went into the provision of young officers for the army. A military mission was sent to France and then to the United States to study the methods of training used in those countries. Meanwhile, the Air Corps, the Army Ordnance Corps and the School of Music were allowed to take in a small number of cadets. The very first group of cadets for the army were enrolled in the Army School of Instruction and thirteen 2nd Lieutenants were commissioned in 1929. For me it is a sobering thought that I knew and even served with a few of those first officers. This serves to demonstrate just how young our Defence Forces are and how much has been achieved since those confused and difficult early days following independence.

The Military College as we know it today was finally established in 1930 to replace the existing training arrangements and the Cadet School was incorporated as one of the three departments of the college. Since its establishment, the Cadet School has produced classes of commissioned officers more or less annually for the forces. Intended to fulfil the projected needs for a flow of young officers to replace the losses (retirement, resignations, deaths, etc.), the size of the classes has varied both due to the demands of the forces and the restrictions of the Department of Finance.

With the advent of the Korean War (1950–53) a frisson of anxiety about defence rippled through the government. A new recruiting drive for the regular army was set in place and the terms of enlistment were made more attractive. The written examination when applying for a cadetship was also dropped. It became simply a matter of writing to the Department of Defence for an application form, which I did promptly. Having submitted the application form to the department, I was called to St Bricin's Military Hospital, Dublin, in September 1950, where I was required to undergo a rigorous medical examination and an oral Irish test. Soon afterwards I had to submit to a long and detailed interview in front of a large board of officers.

In those times sport in any form had become very important to the forces, so my background in swimming was fortunate. My main sport was competition swimming and life-saving at which I was reasonably good, having an assortment of Clare and Munster championships to my credit. Although I did not know it then, swimming had a very high profile in the Defence Forces. My service, short as it was in the FCA, did no harm to my chances either. (In fact, it was many years later when I discovered that I had been under consideration as a potential officer in Ennis Battalion FCA.) Needless to say, I was delighted to be informed by post soon afterwards that I had been awarded a cadetship and that I was to report to the Military College on 21 November 1950.

The 25th Cadet Class: 1950 to 1952

On a bright Tuesday morning in November, I boarded a bus at McBirneys on Aston Quay, Dublin, and bought a one-way ticket to the Curragh Camp, sitting back in a state of mild nervousness for the hour-long journey. After a while I noticed another young man of my own age who also had that certain look about him and we ended up introducing ourselves as we got off at the Post Office in the centre of the camp. He was Kevin Duffy from Dún Laoghaire. We became firm friends, both of us ending up in the Artillery Corps after commissioning.

As we tramped up towards the Military College, I found myself lost in wonder at what I was seeing. It was not at all what I had expected. The term 'camp' suggested something like what I had already seen in Lahinch and Youghal. Yet, here I was walking through what could only be described as a regular town with large, permanent, mostly red-brick buildings, civilian shops, a cinema and the other conveniences typical of the average Irish town. The large gymnasium doubled as the garrison church until the present fine structure, St Brigid's, was built.

By about 16.00hrs, the new cadet class had gathered in the billiard room in the cadet mess. There were thirty-four of us for the army (six more were due to join us in January) while three others were destined for the Naval Service as the 4th Naval cadet class. The Naval Service allowed their cadets to spend a limited number of weeks in the Cadet School for what was described as a 'saluting course' before transferring them to the naval base in Cork and then to Britain for training with the British navy. Specialist direct-intake categories for other corps such as engineers, dentists, chemists or doctors were also treated to a similar brief 'saluting course' before commissioning.

All the new cadets gathered there were around the same age, within a year of each other. Col. J.J. Lillis appeared and moved around to welcome us, and I remember being impressed that he seemed to know each of us by name. He had been the chairman of the interview board in Dublin nearly two months earlier and was at that time the Commandant of the Military College.

The Cadet Master, in charge of the Cadet School, was Lt-Col Seán 'Johnny' MacEoin, a man who had a fairly tough reputation and who was to be avoided if at all possible. Capt. John F. Gallagher, an infantry officer, who quickly became known to us as Jack, or more usually 'Gildy', was to be in charge of our class. He was a native of Belfast, an excellent Gaelic footballer and basketball player, and he quickly showed us that while he was generally fair he was also extremely demanding. He ended his days as the Quartermaster General of the Defence Forces with the rank of Major-General. Capt. Gallagher's assistant was a Capt. Denis Quinn, on loan from the Cavalry Corps – a lovely, gentle and relaxed man.

Cadets were neither officers to be treated with care nor private soldiers to be pushed around or bullied, but the NCO instructors of the Cadet School had developed a middle of the road approach that worked very well. We were controlled and dealt with in a very clever, subtle way, and always addressed as 'Cadet'. Our senior NCO instructor was CS (company sergeant) Peter O'Connor, known to us all as Pedro. He was a very fine soldier and an outstanding shot with the rifle, having been All-Army Individual Champion on a number of occasions.

The No. 2 Section Training Corporal was William Hartley, a small and slightly portly man from Belfast who had a quirky sense of humour. On one occasion we were out on the plains undergoing instruction on a very unwieldy and out-of-date Second World War anti-tank weapon called the Projectile Infantry Anti-Tank. It was a short-range weapon to be fired only from very close quarters as the projectile, a fin-stabilised rocket-like device, was propelled by a very large spring. Someone asked him the obvious and very relevant question: 'Corporal, what do you do if you fire and miss the tank?'

Corporal Hartley rocked on his heels, a typical movement of his, tipped his cap back on his head and replied: 'In that case, Cadet, you put on your gym shoes and run like f—.'

Another popular expression of his was, 'Jaycus Cadet, you will get me and you your ticket', an expression he would use if one of us did or said something that might result in disciplining either for the cadet or himself or both. When a soldier is discharged from the Forces for whatever reason, regulations required that he be issued with a one-way ticket to his recorded home address, hence the expression. However, in the case of a cadet 'getting his ticket', it meant something much more serious altogether. It meant that he had failed to come up to the standards required and was deemed not to be suitable for commissioning.

The course of training for army cadets at that time lasted for two years. For the first year we were expected to live and work under conditions similar to those of privates, living eight to a room, while in the second year as senior cadets, we lived two to a smaller room. In fact the regime was much more demanding than that for privates, and if applied to ordinary soldiers, it would have had the effect of driving many of them out of the service. The Cadet School was a pressure cooker, deliberately designed to test and to mould all kinds of unlikely young males into competent leaders for all branches of the army.

Our class was divided into five sections of eight cadets each, with each section living in its designated billet. There were fairly basic toilet and washing facilities, shared with the section on the other side of the corridor. I was in Section 2, along with Cadets Mick MacGreal, Jack Spillane, Frank O'Donovan, Barney Dobey, Paddy Goggin, Gerry Kenny and Seán MacNiocaill. The billet was centrally heated, had a floor covering of lino and each cadet had a metal locker and an overhead rack on which were placed the webbing and the steel helmet on issue to each cadet. The lighting was by bare overhead bulbs, we had a chair each and had to share two small tables. The accommodation was not exactly designed for comfort.

In our first week as cadets, we were brought into the main

lecture hall to be addressed by Capt. Jerome, the CO of the Naval Service. While three of our class, Cadets Joe Deasy, Jackie Reville and Pat O'Mahony, had enlisted specifically for the Navy, he was appealing for additional volunteers from our group. He got no takers, although I was very tempted.

We were issued with our bull's wool uniforms, and another called a fatigues uniform, poorly made in khaki twill, for use only when working on especially dirty jobs. We were given many items of clothing and equipment that were new to me, items never issued to members of the FCA. We were not issued with pyjamas, we had to supply our own, even though at least one of our class always slept in his 'greyback', a collarless grey shirt issued to all soldiers. Another item was called a 'wobbler', in reality a shaving brush used by soldiers everywhere not for the application of shaving cream (many of us did not require a daily shave anyway), but as a device for cleaning dust and dirt from rifles in advance of inspections.

Most intriguing of all, we were informed that each one of us would be issued with a 'housewife'. The reality was quite different to expectations, however. The 'housewife' was simply a small cloth roll containing sewing needles, thread, spare buttons and a thimble, designed to enable the soldier to do his own running repairs rather than bothering the unit tailor with trivial matters. We were required to buy our own blanco (cleaning powder for the webbing equipment), brasso, brown and cardinal red polishes, as well as whitener for the gym shoes. Cardinal red was used solely on the scabbards of the bayonets, but it was also used on each other from time to time during episodes of high spirits and exuberance.

The army had, and still has, a great belief in the power of the service number, no doubt as a result of experience gained over the years. Each and every item of personal kit and equipment had to display the military service number of the owner. On leathers and metals, the number was stamped, using metal stamps, while on soft clothing items, white cloth tapes were issued on which one's number had to be stamped in black ink. They were then sewn on to socks, shirts and underwear. The process of numbering all our kit consumed a lot of time and energy during our first week.

Training got under way promptly, with the early emphasis on foot and arms drill, saluting and the care and presentation for inspection of our large quantities of kit. The typical week ran from Monday to Saturday with sports training on Wednesday afternoons and a half-day on Saturdays. Saturday mornings were devoted to inspections on the Barrack Square and in our billets, lecture halls and section training rooms. The day started with reveille at 07.00hrs followed by Check Parade on the square at 07.30hrs with dinner at 12.30hrs and tea at 17.00hrs.

For movement around the camp, each cadet was issued with a bicycle. These sturdy bikes had been used in very large numbers during the Emergency, when a number of Cyclist Squadrons were formed. Braking was by means of a back-pedal brake and to slow the bike, or to bring it to a halt, the rider simply stood on the pedals, something that required a bit of skill on a steep slope or while moving at speed.

Needless to say, the army had developed a drill for bicycle parades also. Initially, we formed up in twos and marched off by pairs until the order 'mount up' was given. When at the destination, the bikes were parked in line and in pairs resting against each other. Occasionally, when cycling home and where there was no school supervision, the forty cadets often ended up in a 'Tour de France' style race back to the Military College.

For the first year of their training, cadets received the same pay as for a private recruit and in the second year the pay rose to that of a three-star (a fully trained) soldier. We wore the soldier bull's wool uniforms but with a white and green band around the peaked caps for both years. In our second year we were issued with the officer uniform and Sam Browne belts, but still with the white and green band around the cap.

The arrival of the officer-pattern uniform was greeted with great enthusiasm as it was an important indication that we were getting closer to being commissioned. In our second year, because of the superfine uniform, we were regularly required to provide guards of honour for visiting dignitaries, ministers for defence, bishops, generals and for commissioning ceremonies for our senior cadets.

While we were out on training exercises, our billets and toilet facilities were inspected on a daily basis for cleanliness and to ensure that all beds were made up in the prescribed manner. Sanctions were applied if our work was not up to standard. All the smaller items of kit and equipment had to be stored in a wooden kit box. Each shirt, towel and sock had to be folded and displayed in such a way that the serial number was visible, while the other items had their allotted places from which no deviation was permitted. The structure of the kit box required each owner to cut up pieces of light timber in order to shape and fix each item in its place in the box. I was certainly not a carpenter and my efforts never reached the standards set for us by the long-service soldiers. It was rumoured that some old soldiers – the 'old sweats' – had two full sets of kit, carefully accumulated over the years, one of which never left the kit box and was only trotted out for inspections.

One aspect of the training day was the emphasis on the absolute need to be on time. It was drummed into us that one is only on time when five minutes early. The other absolute was to be correctly dressed for the task at hand. The training programme clearly specified the appropriate 'dress' for each planned activity. For all lectures, cadets had to present themselves in the normal working uniform with leather belt and peaked cap. For foot drill on the square, the dress might include web equipment, bayonet and rifle. There was an endless variety of dress required for wet weather (groundsheets, a large rubberised canvas garment that could also be used as a rudimentary tent, had to be carried); for the gymnasium – singlets and knicks; for swimming parades – swim togs, and so on. It was necessary to consult the programme carefully otherwise you might have a scramble to change at short notice, or otherwise suffer the embarrassment of being incorrectly dressed for the task at hand. The programme would sometimes mean that the class would complete, say, a five-mile run, and immediately afterwards, be required to change into bull's wool with cap and belt and to sit, bathed in perspiration, for forty-five minutes to endure a talk in a heated lecture room.

Saturday morning was devoted to a major inspection parade taken by the Cadet Master, Lt-Col MacEoin. Unusually, during the first six weeks of our training, there were four cadet classes in the Cadet School – a total of some 120 cadets. The Cadet Master, if nothing else, was very thorough and he always proceeded slowly and with great attention to detail. As each class was inspected, it was dismissed from the parade, but as the 25th class was the most junior, we had to wait for perhaps ninety minutes before it was our turn.

We would have been standing at ease, looking to our fronts without being permitted to move at all, except very discretely. Each cadet would be dressed in full webbing kit with bayonet, water bottle, rifle and steel helmet. On his back was the haversack in which was his groundsheet, neatly folded. It was very demanding having to stand dressed like this and immobile for such a length of time, but fortunately we were young and fit. After a while, the practice of overly long inspections gave way to a more lenient regime, helped, as it undoubtedly was, by the commissioning of the 22nd cadet class.

The junior class – ours – were allowed one weekend off per month, the weekend starting after parade on Saturday morning. In our second year, we were allowed every second weekend off.

The luckier cadets who lived locally or in the Dublin area had no difficulty in making a dash home for a few hours of 'civvy' life and food. Others like myself, from further afield, had no chance of such relief, so we had to make our own amusements. Having been a keen swimmer, I quickly became a member of the Curragh Swimming Club, probably the most successful club in the country at that time. It was easy for me to spend long hours at the pool at night or at the weekends. Under the coaching of Sergeants Tommy Cullen and Pete Madden, I would complete a routine of twenty lengths breaststroke, twenty lengths legs only and twenty lengths arms only. This schedule was regarded as quite advanced at the time, but of course in relation to the demands placed on the modern swimmer, it was only child's play.

Swimming was hugely popular in the Curragh and galas were held regularly between the Curragh Swimming Club and various clubs or combinations of clubs from around the country. These were competitions that we always seemed to win, even managing to beat a combined English universities team on one occasion. As the club was a civilian club, it included many fine women swimmers, most of them daughters of ORs from the camp, some of whom were national champions. The popularity of these galas was increased by an incident where the neck strap of one of our lady backstroke swimmers snapped in the middle of a race!

On the establishment of the Cadet School camera club in the winter of 1950, I became an enthusiastic member. We were given lectures from many of the top camera experts in Dublin, plus assistance and advice in the purchase of cameras and darkroom equipment. I spent many happy hours over the weekends developing and printing my photos, eventually purchasing my own darkroom equipment. It was a very fortunate expertise to have acquired and I put it to good use later when overseas service commenced.

The syllabus of training for cadets covered all the usual military skills and crafts: physical training, unarmed combat, obstacle course training, night compass marches cross-country, military history, military law, Defence Force Regulations, as well as some more unusual topics such as courtesy and etiquette. We trained in and fired most of the weapons on issue to the Forces at that time and threw live hand grenades. The over-all intention of the syllabus was to qualify us as infantry platoon leaders.

Providing the weather was reasonable, time spent on the ranges was enjoyable, or at least tolerable. On one occasion, a cadet complained to Capt. Gallagher that the barrel of his rifle was bent, he could see it clearly and that this could explain his poor shooting. He was quite serious about it too. Mind you the rifles in use dated from 1917 or 1918 and considering the use and abuse that the same weapons had to put up with over the intervening years, it was not at all an improbable argument. Capt. Gallagher was not impressed with his reasoning or with his excuse.

After-hours work included preparation for the multitude of lessons, lectures, reading of military history and the addition to our copies of Defence Forces Regulations of any amendments to military regulations. In addition we had to make time for games, such as visits to non-military establishments like Clongowes Wood and Newbridge Colleges with whom we competed in an annual Triangular Competition in rugby, athletics and basketball. The subject that gave most of us a genuine cause for worry was military history, principally because the Cadet Master himself, Johnny MacEoin, conducted all the instruction on this subject. We had access to the Military College library and were encouraged to use the county library system. However, the life we led was not really conducive to serious reading or deep study of any subject, even military history. Our days were intensively physical in nature, leaving little energy for late night reading and note-taking.

Much stress was placed on obstacle course training, designed to improve our ability to cope with complex obstacles and how to overcome them at speed and (theoretically) under enemy fire. The obstacles were designed to test individual balance and technique but also how we functioned as a cohesive group. On one occasion while training on the obstacle course at the Military College, Frank O'Donovan landed awkwardly and rolled over, shouting that he had broken his ankle. We just laughed as it had seemed like a very simple fall – but he was right. He hobbled back to the lines, but later some of us had to carry him to the Military Hospital, fortunately only about half a mile away. After some weeks in hospital he was back with us but on light duty only. This meant that he made his way to all lectures and indoor activities at his own speed and was excused all parades and physical tests until fully recovered.

There was a huge emphasis on games and fitness and practically every cadet was skilled in some sport or other. Cross-country races, road runs, boxing matches, rugby and in particular, all the GAA games, were very much part of the training and the after-hours life of all cadets. Cadets featured in all the competitions between the seven barracks in the camp proper, as well as Magee Barracks in Kildare and the Army Apprentice School in Naas, while the better ones were selected to play in competitions at Defence Forces level against the other Commands.

On one occasion, when the Military College was playing the Cavalry Depot in hurling, a prominent member of the College team, a young officer, was injured. One of the many onlookers, Capt. Johnny Stapleton, later to become Director of Cavalry, ran onto the pitch to see how he was. After a brief assessment he returned to the sideline, announcing loudly to the general onlookers, 'He'll be OK, he was only hit on the head.'

On another occasion, I was watching from near the Kildare goal during a soccer match played on the Military College grounds, refereed by Capt. Jackie Jones. It was a dull and boring game, played with more perspiration than inspiration, between the Artillery Depot and the 3rd Battalion. A small number of gunners had assembled on both sides of the Depot goal mouth. On one occasion, a slow ball out-manoeuvred the goalie and was clearly destined to go into the net close to the left-hand post. An anonymous boot appeared and deflected the ball around the post. The referee blew for a goal kick. There was uproar from the 'Bloods' – as the members of the 3rd Battalion like to describe themselves – but the referee had no intention of changing his mind.

When free to do so, I played a lot of tennis as a member of the Curragh Lawn Tennis Club. In June 1951, Cadet Gerry Corbett and myself were selected with some officers to represent the Curragh Camp in the All Army Tennis Championships in Cork. Myself and Gerry travelled third class by train to Cork – the officers travelling first class – where we had a few blissful days, living in officers' quarters in Collins Barracks and dining with the commissioned officers of the 4th Battalion. The Lawn Tennis grounds lay across the road from the barracks and each time we passed through the gates dressed in our superfine uniforms and wearing Sam Browne belts, the MPs gave us their best salutes. They did not have to do so as we were not commissioned, but they were obviously unsure how to deal with cadets. They might never have come across such strange entities as officers without rank markings and with green and white bands on their caps. We did not correct them either as we were delighted to be getting our first salutes well ahead of commissioning.

On return to the Cadet School at the end of the week, I was brought down to earth with a bang. My section, Section 2, was confined to quarters for the weekend as they were deemed not to have properly cleaned their rooms or toilets. As soon as one's back was turned …!

As well as the physical challenge of the training, our class came under a certain amount of emotional stress. The members of the 23rd cadet class suffered under a more severe regime, with many of them discharged for quite trivial reasons. The treatment of that class had a traumatic effect on both the 24th class and on ourselves – it created a tension that never really eased until a new regime was installed at the top. Artillery officer Lt-Col Bill Donagh became our new Cadet Master in place of Johnny MacEoin and the School Commandant, Col J.J. Lillis, was moved to a new appointment in Defence Forces HQ and replaced by Col Dan Bryan. Both officers brought their own standards and values to their new responsibilities.

In order to understand fully the duties and responsibilities of how the rest of the army functioned, in our second year we spent an introductory period, usually of a week's duration, with most of the corps of the army – Supply and Transport, Artillery, Cavalry, Engineers, Signals, Ordnance and so on. In our time with Supply and Transport, we learned of the supply systems within the Forces and maintenance methods for the fleet of vehicles. We were trained in the techniques of double de-clutching and were taught to drive the many different types of vehicles in service at the time. The final part of the truck-driving test took place on a steep slope where a matchbox was placed under a rear wheel. The driver was required to take off on the slope without crushing the matchbox! The Air Corps week was popular with everybody because it was near Dublin and because we lived and dined in the officers' mess. Apart from short flights and many lectures, we were taken up to Gormanston and treated to a very effective air-to-ground firepower display by a flight of Seafires.

However, probably the most popular corps experience was at the Cavalry School. Rather than horses, here we were taught how to ride motorcycles. The motorcycles were elderly wartime BSA 500cc bikes from which most of the breakable items, such as lights, had been removed. The training took us from simple starting up and maintenance, to cross-country riding on the trickier parts of the Curragh Plains and long-distance convoy driving in Kildare,

Carlow and Wicklow. The senior instructor was Squadron Sergeant Barry, an elderly man with a heavy Waterford accent, who had an endless enthusiasm for the BSA motorbike. It was great fun and although there were many crashes, none were serious.

During our years of training, every day and in every way, each cadet was being tested and reported upon, and he was regularly placed in a position where he had to make decisions and to issue orders to deal with numerous surprise situations or emergencies. He was required to give lessons on a wide variety of weapons and subjects such as map reading or fire control orders, or he might be placed in charge of conducting small unit tactics. For lessons, he would usually be addressing the members of his own section.

These stressful occasions would sometimes create unintended hilarity. While taking weapons class, Mick Considine, from Gort, was giving a lesson on the care and cleaning of the rifle. These lessons were delivered in front of a small assessment panel of his classmates, who would be asked afterwards for their comments on the lesson. At the end of the lesson, Mick was asked how much oil should be put in the barrel of a rifle before placing it in storage. Mick brought the house down with his reply: 'Oil in the barrel should be like perfume on a woman, sensed but not seen.'

Two other funny incidents from my training stand out in my memory and are worth recording here. A thirty-six-hour non-stop endurance exercise was held that started with a tactical route march in full kit from the Curragh into Glen Imaal, where we had to dig slit trenches in a defensive situation by night. We followed that with a 'section in attack' test for each of us the following morning, all without any opportunity for rest or sleep. This was the age of chlorophyll, a green substance that was included in every product and regarded as the saving of mankind! I was so tired at the morning ablutions on that exercise that I wondered why the chlorophyll toothpaste tasted so strange. On closer examination, I found that I had managed to shave with the toothpaste and clean my teeth with the shaving cream, as both were the same colour green.

When it came to the turn of Mick MacGréil to command the section in attack on the same exercise, he carried out all the preliminaries without fault, but he chose a particularly dense hawthorn hedge and ditch from which to conduct the final assault on the 'enemy'. (The 'enemy' typically comprised one or two of our NCO instructors firing 'blanks' in our direction from a hidden position.) As Mick was the first to arrive, he chose the only available gap in the hedge, ordering the rest of us to spread out at intervals to his left and right. He shouted out his final orders – 'we will attack and kill all enemy there' – then, pointing in the direction of where the enemy lay, he ordered, 'fix bayonets, charge'. Being the only one of us able to get through the hedge, he disappeared across the field bellowing 'bullets, bullets' (i.e. fire from the hip), completely oblivious to the fact that he was on his own. The rest of us just collapsed into the wet ditch with laughter, unable to follow him.

With the two years of training almost complete, we were allowed to hold a commissioning ball in the cadet mess a few weeks before our actual commissioning. Vast amounts of time and thought went into converting the mess into something more like an Aladdin's cave. We built a covered walkway leading from the billiard room, where the guests were received and aperitifs were served, to the mess itself. But as much attention and energy was devoted to the problem of inviting girlfriends to the ball as to the manner in which the mess was prepared. For those who lived in Dublin or in the local area this did not present much of a problem, but for those of us who came from far-away places, it was a major logistical problem, assuming that one had a girlfriend in the first place. The daughters of serving officers in Kildare and who might only have been met once at a tennis or swimming club social were in great demand. However, it was a most enjoyable occasion and it all went smoothly.

Customarily on the final night before commissioning, each class did something silly or out of the ordinary. In our case we attacked the junior class, emptied all our refuse bins in their rooms and applied cardinal red polish to as many unfortunates as we could seize. Later we held a noisy midnight parade on the square dressed in our army long johns and helmets.

The cadet course was long and arduous, and because of the stresses and strains and the constant struggle, shared equally between the members of the class, a very special bond of friendship was formed, a bond that has lasted, not just while in service, but for the rest of our lives.

I had enlisted on 21 November 1950 and was discharged on 23 November 1952 for the purpose of being appointed to commissioned rank. Some weeks before commissioning, we had been invited to express our preference for a corps posting. In common with the rest of the class I opted for the Air Corps first, and in my case, Artillery second. Unfortunately for our class, and we did not know this at the time, the Air Corps had just introduced a short-service commission scheme for pilots who would enlist for a period of five years before discharge. Consequently, no member of our class was posted to the Air Corps, a matter of disappointment to many. However, I was very happy to be posted to my second choice of the Artillery Corps and never regretted it. Following commissioning on 24 November 1952, seven 2/Lieuts were appointed to the General List, Artillery Corps. These were Noel Bergin, Jerry Healy, Kevin Duffy, Pádraic O'Farrell, Willie Phillips, Mick McMahon and myself.

Chapter 3

THE GUNNERS

The Artillery Corps

In the 1950s, the Artillery Corps – the second largest corps in the army – was a vibrant and lively organisation with a great variety of tasks. It was divided into four branches: Field, Anti-Tank, Anti-Air and Coast Defence. The Anti-Aircraft Training Regiment, as it was then termed, incorporated FCA batteries in Dublin, Cork and Limerick. The CDA was even larger, with forts from Duncannon around the south and west coasts to Lough Swilly in Donegal.

The Artillery Corps consisted of a small Directorate, the Depot and School, three field artillery regiments (regular units), seven independent FCA field batteries, CDA and the 1st Anti-Aircraft Training Regiment, based in Magee Barracks, Kildare. The anti-tank element, the smallest and least developed branch, was represented by an anti-tank troop with four 17pdr guns in each of the regular regiments.

Over the centuries, as artillery support weapons developed, they came to be classified as 'field', 'medium' or 'heavy' artillery that today would equate roughly with 105mm, 155mm and 175mm guns respectively. The term 'field' came to be associated with artillery batteries from the days when they provided close intimate fire support to their associated infantry battalions. It would operate 'in the field', close to or even in front of its infantry – as in the early years of the short-range muzzle-loading cannon. Apart from one battery of antiquated 60pdr guns, long since disposed of, the corps was never equipped with either medium or heavy artillery weapons. Initially composed of eight guns, today, because of the development of faster firing and more accurate field guns firing heavier shells over longer distances, a battery is composed of six guns. The present standard equipment for all field batteries is the 105mm light gun.

An artillery weapon is referred to by many terms such as cannon, piece, gun or equipment, and to add to the confusion, some are categorised as gun-howitzers or howitzers. A howitzer fires a shell in a lobbing manner, designed to clear steep hills or to fire into deep and narrow valleys. The British Second World War 25pdr was designed to combine the qualities of both a field gun and a howitzer and was thus referred to as a gun-howitzer.

The Artillery Corps had originally been a mounted corps. Many of the officers and all the NCOs and gunners were horse soldiers, dressed in riding britches and wearing spurs. They wore small arms ammunition leather bandoliers diagonally across their chests. In addition they wore white lanyards on their left shoulders, a reminder of the days when gunners had to use lanyards to fire some of the earlier artillery weapons. One of the 'myths' solemnly told to us in our early days of training was that the biggest and strongest recruits were generally sent to the Artillery Corps. The argument was that strong men were needed to deal with the teams of horses, to manhandle artillery pieces into and out of position, or to lift and carry heavy boxes of ammunition. This was not as far-fetched as it might seem, as physically the young Irish male in the first half of the twentieth century tended to be much smaller and lighter than the soldier of today.

During the late 1930s, all the field artillery weapons were converted from solid to pneumatic wheels, the horses were retired to pasture and the guns were towed by specially designed vehicles. This had the effect of increasing the speed and mobility of the batteries. By 1939, all towed field artillery in the Defence Forces were 'shod' in pneumatic tyres at a time when many continental armies persisted with wooden-wheeled, horse-drawn artillery.

The Young Officer's Course

Having completed our commissioning leave, seven young 2nd Lieutenants reported to the Artillery Depot in Magee Barracks, Kildare to commence the basic training course for young officers, known unsurprisingly as the Young Officer's Course. While all the corps and services have their own schools, housed in mainly unsuitable buildings, the 'Tillery', as it was often called in the early years, boasted a new barracks for its depot and school in Kildare town. The new barracks also featured easily the largest barrack square in the Defence Forces, designed to hold large concentrations of horse artillery units for parades and training. The barracks was eventually named Magee Barracks after Gunner Magee, an Irish member of a gun crew fighting with the French at the Battle of Ballinamuck in County Mayo in 1798.

Our principle instructors were Commandant Bill Rea, the School Commandant, and Commandant Ned Shortall, both of whom had received training in Britain in the latest artillery techniques. Another was Captain Tommy Wickham, whose speciality was battery and regimental survey. The chief NCO instructor was Battery Sergeant Louis Carroll, a lovely old gent, who was very fond of his pipe and who behaved like a kindly grandfather to young officers. The NCO instructors were all very experienced and gave us a great grounding in what was a long course of complicated and detailed training. Safety took a prominent place in everything we did – a mistake could be very dangerous during live firing practice.

The four-month long Young Officer's Course introduced us to all the field guns used in the corps at the time – the 3.7in and 4.5in howitzers, the 75mm, the 18pdrs (all versions) and the 25pdr. (The 'pdr' refers to the weight of the projectile in pounds while the 'in' refers to the diameter of the bore (or mm) at the breech.) These weapons were mostly from the First World War era and only the 25pdr gun-howitzer dated from the Second World War.

During the course we had to learn the drills and duties of each member of the detachment for each weapon, how they functioned and how they were maintained by the gunners and by the artificers of the Ordnance Corps. We covered all details of the various ammunitions, as well as the principles of how field batteries were deployed and directed in action. We received instruction on the plotting boards where the grid reference of a target, sent down by radio from an observation post, was turned into the necessary bearing (a corrected compass direction to the target), range (distance from battery to target) and elevation (the vertical difference in height between the battery and the target) to be placed on the sights. We learned about the specialised artillery radio sets and the radio procedures peculiar to artillery units. Long hours were spent out in the Kildare countryside practising the drills and techniques of bringing a battery into position prior to firing, coupled with the preparation of fire plans for both attack and defence situations. We also conducted endless simulated engagement of targets on what was called the raikes range, a training device intended to prepare the observer for the real thing in Glen Imaal.

The raikes range was essentially a large-scale model of a selected piece of terrain, beautifully laid out on canvas over a wooden frame. Measuring about 14 x 12 x 7 feet, it showed roads, fields, houses, churches, bridges and woods, essentially all the features usually seen on a typical piece of Irish countryside. It was the predecessor to the present-day sophisticated computer-controlled indoor simulators. These new simulators use large screens to show the terrain on which the exercise is being conducted. A wide range of conditions and realistic sounds can be produced, including night shoots or the engagement of moving targets, subjects that were difficult or even impossible to simulate on the old raikes ranges.

Our first live shoots on the artillery ranges in Glen Imaal were times of some tension for us, but we received a lot of surreptitious help from the instructors and the experienced crews to help ease our way. Each officer conducted one shoot from the OP and was part of a crew for another shoot.

When we had completed the main part of our field artillery training, we switched to training with the 1st Anti-Aircraft Training Regiment, known today as the Air Defence Regiment. We trained on the 3.7in AA gun, range finder and the predictor, a large, ingenious and very out-of-date mechanical 'computer' used for predicting the future position of a target aircraft. We also spent time on the Mk IV radar sets, both in barracks and on the Curragh Plains, for which the Air Corps sent an aircraft to act as a target.

Later, we moved to Gormanston Camp to undergo further training in anti-aircraft artillery where much of our instruction was given by reserve officers of the 'Ack Ack'. This was the term used during the Second World War to indicate anti-aircraft artillery, the personnel of which had participated in the air defence of the country during the Emergency. They had fired in anger a number of times on aircraft, irrespective of nationality, that wandered into Irish air space. Getting on in years, these officers were still quite enthusiastic about their 'trade'. However, as they were doing their annual three weeks reserve training, they were also quite intent on enjoying each other's company and re-living the experiences of the war years. One of our instructors, Capt. O'Brien, known to us as 'Gunga Din', had risen to be a senior member of a government department by then. He had earned the nickname because the famous poem of the same name by Rudyard Kipling was his standard contribution to mess parties.

During this training, we did not fire the 3.7in anti-aircraft guns but used the more modern 40mm Bofors L60s. The Air Corps provided an aircraft to tow a drogue target (a canvas target that looked like a windsock) up and down at a fixed height some distance offshore. However, despite our best efforts, we managed to score only one hit on the drogue.

The final section of the course took us to the headquarters of Coast Artillery on Spike Island in Cork harbour, where we spent a most interesting week. Lt-Col D.J. Collins was OC of Coast Defence Artillery at that time with responsibility for all the forts around the coast. Ireland had coastal forts in Duncannon, County Wexford, Cork harbour (3), Bere Island, County Cork (2), Ardmore Head, County Kerry and the two northern forts on Lough Swilly, County Donegal. By 1953, most of them were unmanned with only a civilian Charge Hand and a small number of maintenance workers in situ.

In Coast Defence Artillery, each of the larger weapons, the 6in or 9.2in gun, was commanded by an NCO with the rank of BQMS, but known to all in the corps as a 'Master Gunner'. While we were exercised in the gun drills for the 6in guns, we did not actually fire any of the CDA weapons. I was intrigued to be told that when firing practice was held in the past, all those living around Cork harbour had been advised to open their windows as a precaution against the shockwave.

In the 1950s the concept of Coast Artillery was in critical decline. The very term 'Coast Defence' was a misnomer anyway, it should have been harbour defence, still a valid concept today. Most of the forts have been retained for summer training camps by the FCA and less frequently for use by regular units. The last

Coast Artillery shoot was conducted at Fort Dunree (Donegal) in July 1967.

During the Young Officer's Course, in addition to training with artillery, we were also introduced to the delights of garrison duties in Magee Barracks, such as that of Orderly Officer – a twenty-four-hour duty. I performed the duties of Barrack Orderly Officer on many occasions in Magee while on that course. Among the many duties to be performed during the twenty-four hours was to ensure the closing of the NCOs' mess at 23.00hrs. On one particular night, the bar shutters had already been pulled down as I arrived in by the back door. While I was collecting the night's takings and signing for them, I overheard the barrack Sergeant-Major speaking to his NCO friends in the lounge on the other side of the shutters. I did not hear his complete speech but I was able to understand that he was speaking in quite a bitter tone, saying that this was 'only an officer's army, they get the best of everything, NCOs get nothing'. It is quite possible he knew that I could hear him and for all I knew, he might have wanted me to hear him. Rather than listen to any more, I quickly let myself out. I never mentioned it to the adjutant, or took any action myself, as perhaps I should have.

However, I believe that it was a fortuitous event as it influenced my attitude to all my subordinates. I am satisfied that it opened my eyes to my relatively privileged position as an officer compared to that of the NCOs and lower ranks in a way that I had not considered before. The morale of the Defence Forces was certainly at a low state in 1953 and NCOs must generally have felt very much neglected or bypassed by officers. I had heard many stories about the brutal disciplinary regime for officers during the Emergency, where they could be harshly disciplined for quite trivial matters. So it was quite understandable that an officer would have developed the habit of protecting his career by insisting on doing even a quite menial task himself. As a result, I believe that some officers became so conditioned by their experiences that they had the greatest difficulty in delegating responsibilities to their junior officers or to NCOs. For example, in one of my overseas units, an elderly and experienced QM with the rank of Commandant spent all his waking hours working in the QM stores he had just taken over from his predecessor. He insisted on checking every item of stores himself, a mammoth task that he could easily have delegated. The pressure became too much for him – he lasted only three or four weeks in the mission and had to be repatriated.

In Cyprus with the 41st Battalion, I was sent to the British base at Dhekelia to draw additional ammunition for the mortar troop. I was very impressed that it was a warrant officer who dealt with me throughout, merely having to get the signature of a duty officer to authorise the release. A warrant officer does not hold a commission but would have received specialised training to enable him to operate at a level between officers and NCOs. The Defence Forces do not have a warrant officer system, but within their areas of training and experience, our NCOs are better than officers at carrying out many tasks. During UN missions our NCOs quickly proved that they were absolutely superb. Once they were given the opportunity to prove themselves, they responded in a most effective manner, making a great impression on the other nationalities with whom they were dealing.

As our group approached the end of the course, we debated where we were likely to be stationed – not that we had any say in the decision-making process nor were we invited to express our preferences. Such matters were decided by the Director of Artillery in consultation with the OCs of the Commands and the Adjutant-General. At the time, popular opinion had it that, of all the available artillery stations, Columb Barracks in Mullingar was regarded as the least attractive. At the end of the Young Officer's Course, we were informed of our appointments – Pádraic O'Farrell and I were posted to the IVth Field Artillery Regiment in Columb Barracks, Mullingar. I am happy to state that, contrary to expectations, this posting proved to be a very fortuitous decision for me.

Chapter 4

COLUMB BARRACKS, MULLINGAR

Columb Barracks was built in 1815 as a replacement for two previous fortifications in Mullingar on a site purchased from the Earl of Granard. It includes a right of way leased from a Mr Fulke Southwell Greville Nugent for a period of no less than 10 million years – the longest in the world – recognised in the *Guinness Book of Records*. It was named after a Free State soldier, 20-year-old Company Adjutant Patrick Columb, who was killed in Mary Street, Mullingar, when attempting to free nine soldiers held by the anti-Treaty forces.

On 13 July 1953, 2/Lieut Pádraic O'Farrell and myself were met in Kildare by a gunner from IVth Regiment and driven to Columb Barracks. We were given a warm welcome by Lt-Col D.J. Cody, the Commanding Officer, who was due to retire shortly afterwards, and introduced to the officers of the unit. Another smaller unit, the 4th Field Company, Supply and Transport Corps, shared the barracks and the duties with the regiment. The IVth Regiment was composed of HQ Battery and the 8th and 15th Field Batteries. HQ Battery provided all the administrative elements of the unit.

Every officer in the Defence Forces has to have an appointment – an allotted place in the organisation of the unit to which he is assigned. This is based on the 'Establishment' – the number of officers permitted by regulations for that corps or unit. In my case, I was posted as 'Left Section Officer, HQ and 4th Anti-Tank Battery, IVth Field Artillery Regiment' and Capt. Pat Kavanagh was my battery commander. HQ Battery had responsibility for about 160 soldiers, including a small caretaker detachment at Fort Dunree – the Coast Artillery Fort on Lough Swilly in County Donegal.

The Battery Sergeant – the senior NCO in the battery – was BS Hughes, known to most as 'Slippy' Hughes, possibly because he had a fondness for wearing his gym shoes and uniform when off duty. The battery clerks were Cpl John Collins and Gnr Bob Gander. Apart from Capt. Kavanagh, I was the only other officer in the battery.

The regiment itself was well up to strength and Lieut Liam Donnelly was bringing a platoon of recruits to the end of their training. An early surprise for me was the custom of holding literacy classes for the small number of soldiers who were so under-educated that they could barely sign their names on the payroll. I discovered later that this practice was common across the units of the Defence Forces – such was the low standard of literacy among the young recruits in the 1940s and 1950s. Another practice that has fortunately died out, and that angered all serving personnel, was the frequent habit – no doubt well-intentioned – of judges in the lower courts telling a miscreant that he could 'take six months or join the Army'.

Life in Columb Barracks was pretty good. We were lucky to have a fine gymnasium for a wide spread of games and other indoor functions. However, it was badly in need of a modern officers' mess, as well as a new cookhouse and dining hall. The standards of cooking across the Defence Forces was not all that it could have been in those days, but in Columb Barracks, we were very lucky to have Cook Sergeant Dick Roche in charge. Despite the antiquated cooking equipment and the inadequate ration scale, he performed wonders for his charges.

At Christmas, the officers and senior NCOs came into barracks to serve Christmas dinner to those unfortunates who, for whatever reason, be it duty or because of family circumstances, were required to remain in barracks. It was in Mullingar that I first heard the term 'Barrack Rat'. This term was applied to elderly, and typically unmarried, NCOs or gunners, whose only life was the military one and who rarely appeared in public dressed in civilian clothes. They left the barracks only when it was essential and availed of annual leave with reluctance.

Religion featured strongly in the daily routine. When the Angelus was blown at 12.00hrs, all those in the open or under training came to a halt, removed their caps, bowed their heads and remained motionless, not resuming whatever they were doing until the call had ended. However, Columb Barracks did not have a resident chaplain even though it boasted an excellent chapel. On Sunday mornings, therefore, a mass parade was held to march to the cathedral in Mullingar town. When the Lenten Missioners came to Mullingar, a mini-mission was also arranged for the barracks. Single officers like me had the company of the preachers for meals in the mess and they were usually very interesting and great fun, not at all the ranting, roaring preachers of the pulpit.

Despite having just finished our training in the school, our new unit saw us commence further training almost as soon as we arrived. The year 1953 saw 8th Battery firing 18pdr field guns for the very last time in Glen Imaal. The battery was then re-equipped with new French-made 120mm mortars and new Landrovers to tow them. While the vehicles were very welcome, we regarded the heavy mortars as infantry weapons, although it has to be said that over time the entire corps came to accept them, however grudgingly.

Commandant Mick Sugrue, second-in-command of IVth Regiment, who had previously served in Coast Artillery as the first and only CO of Fort Shannon at Tarbert, took to the development and training in these new weapons with great energy. He was assisted by Lieuts Tom Ryan and Pádraic O'Farrell, Sgt Brennan and Gnrs Craig and Columb. The French system of control for these weapons had not been purchased, so it was necessary to adapt our own artillery fire control systems to the new weapons. This involved a huge amount of work, but it is fair to state that the work done in Columb Barracks in that first year – with the close assistance of the Ordnance Corps – proved to be highly successful. New artillery plotting boards and associated instruments were manufactured by the Army Ordnance Corps. The mortars were then successfully test-fired for the first time in May 1954 by 8th Battery at a location near Oughterard, County Galway.

As part of the continuing assessment of the potential of the new weapons, a full war-time battery of twelve mortars (three troops) was fired in Glen Imaal the following year.

Despite these new training challenges, barrack routine continued without interruption. Command inspections were an annual event and many weeks were spent in preparation: every aspect of barrack life was reviewed, every hole and corner was cleaned and painted. For weeks before the big day, flocks of staff officers pried and poked into every aspect of barrack administration. On the big day, the regiment and the transport company would be drawn up on the square for inspection by the OC Western Command. In the afternoons, kit inspections were held, where each soldier and NCO had to lay out his entire kit on his bed.

During one inspection in 1955, when I was Orderly Officer, I happened to be up at the north-east corner of the barracks where I had a view along the rear of all the regimental billet blocks. To my astonishment, when HQ Battery had been inspected and the staff officers had moved on the 8th Battery building next door, I noticed two of my soldiers appear from the rear door carrying a bed on which was laid out a complete kit. As I watched with disbelief, they scuttled along the back of the building, past the 8th Battery and disappeared through the rear door of the 15th Battery billets. Clearly, an agreement had been reached with a desperate soldier in that battery to supply him with a perfect kit which he would pass off as his own! I did not interfere, as it was considered to be fair game to deceive or to put one over on the inspecting staff, but I often wondered if any money had changed hands.

On another Command inspection by Col Seán Collins-Powell, the heavens opened as the parade began. To his credit and to our dismay, he ignored the downpour, even when he had his arm raised in salute for the march past at the end of the parade. As we passed by, I pictured, with some satisfaction, the rain running down inside his sleeve and into his armpit, as it was in mine! He and his staff were taken into the officers' mess immediately afterwards where they were given civilian clothes by us living-in officers. The inspection staff continued as best they could in 'civvies', but the entire effort faltered after that, much to everybody's relief.

The Orderly Officer had responsibility for the security of the barracks or post, the personnel, routine and all activities that took place for a period of twenty-four hours. It was a duty that all junior officers had to carry out (the frequency depending on the number of officers available) and one that I did not particularly enjoy, because we were required to wear riding britches and leggings until after flag-down, a throw-back to the days of the mounted soldiers. The wearing of britches and leggings was a form of torture to me, because mine did not fit very well and severely restricted my ability to run. One of the duties was overseeing the raising and lowering of the flags. A guard, consisting of a corporal and four gunners, was mounted just before flag-down at sunset. From this guard a stickman was always selected who was the soldier adjudged by the Orderly Officer to have been the best turned-out of the four gunners on parade. He was then released from duty.

Pay day was a major event where all ranks from sergeant-major to the newest recruit had to appear to collect their pay in cash. The pay roll listed all the credits and debits for each soldier and contained a column on the right where the recipient had to sign. The pay rolls were made out manually in those days on a vast army form on which the soldiers of HQ Battery plus attachments were listed. Three copies had to be made out in pen and ink, using carbon sheets. It was a matter of great joy to Gnr Gander, the battery pay clerk, therefore, when a directive arrived to state that the Department of Defence was providing ballpoint pens to each unit to be used solely and exclusively for the compilation of the pay rolls. Needless to say, that restriction did not last very long and we all became equipped with these wondrous devices.

The pay roll was a huge and intricate document, in the old days of pounds, shillings and pence, and totting up was only for the experienced. Paying out in HQ Battery was a complex affair as so many soldiers were here, there or anywhere and would not be home until late or even the following day. To cater for additional visiting soldiers or for unexpected claims for allowances the Command Cashier always provided more money than was required. This meant that there was always a surplus to be lodged after payout on Fridays. When the payout was finished, the clerks and myself would take turns at the totals, and where we failed to agree, I had to send for my Battery Commander, Pat Kavanagh. Capt. Kavanagh had an astonishing flair for figures – he could do a tot-up at speed for perhaps forty names and would always be correct. Typically, we had five pages of pay rolls to be counted with perhaps thirty names or more on each page, with six or more columns to be counted (pounds, shillings and pence). After agreement was reached between those counting up the figures, I was able to depart for the bank with a happy heart to lodge the balance.

On Friday mornings, the four cheque-holding officers were driven down to the bank to collect the appropriate sums with an armed military policeman as escort. HQ Battery always had the largest payout, having the most soldiers and the longest serving NCOs and gunners. On one particular Friday, I was delivered of a very severe shock. When I returned to the battery office to commence the payout, it quickly became obvious that I was seriously short of cash. On checking, it amounted to £100, a huge sum in those days. Cpl Collins and Gnr Gander did a check, but there was no mistake, I was in big trouble. I phoned the bank, only to be informed that they would not be able to help me until after closing time at 15.00hrs.

I had to explain what the problem was and then to walk past the long line of soldiers waiting outside the office, whose expressions ranged from the shocked, to the suspicious, to the angry. It was, for the married men in particular, a serious problem, because it meant that they had to go home to their families for dinner without their eagerly awaited pay. At that time, I was the owner of an elderly Ford car, and I spent much of the lunch hour wondering how much I might get for it. Fortunately, there was a happy ending. The bank reported that they were in surplus by £100 pounds – a sum that I promptly collected and paid out to a very relieved soldiery. They were not half as relieved as I was though.

Another memorable incident connected with pay happened to me when I was in Athlone one Friday morning for some business connected with my job as Barrack Welfare Officer. The Barrack Welfare Officer was a kind of entertainments officer who organised film shows, concerts, competitions and dances for the ORs of the garrison. He kept the accounts and dealt with the Command Welfare Officer in Athlone. Whilst in Athlone, I received a telephone call from Mullingar. I was to collect a supplementary pay cheque from the Command Cashier and return to Mullingar as quickly as possible. My driver was Gnr Delaney, a lanky old soldier, and when I said we were in a hurry, he took me at my word. He was driving what we called a 'Bugchaser', a cut-back Ford saloon, one of hundreds that had been converted during the Emergency into a jeep-type all-purpose vehicle. In the Artillery Corps we used them as radio vehicles. Because it had a V-8 engine and was much lighter than the saloon it had been previously, it could travel like the wind. Gnr Delaney drove fast, reaching up to 70 miles per hour at times. The vehicle did not have doors or seat belts, indeed the passenger had nothing to hold on to except his cap, so it was a rather stressful experience for me. Fortunately, the road traffic was very light in those days and Gnr Delaney was an excellent driver, so we got the essential pay cheque to where it was needed in time. I could of course have ordered him to slow down, but I was too concerned about my image and what all the drivers would be saying about me afterwards!

During the winter of 1953–54, the regiment saw action in a rather unexpected way. The winter was an unusually wet one and the Shannon river burst its banks, flooding a wide tract of land above and below Athlone. Considerable hardship ensued, roads and bridges were damaged and the lives of some members of the farming population were in danger. The OC Western Command, Colonel Seán Collins-Powell, declared an emergency and ordered his units to carry out patrols using four-wheel-drive 3-ton trucks. These were the only vehicles capable of 'wading' through the deep waters of the flooded roads. Small patrol teams were formed and routes were allotted.

Each team was composed of a junior officer or senior NCO, a driver, a medical NCO and a private, while each truck was equipped with a Motorola radio, specially donated by that company as their contribution to the relief effort. Many residents had already been taken to Athlone for temporary accommodation and supplies were brought to those in need. The Red Cross was involved from the beginning but they did not have the vehicles to negotiate the flooded roads.

To my delight, I was called up after a week. My patrol beat lay to the south of Athlone on the eastern side of the river in the Ballinahoun area. While the waters had subsided somewhat by the time I got going, I was surprised by the extent of the flooding. I met with some of the unfortunate farmers and came to understand their many difficulties. As it was coming up to Christmas, the Red Cross provided special fare for those in need to reflect the season and we had the pleasant task of delivering some minor cheer to those who needed it badly. My team called on a daily basis to one elderly farmer whose small cottage had been flooded to a depth of about two feet. He had brought in a large quantity of stones to raise his bed above the water level. He did the same for the fire, which he kept going around the clock. He absolutely refused to let us take him into Athlone where he would have a damp-free bed, a warm shelter and plenty of company.

My tour of flood duty only lasted two weeks, but it was a welcome break from the routine of the barracks and allowed me the comfort of a pleasant room in the centrally heated mess in Athlone. It was deeply satisfying to have played even a small part in the operation while using one's training and equipment in a positive manner to assist members of the local community.

It was around the time of my return from Athlone that I nearly burned down the officers' mess in Columb Barracks. We did not have central heating in the mess in Mullingar, having to rely on open fires or electric fires to dispel the cold and the damp. One evening, before going down town, I had the electric fire switched on, casually pushing it back a little from its position near my bed. When I returned later that night, there was a small amount of smoke and a strong smell of scorching in the room. I quickly discovered why. In pushing back the fire, I had foolishly placed it immediately under my army greatcoat which was hanging on the wall overhead. Nearly the entire hem of the coat had been badly singed. Fortunately, the coat did not catch fire. The regiment had an excellent unit tailor, known to all as 'Stitch' Murray, an amiable old gunner, and he did a first-class job for me in making the greatcoat serviceable again. There was only one problem – the coat was now a knee-length coat at a time when by regulation it should have extended to well below the knee. For a long time, I remained in dread of inspections where I might have to parade in my 'shorty' greatcoat. It was not uncommon for an inspecting officer to demand that, following the morning parade, all ranks were to return in the afternoon wearing their greatcoats. Happily, that did not occur, but by coincidence, some years later, the permitted length of greatcoats was raised to knee level. I just happened to have been well ahead of the fashion!

In January 1954, I was nominated to undergo a Physical Training Instructors course at the Army School of Physical Culture (ASPC) in the Curragh Camp. The course ran from January to May. The ASPC was a branch of the General Training Depot in the Curragh and it was located in the large and unsuitable gymnasium (formerly a riding shed). Comdt 'Donie' McCormack, a cavalry officer, was the officer commanding and the other instructors were Capt. Joe O'Keefe and Lieut Mick McDonough. The senior NCO instructor was Company Sergeant Mickey Gray, a multiple boxing champion at army and civilian level. Capt. O'Keefe was a multiple army champion at the long and high jumps and pole vault, while Capt. McDonough had many army titles in field sports to his credit also.

The Physical Training Instructor's Course was very popular with the NCOs because it gave them an important lead into employment in civilian life after service, but us officers were not so impressed. The class consisted of three officers and sixteen young

NCOs drawn from units and formations across the Defence Forces. The three officers were Lieut Cathal O'Leary, a first-class and practising Dublin county footballer, Lieut Mick Tallon and myself. All of us were already qualified as PT leaders from previous courses, so the emphasis throughout the course was to turn us into instructors. During the next five months, the course of instruction covered all the field sports, including the pole vault, the high and long jumps, the hop, step and jump as well as the javelin, the discus and the shot. We also spent a lot of time in the gym doing groundwork, the pommel horse, the horizontal and parallel bars, as well as boxing.

The course, as was the custom, went to Glen Imaal for the final three weeks for general fitness training. Here we carried out all sorts of free fitness and endurance exercises. One such involved moving along the course of the Slaney, using our vaulting poles to cross and re-cross the river as we went. The river was quite small within the Glen, but we eventually arrived at a section where no member of the class succeeded in crossing it. As it happened, just then Capt. O'Keefe arrived to inspect the training, clad as he always was, in immaculate tracksuit, white shoes and a neat white polo-neck pullover. Somebody asked him to show us how to vault across such a minor obstacle and, to our surprise, he agreed – he was the Defence Forces champion after all.

He carefully checked the take-off point, the run up line and the landing point and then confidently commenced his run. He vaulted faultlessly and got his feet on the far bank, but no further. He was left holding onto the upright pole in the middle of the river. He was stalled – he could not go forwards or backwards. He slowly slid down the pole and splashed into the deeper part of the water, quickly standing up with a sheepish grin on his face. By then we were howling with laughter, but we applauded him as he dragged himself out and left for Coolmoney House to change. He took the whole affair in the best of good humour.

It was a tradition that all PT courses ended with a quick climb up to the top of Lugnaquilla, Ireland's third highest mountain. Unfortunately, on this occasion, the climb on 5 May ended in tragedy. Although it was raining and the upper half of the mountain was covered with cloud, we voted to go ahead anyway. All went well until we got into the cloud, where we found ourselves in a raging snowstorm. On a very steep section near the top, we were moving in single file when I happened to look up and I saw somebody fall over. Rushing over to the figure, I recognised Cpl J. Mulvaney, a member of the 2nd Battalion in Dublin, and discovered that he was unconscious. Despite the howling wind, I managed to get those ahead of us to stop and turn back. When Comdt McCormack arrived, he aborted the climb and ordered us all to descend, sending some ahead to raise the alarm. We took turns to carry Mulvaney, but it was very difficult and slow work. Eventually we arrived at the foot of Camera Hill where a rescue group with an ambulance was waiting for us. Mulvaney was placed in the ambulance and driven to the Military Hospital in the Curragh. Sadly, we were informed later that evening that he was dead on arrival at hospital, which destroyed any of the happy feelings we might have had as we approached the end of the course. Just before the course ended, a number of instructors and students climbed back up the mountain and placed a wooden cross at roughly the spot where the Corporal had collapsed.

On return to the IVth Regiment after the course, I was required to conduct PT training for the ORs, something they heartily detested and would go to a lot of trouble to avoid! My assistant was Sgt Tom Muldoon, a qualified PT leader and a lovely old gent who had a genuine interest in PT and sports.

Life continued on as usual for some time. However, the following year, saw me involved in a number of unusual experiences. The first of these was due to the very poor summer, which left the harvest in grave danger of being totally lost. The farmers appealed to the government for assistance and the army was tasked to give whatever assistance was possible.

My first task was to assist with a threshing operation at a farm some twenty miles south of Mullingar. Travelling in a six-wheeler Morris, I brought a group of six soldiers to the site of the threshing. The farmer was using a large threshing machine driven by an endless belt coupled to a small tractor. The soldiers were mainly employed in forking up the sheaves of wheat to those on top who fed it into the machine, while others helped in carrying the sacks of grain to the barn.

On another mission, the soldiers were picking potatoes, a muddy and back-breaking chore. I at least enjoyed myself as I had landed the task of driving the tractor to deliver the sacks of potatoes to the barn. We had again travelled to the farm in a Morris six-wheeler which broke its fan belt just as we arrived. I sent a message to the barracks requesting a mechanic and a new belt. Help arrived in a Willys Jeep, which in turn broke down, so I had to send once more for assistance. We eventually arrived back to barracks about 20.00hrs in an embarrassing threesome – a Quod gun-towing vehicle towing a Morris six-wheeler towing a Willys Jeep. I was glad it was dark!

Also in 1955, a military pilgrimage to the Marian shrine in Knock, County Mayo, was organised by the head chaplain to the forces. In the case of the garrison of Columb Barracks, we set off by train from the local station, travelling non-stop to Knock. I found myself stuck with about five other officers, of whom the senior was Comdt Denis O'Callaghan, OC 4th Field Company, Supply and Transport. Denis was a thorough gentleman and had been a great hurler in his day, but he was also extremely religious. Being the senior officer in the carriage, he kept the rosaries going as we rattled across the country to Knock.

It was a great relief when we de-trained at Knock. To my surprise, the band of the Western Command under the baton of

Lieut Jim Magee was waiting to play for us all the way from the station to the shrine. As we marched along, the long rows of stall-holders, who clearly had been surprised by our arrival – it was mid-week – threw open their tin-roofed shacks in the hope of selling us some souvenirs. They did not realise that soldiers were unable to drop out of the parade and browse through their wares, or because of very poor pay rates, had little to spare for such items. Of the service I can remember little, but I did ensure that I was not in the same carriage as Denis O'Callaghan on the return journey to Mullingar that evening!

These experiences may have been unusual, but the next challenge was of a more serious military nature. When the IRA border campaign, as it was called in the papers, began in 1956, I did not pay much attention. However, one afternoon in January 1957, about 16.00hrs, an order was issued by the adjutant to close the gates and confine all members of the garrison to barracks. This was extremely unusual – even the married personnel could not go home to their evening meals with their families.

I was sent for by the CO, Lt-Col Jimmy Dolan, who informed me that I was to take a platoon of forty soldiers to Donegal for duty on the border and that we would be away for up to three months. We would be using Rockhill House as a base. I was allotted six Landrovers and a 3-ton truck, and we spent the night drawing personal weapons, ammunition and equipment. We were also issued with a substantial quantity of entrenching tools, sandbags, barbed wire and fuel in jerrycans, as well as some spare parts for the vehicles.

Rockhill House, on the outskirts of Letterkenny, had been an occupied post during the war years. Since 1945, it had been the HQ of the local FCA battalion, at that time commanded by an Artillery officer, Comdt John L. O'Brien. Further north from Letterkenny, on the eastern side of Lough Swilly, lay Fort Dunree, a Coast Artillery fort. I had visited Dunree on a number of occasions previously for administration purposes. Thus I was reasonably familiar with the area even though I had never seen Rockhill House before.

There was a great emphasis on security – no word of the re-occupation of Rockhill House was to be leaked as it was feared that the IRA might attempt to burn it or attack Finner Camp, or both, to prevent us from using either facility. We departed for Donegal at 04.00hrs next morning, calling for a meal and to refuel at Finner Camp, outside Bundoran. Finner Camp at that time was essentially a summer camp for the FCA units of the Western Command, run by Company Quartermaster Sergeant Jim Grant and Private 'Dixie' Bowe. We continued on and arrived at Rockhill House outside Letterkenny without any problems. The company commander was Capt. Dermot Byrne and he brought two more platoons from the 1st Battalion, Galway, to form a composite infantry company. Our task was to provide security to An Gárda Síochána in dealing with the IRA campaign in County Donegal.

The residents of Letterkenny gave us a warm reception. They were delighted to see us and for a while soldiers in uniform were given free entry into cinemas and dance halls. The arrival of a company of 130 soldiers was a great bonus for the businesses, bars, cinemas and dancehalls in the town, not forgetting the demands for petrol, fresh food and so on.

Our area of operations was large, covering the entire border from Lough Swilly down to the River Erne at Ballyshannon. We had no authority to set up road-blocks on our own or to arrest anyone – we were there strictly in the role of 'aid to the civil power'. Duties were heavy, with demands from the Gardaí for support almost on a nightly basis, while the post itself also had to be protected. While most of the escorts were humdrum affairs, there were occasional moments of excitement. On one occasion a report had come to Gardaí that there could be IRA men in a schoolhouse in a certain location. I tactically arranged my group while an unfortunate young Garda was hoisted up to climb in through an open window of the schoolhouse. There was nobody inside of course and we were all disappointed.

On another occasion we rushed down to Ballyshannon, as there had been a threat that the ESB generating station at Kathleen Falls, located up river from the town, would be blown up. I walked across the top of the dam with some Gardaí while they searched for explosives, but nothing was found.

One morning, having just completed a twenty-four-hour duty, I was getting into bed when a shot rang out, followed by the sounds of shouting and the noise of vehicles being moved. I dressed in a hurry and when I arrived down to the guard-room, I was told that there had been an accident. One of my corporals, Johnny Farrell, had been shot and taken to the local hospital. He had been standing in the doorway of the guard-room watching the off-going guard being stood down. In unloading his submachine gun, the corporal of that guard accidentally fired off one 9mm round. By the most freakish of accidents, the round struck the tarmac to his right, ricocheted up into a large tree near the front of the guard-room, changed direction a second time and struck Farrell in the chest.

I quickly went to see him in the local hospital and he seemed happy enough, able to talk and so on. But the bullet had lodged behind his chest bone and the local hospital staff did not have the facilities to deal with it. The doctors wanted to send him to Altnagelvin Hospital in Derry, where sadly, they were only too familiar with gunshot wounds. Instead Corporal Farrell was removed to Dublin by ambulance (the Defence Forces did not have any helicopters then) and tragically he died some three weeks later.

Out of the blue, in early March I was informed that I was to undergo an 81mm Mortar Instructor Course at the Military College. Lieut Liam Donnelly arrived from Mullingar to relieve me at Rockhill House. It was an enjoyable course during which we did some firing in Glen Imaal. On completion of the course I returned to Columb Barracks, where I discovered that we had a new Transport Officer. He was Capt. Gerry Kenny, an elderly captain, known to all as 'Adler' Kenny because of his love for Adler cars. He had no less than three beautiful cars, all of the same model, in a shed at the rear of the mess, where he spent his spare time repairing and painting them. They were in excellent condition and he eventually sold one to Lieut Noel Clancy who needed a car to get him to Dublin for weekends. It should be said that all three cars were painted in the same colour, carried the same number plates, but only one was taxed and insured. In carrying out a test run in the car he was hoping to buy, Noel was driving along the main street in Mullingar, when to his horror, he passed Gerry Kenny going in the other direction in an identical Adler!

Gerry was a lovable but grumpy eccentric. At a mess meeting where, as the mess secretary, he was recording the minutes, a major debate had taken place over samples of wallpaper to be used in re-decorating the anteroom. During the argument, one officer suggested that a particular sample of wallpaper was what you might expect to see in the bedroom of a 'lady of the night'. Another officer interjected with something rude. The following month, as the minutes of the previous meeting were read, Gerry said, without batting an eye, 'at which remark Lieut R— replied, "Well f— me, how would you know?"' There was a huge burst of laughter but the CO got very upset and ordered him to delete the offending comment immediately. Shortly after, Capt. Kenny was replaced as mess secretary!

During my years in Mullingar, three major exercises were held, in two of which I was involved. One was called 'Ex Fuchsia', an outright disaster of an exercise from the outset. Ex Fuchsia was intended to get the soldiers out of barracks and their routine existence, and offer some fitness training and experience in logistics. It involved an under-strength battalion with a field battery in support. The weather quickly developed monsoon-like patterns and the entire exercise was carried out under conditions of considerable discomfort. To make things worse, I developed some sort of bug and when taking some of Comdt Pat Kennedy's secret 'mist' at the medical tent in a field near Ballinasloe, I collapsed and was sent immediately to the Military Hospital in Athlone. I recovered in a day or two, enjoying myself hugely as I was the only patient in the officers' ward.

A much better exercise was 'Ex Youghal', held in July 1956. The Eastern, Western and Southern Commands were each required to provide a battalion to the exercise. The Western Command at that time possessed only two infantry battalions, each of which provided a marching company. The IVth Regiment was required to provide a marching company to make up the numbers, while also providing a troop of heavy mortars. While it was a much larger exercise, the aims were similar to 'Ex Fuchsia' and perhaps also intended to emulate in a very small way the largest military manoeuvres ever carried out by the Defence Forces back in 1942.

Training for this exercise began many weeks beforehand and a detailed log was kept of mileage marched by each person involved. I covered seventy-four miles in the many practice marches, all of which took place on the back roads in the vicinity of Mullingar. Capt. Tom Maher was our company commander and although not exactly in the first flush of youth, he surprised us all by how well he stood up to the challenge. Our battalion finally gathered under canvas in Athlone and the following day we were transported to the village of Golden in Tipperary. There we were inspected by Lt-Col Johnny MacEoin, my former Cadet Master, who was the Commander of the composite unit.

Each day of the exercise we marched about fourteen miles, taking a break every hour, after which a different company would take the lead. The large administrative rear party and the mortar troop, under the command of Capt. Joe Higgins, would drive past our column during the morning and when we had reached our destination in the evenings, the tents were already set up, the footbaths containing crystals of potassium permanganate were prepared (for those with blisters) and the dinner was nearly ready.

From Golden, our company marched to Cahir and camped in the grounds of Cahir castle. The following day we marched into the mountains, spending about eight hours in a damp field high in the 'Gap' as it was called, close to the monastery at Mount Mellary. There we had a break of half a day while the entire battalion was given – one company at a time – a conducted tour of the monastery. That evening, we left for a night march down hill through Campfire where we crossed the River Blackwater, entering our campsite in darkness. The following day we marched into Youghal, ending up in a huge field on the Cork road. The battalions from the other Commands arrived during that same day.

To my delight I was to be in charge of swimming parades on the nearby beach, where I spent a lot of time as the troops were rotated through for a much-needed wash. Earlier, I had been nominated as the battalion photographer by our CO and was given the use of the Western Command Welfare 16mm camera and a supply of film. I used the camera as much as I could and managed to capture the military parade by the composite brigade that was held the following day through the centre of Youghal. After the exercise concluded I returned the camera and film to the Command Welfare Officer in Athlone. I have since lost track of that film and can only hope that it is in protective custody somewhere.

My time in Mullingar was running out. Every artillery unit had occasional visits from the Director of Artillery. While it did not inspire a reaction comparable to the threat of a Command inspection, it was nevertheless a time of tension for some. One of the purposes of his visit always related to officers and their possible transfers to other stations as part of their career development. This seriously worried the married officers. They had invested in houses in the town and had children attending the local schools and were therefore in fear of a possible relocation with all that entailed.

Being a single officer, I did not have such worries. However, when my transfer to the Artillery School in Kildare was announced in 1957 after one such visit, it still came as a shock. While I felt that the life of an instructor in gunnery might have its own attractions, I was genuinely sorry to leave the IVth Regiment, all the NCOs and soldiers that I had come to know and like, and to leave my friends in the musical society, the swimming club and the tennis club.

It is often said that your first station is the one that you are never likely to forget, the post that makes the most impression on you. I believe that this was certainly the truth for me. I have always retained a great affection for Columb Barracks and a very special place in my memory for an excellent unit, filled with so many close friends.

Chapter 5

AN INSTRUCTOR IN GUNNERY

My transfer, in September 1957, from the active and varied life I had been living as a happy member of the IVth Regiment was a surprise, but Magee Barracks was a modern, attractive station, familiar to me since undergoing my Young Officer's Course.

I quickly settled into the normal regimental duties at Magee Barracks – Orderly Officer, member of mess audits, annual range practices with the ORs of the barracks – all activities I was quite familiar with from Columb Barracks. The School Commandant was Comdt Bill Rea, a man for whom I quickly developed a great respect and affection. My main initial involvement at the school was in the training of young soldiers who had been nominated by their units as potential non-commissioned officers. Not every corps of the army trained their own NCOs, but the Artillery Corps was big enough and was sufficiently technical to warrant it. I became an assistant to my former battery commander, Capt. Pat Kavanagh (who had also been transferred from Columb Barracks), in the running of my first PNCO course.

On completion of one such course, I was given charge of later courses with the assistance of other officers such as Lieuts Jim Murphy and Brian O'Connor. Throughout this training, I was very conscious of my responsibility for turning out competent corporals and aware of the foundation it could give them for progress in their careers. While the syllabus of training was fairly specific as to what must be done, there was a fair amount of leeway permitted as to what extra training could be slipped in, time permitting.

In 1959, a number of IRA prisoners escaped from the Detention Camp in the Curragh. The alarm was sounded in Magee Barracks and the existing PNCO course was utilised to the full. Lt-Col Arthur Dalton, OC 1st Anti-Aircraft Regiment, in the absence of the Barrack OC, Lt-Col Maurice McCarthy, took charge and directed operations. As we had only one ancient barrack truck available on the day, driven by Gnr Brabazon, officers were detailed to use their own private cars to carry armed soldiers to the various crossroads in the Magee Barracks sector of the cordon around the Curragh Camp. We failed to capture the escapees, but it was a useful exercise for all involved, and while it disrupted the training, the exercise only lasted about thirty-six hours.

Apart from the training courses and the normal barrack security duties, I was involved as often as possible in the live firing exercises that took place in Glen Imaal. In those days, Glen Imaal was a beautiful, but fairly empty place where the problem of hill walkers and tourists had not become the issue that it is today. However, on one occasion, just after the range officer had declared the range to be free, and firing was about to commence, somebody noticed a small blue tent half hidden in the scrub not too far from the intended target area. The range officer was dispatched to eject them as quickly as possible. The entire party at the OP were entertained by the sight of a young man and a young woman scrambling to get themselves dressed, to collapse their tent and to get themselves out of the range and out of sight as quickly as possible. The comments at the OP were rich, but unrecorded!

As well as tourists there were other occupants of the Glen whose safety had to be ensured. The Chief Herd of the Glen, in those days old Tom Keogh, was required to round up all his sheep and place them in a safe corner of the Glen before exercises were due to start. The Head Forester, if he had workers clearing or planting trees in or close to the range boundary, was also required to withdraw all his workers to a safe location for the duration of the firing practices.

There is an amusing story told about Tom Keogh when he was working up near the northern end of the range in the forest. A group of Fianna Éireann boy scouts appeared in the Glen, marching up over Leitrim Hill, clearly heading for the crest of Table Mountain. Tom Keogh told them to be careful, as they might wander into the artillery danger area.

'We are not afraid of the f—g Free State artillery, we will do what we like.'

'If you get a shell up your arse, it won't matter who fired it,' Tom replied.

Not surprisingly, the corps was going through a major transformation at this time, mainly as a result of the development of new weapons and tactics during the early days of the Cold War. One of the earliest changes in corps practice related to the use of anti-tank artillery. All live firing anti-tank practices were conducted in Glen Imaal where a towed target facility was available. Every detachment in a battery was tested on firing at a moving target. The target, a large wood and canvas frame on which was depicted the outline of a tank, was mounted on a trolley running on rails. Firing over open sights at a point-blank range of about 200m, each detachment was expected to get off up to three or four rounds during the short time it took for the target to move across its front. It was a noisy, exciting practice, the results were clearly visible to the crews and it generated a great rivalry between detachments.

For control purposes, an officer or an NCO was placed in the engine house, where a civilian member of the Board of Works staff from Coolmoney Camp operated the engine that towed the target. The commands were sent by field phone to the engine house, to advance or retire the target or to vary the speed as required. The rounds (projectiles) used were called 'plugged shrapnel', and they passed through the canvas target and broke up with great violence, rather than exploded, on the sloping ground to the rear.

I was present on the gun line at the firing point on one occasion when there was a lull in firing. A relative silence descended, probably while the target was being replaced, when a very odd event took place. A rabbit appeared from under a furze bush very close to the gun on the left of the line. A corporal from the 1st Regiment spotted him and in one clean movement, he swept his helmet off and threw it 'frisbie fashion' at the rabbit, killing it instantly. This act was greeted with loud applause from the assembled gunners.

Another type of practice that put a lot of pressure on the NCO in charge was called a 'Single Gun Engagement'. This procedure arose from the need of a supported infantry unit for a heavy weapon to destroy a difficult strongpoint or perhaps to engage a sniper firing from a house or bunker. The support battery would send forward a reinforced detachment (typically a double crew) to a designated rendezvous in response to a request. There the target would be pointed out to them. The No. 1 in the team then had to do a reconnaissance and to make out his plan of how best to carry out the engagement. He would select the best firing position from which to engage the target and then select the most suitable route in and out. All actions were to be carried out in the shortest possible time before the enemy could react to his presence.

The entire engagement was performed at a breakneck pace. Five or six rounds were typically fired with the No. 1 having to make his own adjustments by direct observation until he struck the target. Once the target was struck, the detachment hastily withdrew into concealment. It was an exciting exercise, it presented a great challenge to the NCO in charge, as he was required to show his skills in a very different way to the normal routine, and it did wonders for his confidence as a No. 1.

However, like the anti-tank practices described earlier, this form of firing came to an end with the emergence of specialised anti-tank weapons and the many forms of shoulder-fired bazookas, recoilless rifles and wire-guided rockets. These highly effective and mostly portable weapons enable the average infantry soldier to engage an armoured vehicle or a strongpoint without having to send back to his support battery for assistance.

The 'Greyhound Battery'

In 1959, following a re-organisation of the Defence Forces, three new FCA field artillery regiments were formed and one of them, the 6th Regiment, was based at Magee Barracks. Comdt Ivor Noone became the CO of the new unit, Capt. Des Duff was the Administrative Officer while Lieuts Johnny Hall, Mick McMahon and myself were designated as the Training Officers to the three batteries. The batteries had previously existed as infantry battalions located in Newbridge, Naas and Edenderry, respectively. They were now to be designated as the 5th and 6th Field Batteries and the 11th Heavy Mortar Battery. To my delight I was appointed as the Training Officer to the 11th Battery based in Edenderry. However, due to officer shortages, I was still required to perform these new duties while continuing to serve as an instructor in gunnery in the Artillery School.

The proximity of Magee Barracks to Edenderry was a huge advantage to the new regiment, as they could make use of the excellent facilities of the Artillery School accommodation for weekend training camps. In the 11th Battery, Sgt Joe Flanagan was the senior training NCO, Battery Quartermaster Sergeant Handibode was responsible for the administration and the Training Corporals were Jack Keogh and Alec Kieran. Gnr Tommy Lawrence was the only regular driver allocated to the battery and he drove the battery minibus.

A number of soldiers in some of the smaller training centres did not like the change and left the FCA. This was not a disaster because artillery training requires a certain minimum number of gunners to be viable. Using the battery minibus, we started to collect personnel from outlying centres to bring them into the old workhouse in Edenderry for collective training. The building was large and quite dilapidated. However, it did provide some large rooms, an outside training field and lecture rooms as well as offices and storerooms.

The battery commander was Comdt Pat Buckley, a school-teacher, while his second-in-command was another teacher, Capt. Johnny Keane. What impressed me at an early stage was just how well and how eagerly they, and all the other officers and senior NCOs, rose to the challenge. The discipline and the teamwork required them to function in what was for them a very new environment, entirely different to their previous infantry experiences.

While I was working with the new 11th Battery, Colonel Cyril Mattimoe, the Director of Artillery, who lived in Kildare, told me one day that when he was a young captain during the Emergency, the corps introduced a new inter-battery competition that had given rise to intense rivalry. He explained that when he was the BC of the old 11th Battery, in order to raise the morale and to introduce an air of urgency to everything they did, he had set up a novel rule. No individual member of the 11th Battery, or no group, was permitted to walk or march when in public view, they always had to move at the double (i.e. to run). As no other artillery unit behaved like this, other soldiers started to laugh at them, mocking their habits and suggesting that they were like greyhounds. Thus they quickly became known as the 'Greyhound Battery' and the morale of the battery soared. Capt. Mattimoe's 11th Battery won the Inter-Battery Shield two years in a row, a truly impressive feat as the rivalry was intense in those times.

When I heard this story, I decided that the modern 11th would also be known as the 'Greyhound Battery'. I persuaded our 'Tiffy' (artificer) to paint a running greyhound on the mudguard of every mortar and every equipment box. In the manner of soldiers everywhere, the men quickly entered into the spirit of the title, which has remained to this day.

A temporary and incomplete training manual was in existence at this time, but following the Planning and Research 1 (PR1) Reorganisation in 1959, a board of officers was established by the Director of Artillery to produce a proper training manual for the 120mm mortar. PR1 was better known to all by its unofficial title of 'Integration' and was a re-organisation of the forces. As a result, the three regular regiments, 1st, 2nd and 4th (the Roman numerals had been dropped by this time), became larger and even more effective, combining as they did the very best of the regular and reserve personnel.

The first board was composed of Lt Col Noone and myself from the school, and Capt. Tom Boyle from IVth Regiment. Although the board commenced work in a great burst of enthusiasm, it quickly stalled as a result of the dispersal of the members through frequent transfers and retirements. One aspect that particularly pleased me about my involvement in assembling this manual was that I had the opportunity of working with Comdt John Woods and technical members of the Air Corps at Baldonnel in developing a technique for the air-lifting of mortars into and out of firing positions. The Alouette helicopters available at the time were just about able to cope with the weight of the weapon and a small amount of ammunition or part of the mortar crew. On 28

June 1967, a demonstration of the new technique was provided for a large audience in Glen Imaal, where a troop of four mortars and their crews, provided by the 19th Heavy Mortar Battery, FCA, were lifted into a firing position, using two helicopters. All went well even though one mortar suffered a minor mishap. The exercise continued with only three mortars, however, and was adjudged to have been a great success.

Eventually the board activities ground to a complete halt, but a new board was appointed some years later and again I was a member. However, it too collapsed and eventually I finished the job myself when in McKee Barracks with the help of the FCA officers and NCOs of the new 7th Regiment. The final printing of the manual was facilitated by the arrival of a modern printing press in Defence Forces HQ. With the expertise of the staff there, the manual on the 120mm Mortar – T.R.367 – was finally produced.

As well as the lack of an adequate manual, another problem arose during my time with the 'Greyhound Battery' that caused huge problems for the mortar crews and great anger in me. A decision was taken to fire 81mm mortar ammunition from the 120mm barrel. The Ordnance Corps manufactured a set of spacer rings that enabled the smaller 81mm barrel to be inserted into the 120mm barrel. The 81mm barrel rested on a large wooden spacer block and when fired, the entire fitting jumped within the larger barrel in an alarming manner. If a misfire occurred – a frequent feature of the 81mm ammunition at the time – the entire structure had to be dismantled. This led to long delays in the firing practices, while also creating a considerable safety hazard for the crew, as the 81mm round was still lodged within the barrel. I protested long and loudly that this ruined many of our early shoots and had a malign influence on the confidence of the gunners in dealing with misfires. This attempt at a sub-calibre arrangement for the 120mm was quietly shelved a year or two later much to everybody's relief.

In the early 1960s a recruiting drive for the army was instituted and I was designated as the Magee Barracks recruiting officer. It was a very low-key affair with a small budget, mainly conducted through the local newspapers. I was permitted to hire a caravan to be placed in selected towns and villages to get closer to our targets, the young men of the communities. On one occasion I found myself with a small team, sitting in a caravan on the main street in Castlecomer. We had placed a number of billboards around the caravan displaying pictures of soldiers and weapons. I had sent the team around the town earlier to visit shops and the pubs to publicise our presence. We were doing very little business and it was getting near 17.00hrs on a cold and miserable evening. I kept delaying our departure for Kildare for as long as possible – I still held some hope of success. We were all inside with the gas heater on full blast trying to keep warm when the door opened and a woman put her head in and said, 'When will the chips be ready?' We were gone in five minutes!

Throughout the 1950s and 1960s large-scale camps were frequently held at Glen Imaal. In those years FCA units were called up for two weeks' annual training. This gave them the opportunity to practise with the regular units while in Glen Imaal. As many as 600–800 gunners would occupy Coolmoney Camp, and the school officers took advantage of this situation and devised a whole series of large-scale exercises. A typical exercise would have a slimmed-down regiment (comprising three batteries, a total of perhaps 250 gunners) drawn up in the grounds of Coolmoney Camp at 06.00hrs. The regimental commander would send his regiment out of the Glen on a long and looping tactical move. His unit would then come back into the Glen by afternoon on different routes. By late afternoon, firing would then normally commence in accordance with a prepared fire plan.

I have a vivid memory of one such exercise. As a junior officer I was sitting in the back of a Command Post Landrover listening to the radio traffic and watching the convoys as we were heading back into the firing range from the south. Coming into the Glen over Ballinabarney Gap, I was looking at a scene that could easily have come from the Second World War. I was able to see long lines of vehicles and guns travelling in convoy on two parallel unsurfaced roads, stretched away into the valley below, leaving plumes of dust hanging in the air behind them as they moved. On arrival into our designated firing position, in this case at Brennan's Farm, the tension and the pace quickened as each Command Post officer struggled to have his battery ready for the time to open fire, as laid down by the School. The vehicles had to be placed and hidden in the 'wagon lines' (this term was a hang-over from the days when the regiment was a horse-drawn unit).

One of the favourite requirements of the School was that the opening engagement of a fire plan would be on a time on target basis. Because of the mix of mortars, guns and howitzers and because of their dispersal across the Glen, different batteries must open fire at different times in order to hit their targets at the same designated moment. The mortars would fire first as they have quite a long time of flight compared to most of the other weapons. Then the howitzers joined in, followed by the 25pdrs, then the 18pdrs and finally the 75mm guns, as these last two have the highest velocities and thus the shortest times of flight.

Such large-scale firing practices were most satisfying and clearly demonstrated the levels of skill achieved by the combination of the regular and the FCA personnel of the Artillery Corps, proof positive of the success of PR1.

In late November 1960, I was taking my lunch in the officers' mess, Magee Barracks, Kildare, when my CO, Comdt Ivor Noone, walked up to me and clapped me on the shoulder. 'Congratulations, Mick,' he said, 'you are going to the Congo – and so am I.'

That evening I was delighted to be told that Capt. Shane O'Connor, my close friend and diving buddy, and for whom I had been best man when he married, had also been chosen. He was to be the Battalion Ordnance Officer. I was to become the Platoon Commander of No. 1 Platoon, A Company, of the yet to be formed 34th Irish Battalion. However, the challenge did not bother me, as like all commissioned officers, the two-year course of training we received at the Cadet School was designed, first and foremost, to make infantry platoon leaders of us.

Chapter 6

ONUC KATANGA – KAMINA

In 1960 the Congo erupted into chaos. The Belgian administration withdrew in disorder and anarchy raged across the country. The United Nations made an appeal for an international military force to intervene rapidly in order to save lives and to stop the disintegration of the country. The Belgian Congo, a vast country, was centrally located on the continent at a time when the Cold War was threatening to spread across Africa. In July 1960 the situation deteriorated when the province of Katanga seceded from the newly independent Republic of Congo. The stability of Africa generally, and the Congo in particular, was considered crucial to the world at large because the flow from there of copper and many other minerals was essential to the heavy industries of the Western world. The decision of the Irish government in 1960 to send two battalions to the UN mission in the former Belgian Congo took both the country and the Defence Forces by storm. Thus began a period of great excitement as overseas service for ORs had never arisen before. Like the great majority of officers, I immediately volunteered. The topic dominated the newspapers and radio (RTÉ television had not yet arrived) and there was no shortage of volunteers.

KAMINA

The US Air Force Globemaster, the main transport plane of the US Air Force, was an impressive but elderly beast. The greater part of the floor space was taken up by the armoured car that was precariously perched at the top of the ramp, held in place both by its brakes and a multitude of chains and straps.

Capt. Bill Manahan was the commander for Chalk 5 with myself and Lieut Des English – platoon commander, support platoon A Company – the other officers on board. The term 'chalk' came initially from the USAF method of designating a flight by using a piece of chalk to allocate a number to everything related to that particular flight. It helped to reduce the natural confusion that takes place at such times. My platoon (see Appendix A) and a portion of the support platoon with some cavalry troopers comprised a total of eighty bodies on board. We each carried personal weapons and ammunition, and a small bag containing personal toiletries and a change of underwear. Before boarding each soldier had been given a plastic bag containing fruit and sandwiches for consumption during the flight.

Following the closure of the cargo doors, each engine was started, one at a time. As we taxied to the end of the runway the entire aircraft swayed, the undercarriage thumped and when the brakes were applied, they squealed noisily in the huge interior. After a pause, the engines roared and the brakes were released for the long slow take-off. The crew at least had faith in what they were doing, but this slow process was stressful for all of us, none of whom had been in such a situation before. When we finally staggered into the air, the collective release of breath in the cabin must surely have been heard up on the flight deck.

As we crossed southern England and flew over Paris, I was lucky to get a beautiful view of the Eiffel Tower and the Champs Elyseé as the aircraft turned south heading for Libya. Tiredness finally made me lie down on the ramp with my head on my bag, where my thoughts turned back to the exciting events of the last six weeks.

The media interest in our 34th Battalion was even more pronounced than it otherwise might have been because of the Niemba ambush on 8 November 1960. A patrol from the 33rd Irish Battalion was ambushed near Niemba in north-east Katanga, and nine of the eleven soldiers, including the platoon commander, Lieutenant Kevin Gleeson, were killed.

In spite of the huge outcry over this ambush, and the subsequent State funeral through Dublin, there was no question of a drop in volunteers for service in the Congo. If anything, it helped to raise the level of interest in the mission.

Both the 32nd and the 33rd Battalions had paraded through the city of Dublin prior to departure and were cheered on by very large and enthusiastic crowds of well-wishers – a scene not witnessed since the days of British rule. Suddenly, and very noticeably, the attitude of the cynics and others who for their own reasons felt that having an army was a complete waste of taxpayer's money, changed to reluctant admiration if not downright envy. For reasons best known to the General Staff, our battalion, the 34th, did not parade in public prior to departure, a matter of disappointment to some, although not to me, as I had participated in a number of Easter military parades in the past.

I reported to Collins Barracks, Dublin, on Friday 2 December and was delighted to find out that my own Training Sergeant, Joe Flanagan, from the 11th Battery, was to be my platoon sergeant. The platoon was very much a mixed bag. Apart from having an Artillery commander and sergeant, we had a corporal and five troopers from Cavalry and one lone gunner. In addition, three of my six corporals were still finishing their potential NCO course in the Eastern Command training depot. They would not be reporting to me for another few weeks. This meant that they would be inexperienced in their new ranks, not a very consoling thought. Finally, no less than seven of the privates/troopers were still at two-star level, which meant they were not even fully trained. All this was an indicator of the strain on the manpower resources at home in attempting to support what was the equivalent of an infantry brigade – three battalions totalling approximately 2,000 men – the bulk of whom were briefly concentrated at Kamina during the weeks of the rotation in January 1961.

As a result of the experiences of 32nd and 33rd Battalion personnel, and particularly after the Niemba ambush, all personnel in the platoons were armed with the Gustaf submachine guns. The standard rifle then on issue was the Second World War Lee-Enfield .303 No. 4, Mk 2 – a single shot bolt-action rifle, much beloved of those interested in shooting competitions. Its replacement with the Gustaf ensured that, should another ambush situation arise, the firepower of a platoon would be vastly greater, albeit at the cost of accuracy on targets at distances of more than 100m. We did retain three of the .303 rifles, as they were necessary to launch our only anti-tank weapon, the Energa anti-tank grenade.

The battalion was composed of a headquarters, HQ Company, three infantry companies and a particularly important feature, an armoured car group. This was a new and valuable innovation, not made available to our predecessors. The vehicles were elderly and each was armed only with a single turret-mounted medium machine gun. Despite the lack of 4x4 drive, poor engine power, poor armour and inadequate weapons, it is fair to say that in the fighting that ensued later on, they more than earned their keep. The surviving armoured cars were eventually handed over to the Armée National Congolaise when the mission was wound down.

However, there had to be a downside to this new organisation – the addition of the armoured car group was provided at the expense of the numbers in the infantry platoons, as a result of which each platoon comprised a total of only twenty-eight soldiers. This was – in my opinion – dangerously below the usual platoon level of thirty-nine.

The battalion commander was Lt-Col Eugene O'Neill, and the second-in-command was Comdt Jack McGuirk, both infantry officers. My company commander was Comdt Ned Vaughan and the second-in-command was Capt. Bertie Murphy, neither of whom I had met before. The company sergeant, the most senior NCO in the company, was Christy Walsh from the 2nd Anti-Aircraft Battery, a very fine NCO who fully lived up to his excellent reputation.

Preparations continued apace. On 20 December our company was brought to Kilbride ranges for battle inoculation firing practices, but these had to be cancelled because of three inches of snow! We received a lecture from the battalion commander in which he made a historical link with the Fianna of long ago. He required us to adopt the battle cry or challenge of the Fianna, 'faire faire' – the word 'faire' meant 'beware or be alert' – and the reply was 'faire hoy'. It was a very interesting connection that he made between the old and the modern armies, and it was adopted with a certain amount of embarrassment by his soldiers, as Irish soldiers are not usually required to respond to slogans or calls from their superiors.

Normally there would be a wealth of information and recommendations flowing from the experiences of our predecessors, but in this case these were very sparse. Before our departure only a few individuals had returned to Ireland from the other battalions, because of sickness or injury. We were, however, issued with a very useful little booklet giving us the basics of Swahili, the most widely used language of the region.

Officers were advised to go to an outdoor sports and camping shop called Milletts in Dublin's Mary Street to purchase 'tropical' kit – khaki slacks, shorts and shirts. These had to be paid for out of our own pockets, as base stores in Clancy Barracks could not provide such items. Like the two previous battalions, we had to travel in our heavy home uniforms, garments uniquely unsuitable for the heat of Africa. The officers travelled in their No. 1 superfine uniforms, peaked caps, Sam Browne belts and brown shoes, complete with submachine gun and ammunition pouches draped across their shoulders. To be fair to the UN, an ample supply of very welcome lightweight uniforms and headgear awaited us in Kamina and by the end of the second day there we were fully kitted out.

Another concern was that while contact between Dublin and ONUC Headquarters in Leopoldville, the capital, was satisfactory, communications between the battalions and their outposts in Katanga were difficult. By a stroke of luck, an Irish engineer, Terry Tierney, working in Uganda, who happened to be an amateur radio fan, overheard an Irish voice calling the Amateur Radio Club using the Curragh Camp call sign one night. He managed, at some considerable personal effort, to bring about a temporary solution to the problem, which was later remedied permanently (see Appendix B).

Shortly before departure each of the companies paraded in their home Commands to receive their pennants. The officers of the battalion were received by the President, Éamon de Valera, at Áras an Uachtaráin on the evening of Friday 6 January and the entire battalion paraded in the Curragh the next day, where the unit flag was brought on parade for the first time. The Minister for External Affairs, Frank Aiken, spoke of the importance of our mission and the Minister for Defence, Kevin Boland, offered us his and the government's best wishes for a successful tour of duty and a safe return home.

Finally, we paraded for An Taoiseach, Seán Lemass, at McKee Barracks on Monday 9 January, where the head chaplain blessed the battalion. Since early December, we had been hounded, prodded, poked at, lectured and issued with more kit than we could readily carry, but we were finally ready for take off. It was a most creditable performance for all concerned, six weeks from mobilisation to departure.

The day for departure, 10 January, arrived. Each Chalk commander was given a manifest listing all the personnel as well any stores to be carried. The manifest was signed by the Director of Medical Services, Col Holmes-Ivor, declaring that all persons on the manifest were vaccinated and free of specified diseases. The Chalk commander was responsible for ensuring that all those designated to be on board were in fact present, not always a sure thing. Soldiers being what they are, there is always a possibility that one might have got carried away in celebrating his good fortune, or even had second thoughts about the wisdom of overseas service.

The entire 34th Battalion was to be flown to Katanga in fifteen flights over a period of three weeks and for those in the later flights, Chalks 13, 14 or 15, the waiting at home must have been very trying indeed. While the earlier battalions had departed from Casement air base in C130 aircraft, our battalion would be departing from Dublin Airport in the older aircraft, probably because Dublin had longer runways.

I had been interested in still photography for years but had always yearned for a movie camera. So, following consultation with Tom Gunn, an FCA Artillery Officer and a professional photographer himself, I bought myself an 8mm movie camera and a large quantity of film. I wanted to record as much as I could of the UN experience on the assumption that I might never again have such an opportunity.

The flight from Dublin to the USAF Wheelus air base near Tripoli was uneventful and smooth although noisy. The flight took

just over eight hours and when we landed and had disembarked into the warm night air, we met our reception committee which was composed of a PFC (Corporal) with a clipboard and a couple of buses, driven by local Arabs. The PFC gave us our instructions in a casual but no nonsense manner. We were bused to a meal at 23.30hrs local time and then to our accommodation billets for some badly needed rest. This was quite a contrast to our departure where we were seen off by the Minister for Defence, Kevin Boland, the Chief-of-Staff, General Collins-Powell and the Adjutant-General, Col P. Hally.

During the night, one of my platoon, Private T. O'Neill, became very ill and had to be left behind in the American hospital at Wheelus. He was repatriated on the next available flight to Ireland. Breakfast was taken in a huge dining-room (chow hall) to the noise of jet planes taking off and landing. Shortly afterwards, we were treated to an unexpected surprise. On the road outside our billets, a British military band arrived and began to play for us, marching up and down, having to compete at times with the aircraft noises. When the band finished playing and was given a fall-out, a number of the bandsmen rushed over to shake our hands and slap the backs of some of their buddies from Dublin. We then had some time to inspect the base as our onward flight did not depart until 18.30hrs.

From Wheelus, the next leg of our journey brought us to Kano, Nigeria, where we had a meal in the warm darkness of a sleeping airport. We reached Leopoldville at 09.30hrs the following day and stepped out into the severe heat of an African summer's day. On attempting to depart for Kamina, the final leg of our journey, our plane made no less than two attempts at take-off but had to abort each time because of an oil pump problem. Our flight crew of five were not at all put out by the delay and seemed very nonchalant about the engine trouble. We finally succeeded in taking off on the third attempt and arrived into Kamina at 19.00hrs after a three-hour flight. It was dark and we were given a meal and taken to our various billets amid scenes of considerable confusion.

Set in the highlands of north-west Katanga, Kamina was a huge base that had been built to provide training for the Belgian Army, Air Force and parachute units during Belgian rule of the area. At the back of it all, of course, lay the desire to provide a western presence in central Africa both as a protection for the important minerals of the area and against the spread of Soviet influence across the continent. It was used, amongst other purposes, for supporting the dreadful civil war in Angola many years later.

Covering 100 square miles, Kamina was divided into two main sections. Base One contained the airport and all the buildings, hangars, workshops, refuelling facilities and so on to support flying and parachute training. Approximately 15kms away lay Base Two, where the infantry and other logistics troops were stationed. Up to 12,000 workers and their families lived in four enormous 'communes' within the perimeter of Kamina. They provided the workforce to grow crops to feed everyone in the base, as well as providing the manual labour for the multitude of tasks from refuelling aircraft to cutting the grass. Our Battalion Commander, Lt-Col Eugene O'Neill, was also the officer in charge for the entire area including the logistics units from India and Pakistan.

He travelled around in a large American saloon with the UN and Irish flags on the bonnet.

With the dawn of our first day at Kamina, we made our way to the mess for breakfast where we met many of the officers from the 32nd and the 33rd Battalions. Once contact was made and old friends greeted, normal routine kicked in and there was much to do. Down in the lines, where the soldiers were billeted, the lightweight green uniforms, UN blue berets and peaked caps were being issued. As we were measuring up for the badly needed uniforms, Comdt Vaughan called me over and said he had a task for the platoon. I was to take my platoon and a section of the support platoon to relieve the guard the next morning at the hydroelectric station at Kilubi, some 80kms north-east of Kamina. The duty would last for one week and we would take over from a platoon of the 33rd Battalion, commanded by Lieut Pat McMahon. Lieut Des English was to accompany me, as well as two cooks and some signalmen.

The journey to Kilubi the following morning took three hours over dirt roads. The landscape surprised me a little, being quite flat with tall grass and small trees – typical savannah country. The rainy season was in full swing – the thunder and lightning was spectacular, as were the frequent downpours. The rain made the dirt roads very difficult and the journey time was much longer than it should have been. However, the heat of the sun was so strong that the roads dried up quickly after each downpour.

The hydroelectric station was impressively large and two Swedish engineers were based there to maintain it in running order. It was built to supply power to Kamina, Kaminaville and other small settlements in the area. A small number of UN police from Kamina were also there to provide additional security. The post was in two parts. The first part was a guard-house down at the foot of the station beside the Kilubi river where an extra large guard – ten ORs commanded by a sergeant – lived. They slept in what had been a large garage, using their sleeping bags on folding stretchers. It was called the Valley Post. The other part of the post lay at the top of a steep hill about a kilometre away where two attractive modern villas were placed. Here the balance of the platoon and the Swedish engineers who ran the plant lived. Lieut English shared one villa with myself and the two Swedes. The remaining members of the platoon, about eighteen soldiers in all, were crammed into the other. Finally, there was a helicopter landing pad in a clearing about 2kms away and each time an aircraft was due, the landing pad had to be secured until it departed once more.

The buildings and facilities were in a very shabby state and the first task was to clean, tidy and fumigate all locations and to familiarise all personnel with the post and with our responsibilities. The second job was to improve the defences. During our week there, the undergrowth was cleared from around the villas and many coils of barbed wire were put in place. Sandbag walls were renewed and extended at the rear to give a greater feeling of security to all. Similar works were carried out at the Valley Post.

Not long after we had taken up our post, a helicopter brought Fr Crean, chaplain to the home-going 32nd Battalion (and formerly a chaplain in the British forces) to Kilubi. Capt. Jack Phelan, Comdt Gus Mulligan and Comdt Mick Gill, the Battalion Legal Officer, had accompanied the chaplain on a trip of familiarisation. Fr Crean was due to depart the following day for Ireland and offered to take letters home. There was a scurry to take advantage of this offer – it meant that our first letters home would be delivered within days.

We soon settled in and a routine developed and rotation of personnel between the two posts was made mid-week. When I realised that the only transport we had was one long-base Landrover that had a broken rear spring and was dangerous to use, I requested a replacement vehicle. To my surprise, it arrived the next day with a re-supply convoy. For the first few days while at the post, it is fair to say that the food was less than satisfactory. As would be normal in any new situation, it took a few days before the supply situation settled down and the fresh food came on stream. At the start we were forced to use a mixture of rations and hard biscuits supplemented with pineapples and bananas bought from the locals.

Our weekly malaria pill was due to be taken during the week – we had all started taking them before we left Ireland. I started a process whereby myself or the platoon sergeant would stand in front of each individual to make sure he swallowed it. Where the circumstances permitted it was done on parade. As a result, not one member of the platoon suffered from malaria over the six months, in fact the incidence of malaria was very low throughout the battalion.

On Tuesday evening, 17 January, we had our first taste of the possible dangers involved in this mission. We received a warning from Battalion HQ that a band of armed Balubas, the dominant tribe in Katanga, were heading our way from the north, burning and looting as they passed through the villages en route. (Such an allegation was seriously off the mark, as I discovered later. The Baluba tribe was from the region and supported the central government in Leopoldville. Only those villages occupied by the Katangese Gendarmerie would have been attacked by them. The Gendarmerie was the army of the breakaway province of Katanga, led by Moise Tshombe. They were led by Belgian Army officers, acting as 'advisers' to the province.) We immediately took all possible precautions, the sentries were doubled and everyone was given a specific place on the perimeter. Des English and I took turns to be up and about during the hours of darkness. As is often the case, nothing happened, the threat fizzled out and we resumed normal duties the following day. Nothing more exciting happened during the rest of our time there.

Our relief platoon, No. 2 Platoon, commanded by Lieut Ray Roche, arrived on Sunday 22 January. Our convoy returned to Kamina without incident. When we arrived, I was informed that B Company was being sent on 9 February to a small coal-mining town called Luena, about 200kms to the south-east of Kamina.

The base provided for a very large variety of sports, being equipped with modern sports facilities as well as boasting a cinema. I found to my delight that my billet was in a fine detached villa with Capt. Jack O'Phelan and Lieut English, each of us having our own bedroom. Our address was No. 135 Korea Avenue, Kalunga, one of a number of luxurious houses that had been built for Belgian officers and their families. An African civilian employee was assigned to our house, a happy young man called Muzeke Dusie, who spoke French and who did all the cleaning and the laundry for us. (I bought a bow and two arrows from him before we left Kamina.) The officers' mess was only about 200m away, across a delightful park with just one obstacle in the way – the base swimming pool!

Before our own Irish packs started arriving we were using American ration packs, designed to provide sufficient nourishment for ten men for one day or one man for ten days as necessary. Many of the tins contained types of canned foods that were not familiar to Irish soldiers. No doubt in designing the contents of each ration pack, a great emphasis was placed on nourishment and basic needs as opposed to flavour and enjoyment. But to the Irish palate, spoiled as we were by fresh food at home, the flavours of the long-life spicy tinned meats, the sauces, the fish pastes, the margarine and the anonymous canned cheeses, were distinctly unpopular. Some of the officers in my company were seen to approach the contents of the cans of meat with great caution and with curled-up noses.

Our own Irish ration packs, once issued, became highly prized by the other nationalities in Kamina. It was even possible to use them (illegally of course) as barter for the most surprising variety of needs, ranging in preference from the allocation of new vehicles to the turning of blind eyes when certain errors in returns or accountancy were discovered!

The packs varied in content and were labelled from A to E depending on the purpose for which they were designed. All the best Irish firms of the time were represented: Bolands, Jacobs, Barrys, Dennys, Mattersons and many others, all displaying their cheerful wrappers. They included tea, salt, sugar, condensed milk, biscuits, luncheon roll, sausages, bacon, salmon, sardines, margarine, (the source of great moaning by the butter purists), powdered potatoes from Batchelors (another source of complaint), matches, toilet paper, boiled sweets and a fruit cake. This latter was to be found in the E pack only.

Other surprises in store for us were the fortnightly issues by battalion welfare of soaps, razor blades and beer. Each soldier was entitled to one bottle of Simba beer per week. This was intended to provide soldiers with a quick replacement for the lost perspiration under the hot sun. It was a little ironic that welfare should be concerned about replacing the perspiration by providing free beer to counter the hot weather, because we had arrived right in the middle of the rainy season. While it was certainly very hot around midday each day, the evenings were actually quite cool and dehydration was not much of a problem.

At the end of January all ranks were paid 1,430 Katangese francs (approximately £10) their first payout, and shortly after that the platoon was given permission to visit Kaminaville, the nearby town. It was a trip they enjoyed as it was their first break since leaving home.

A savings scheme instituted by Comdt Ned Fitzpatrick, the Battalion Welfare Officer, was very well patronised as there were so few outlets in Kamina for the soldiers to spend their money. In January, when we arrived, 100 Congolese francs equated to 14s 4d

Irish or two US dollars. The Katangese franc was 45 francs to the dollar on the black market, which by mid-March had risen to 70 francs. It was suspected that this was caused in part by Belgians and other foreigners who were buying up dollars in preparation for leaving the country.

The one thing we could spend our money on was souvenirs to bring home. The Swahili word 'Mingi' (meaning much or many) came to mean any kind of souvenir and eventually to be associated with the box in which it was to be carried – the 'mingi' box. This was one of the Swahili words that Irish soldiers soon started to use in their daily lives. Swahili, or Kiswahili to be more accurate, is the language of most of the tribes with whom we were interacting and it was impressive that some individuals had acquired a reasonable grasp of the language in the short time in Kamina. 'Jambo' was the usual greeting to which one replied 'jambo sana'. 'Muzuri' meant good, 'muzuri capissa' very good. In retrospect, it is very interesting to see how some of these words of Swahili have been transported by Irish soldiers from one UN mission to another.

However, it was necessary for our mission to have an interpreter. A local man called William Maceko, who had quite good English, was appointed to the battalion when we arrived. A second interpreter was acquired later by B Company. He was an Irishman, Mike Nolan, who had lived for many years in the Congo. He had owned a large coffee and tea plantation and had lost everything when law and order collapsed in 1960. While he had a peaceful time with our battalion, his luck ran out once more when, later that year, he found himself at Jadotville with A Company of the 35th, when they were attacked by Katangese troops and forced to surrender. He survived that event also.

In February, I was detailed to escort an English film-maker called Patterson around the battalion and to facilitate his work where possible. It was a welcome break from duties and it meant that I had a vehicle to myself for three days and could go more or less where I pleased. He was a one-man show, carried a 16mm camera and he told me that the film might be shown in Ireland later on. Despite my scepticism, I actually did see the film in the Adelphi Cinema in Dublin a year or two after coming home. It was in black and white and at the end, amongst other things, it showed our former armoured cars in use by the ANC.

As so easily happens in a military unit, in the stable situation we were experiencing, routine and duties took precedent and became progressively heavier, especially when the Moroccan battalion that had been stationed in Kamina departed in March. My platoon became fragmented as the many duties multiplied. During this period, the battalion was involved in an emergency airlift of food supplies to South Kasai province where a major famine was raging. The same aircraft were also returning many of the Luluas, a small tribe from the north of Katanga, who had earlier fled from the attacks of the Gendarmerie. With the arrival of the UN it was safe for them to return to their tribal areas.

The entire battalion – less B Company in Luena – paraded every morning. Lt-Col O'Neill was very keen on singing as we marched, something we had practised in Ireland before departure. A particular song was designated to each company; in the case of A Company the song was 'Twenty Men from Dublin Town' – this would not have been my choice, as I was from Cork. There has never been a strong tradition of singing in the Defence Forces as our soldiers marched, so it took a bit of coaxing to get them to raise their voices. Mind you, they never had such problems in the canteen.

On one morning parade, I was ordered to march A Company from the parade ground and to lead the singing as we went. Just as we started to move away, the company commander called me over to give me some additional instruction for the day. I turned back to the company, picked up the step and loudly exhorted them to sing the company song. They were not overly enthusiastic about it so I had to remind them that they must do much better or they would spend the next hour practising. They began to improve and it was only then that I realised that I had fallen in with C Company, not A Company!

To keep up company discipline whilst in camp, sports and other training activities were organised at battalion level. One of the essential activities for soldiers was a visit to the rifle ranges. The ranges were very poorly equipped by home standards and the usual targets and repair materials were not available. So, I organised a competition for the platoon. I placed six small squares of paper at different heights on the stop butts and gave each man twenty-four rounds of ammunition for the weapon with which he was issued. Each soldier in turn had to run twenty-five metres, stop, and from a distance of 30m, to fire at each of the six targets in bursts of three or four rounds. We then counted – with difficulty – the hits on the papers and declared winners. The three riflemen complained that they could not fire in bursts, but my response was that they must make up for their disadvantage by speedy reloading. This exercise did not conform to the normal range practices at home in Ireland, but it was practical and it generated a lot of rivalry and good humour. The most accurate shot turned out to be Pte Fennel who was carrying a light machine gun. A new system of firing practices was actually introduced at home many years later that incorporated running between different firing points, but I can take no credit for such a development.

On 1 March, tragedy struck our platoon. No. 1 Platoon was on its second tour of guard duty to Kilubi power station, when my platoon sergeant, Joe Flanagan, was seriously injured in an accidental grenade explosion as he lay sleeping. At first we assumed that the Valley Post had been attacked, but it was quickly discovered that the grenade had been one of our own. With two other soldiers who had suffered minor injuries, Sgt Flanagan was brought up to the helicopter pad where he had a most agonising wait until Comdt Cyril Joyce arrived to give him some relief with a first shot of morphine.

While a lesser man would have died from his injuries, Sgt Flanagan was saved both by his own good health and physical strength, and by the fortunate presence at Kilubi of the company medical NCO. Sgt Maurice Murphy performed wonders with the limited medical kit available to him. He used up all the field and shell dressings that we could collect in the platoon, but unfortunately he did not have morphine, as medical NCOs were not permitted to carry or administer it at that time.

That evening I received a message from Battalion HQ that the sergeant was not expected to survive the night. Now I am not a particularly religious man, but I felt that I had to do something to express my anxiety for his well-being. So I got out my rosary beads and with some of the NCOs, I started to say the rosary. To my surprise the remainder of the platoon at the post joined in with me, even though I had placed no obligation on any of them to do so. We did the same the following evening. On the third morning, to our great joy, we were informed that Sgt Flanagan had rallied and was out of danger. Shortly after this, Sgt M.J. 'Johnno' O'Brien was taken from support platoon and sent to me as a replacement, and a very worthy replacement he was too.

Both of Sgt Flanagan's feet were amputated at Kamina and when he was fit enough, he was sent back to Ireland. He spent some time at St Bricin's Military Hospital where he made a good recovery and where he was fitted with prosthetics. Eventually he left the army and took up a job in the Harp Brewery in Dundalk. He always maintained a cheerful attitude to life and to his misfortune, and was a staunch member of the St Barbara branch of the Organisation of National Ex-Servicemen in Kildare even though he lived in Dundalk. As the years rolled on, I lost contact with him. Thanks to my wife, who spotted his death notice in *The*

Irish Times, I had the consolation of being present at the grave for his burial, the only one there in uniform.

On 8 March, completely by accident, I happened to be at the airport, when Comdts Vaughan and O'Hanlon were preparing to depart on a UN helicopter for Luena to visit B Company. I asked half-jokingly if there was a spare seat and was delighted when they said 'jump in'. It was my first ever helicopter flight as the Defence Forces did not possess helicopters at this time. The villages below us were well scattered, and as we approached Luena we could see that some had been attacked, leaving still-smouldering ruins and with no signs of life.

During the short time on the ground with B Company at Luena we were given a quick tour of the badly damaged town. About thirty Belgian civilians were still there, but there were no locals – they had been driven into the hills by the approximately 1,500 Gendarmerie stationed in the town. The Irish soldiers were accommodated in an abandoned mission convent school in a manner that made us very envious. Comdt George Glendon, the company commander, was very proud of his boast that he slept every night in the Mother Superior's double bed!

I was airborne again a few days later on a recce flight. My platoon had been detailed to prepare for a long patrol to link up with a similar patrol from B Company. The purpose of this patrol was to check the state of the roads and bridges between Kamina and Luena, as well as the attitudes of villagers along the way. The following day, on 9 March, the patrol, commanded by Capt. Bertie Murphy, set off from Kamina on a road made very difficult because of the heavy rains. No. 1 Platoon, with various attachments, provided the main element with a total strength of fifty-three.

A number of times it was necessary to dig one of our vehicles out of the heavy, glutinous mud that kept the convoy speed down to about 18mph. Any inhabited villages we passed through maintained a small sentry post at each end of the village and our interpreter had to negotiate our passage with the locals. They were very wary of us – we were after all white soldiers, and white faces to them equated with Belgians, the Gendarmerie and big trouble.

Our patrols met up at the town of Kabondu-Dienda, a rail junction where a large Gendarmerie force was stationed. They were clearly unhappy to see us. I got shouted at when I produced my camera although I still managed to film my friends from B Company. The Gendarmerie officers, some of them fairly rough-looking characters, eventually invited us to have coffee or tea with them in their HQ and they permitted the boiling up of large quantities of water to make tea for the ORs. It was a strangely stiff meeting as they were unsure of our intentions. Both sides were wary and relieved to say goodbye.

St Patrick's Day was a special event on our base. A major effort went into celebrating the first ever National Day to be celebrated by soldiers of the Defence Forces overseas (if I exclude the Irish officers in UNTSO). Colonel Patrick Hally, the Adjutant-General, arrived from Ireland and was greeted by a Guard of Honour using a special arms drill for the Gustafs that had been developed before leaving Ireland. A dinner for 100 guests was organised and Irish officers were distributed across the room to sit with the guests. Des English and I sat at table with a Canadian paratroop captain, a Swedish lieutenant, Ray Moloney of Associated Press, an Irish woman from Castlebar whose name I never acquired, Miss Joy from UN HQ in Leopoldville, another Swedish captain and finally a Greek UN Field Service employee. On the following day football and hurling games were organised that were of immense interest to all non-Irish, especially to the local workers. We had a swimming gala, a church parade at which shamrock was distributed, and that night, an open-air concert. In a letter I wrote to my family in Ennis on 20 March, I described this as follows:

It was an outdoor affair, with hundreds of chairs laid out in a great semi-circle in front of a specially built stage. A huge bonfire blazed in the centre of the arena. The battalion had produced a number of amusing acts including songs and dances and the pipe band produced a very effective skiffle group. The children of the local schools and the scout troops laid on a really great display. The children marched, danced and sang with a wonderful rhythm and total delight in what they were doing. But it was the group of little drummers, eight- and ten-year-olds, that stole the show. Squatting down over their homemade drums, they produced the kind of sound that we had not yet experienced in Africa. The throb and the pulse of the drums, the seemingly flawless two-part singing and the enthusiastic stamping and shuffling of hundreds of little feet, all lit by the flickering light of the bonfire, combined to make an indelible impression on the onlookers.

The various performances were rapturously applauded by everybody.

Like all good things, our happy hours spent in Kamina were coming to the end, our soldiers were thoroughly fed up with the place and needed a break, and rumours were abounding of a change of location for 34th Battalion.

Chapter 7

ONUC KATANGA – ELISABETHVILLE

Political tensions began to rise between rival factions in Katanga, as well as between UN New York and the caretaker government in Leopoldville. There was a continuing struggle for power in Leopoldville, many tribes in the provinces had begun to fight with their neighbours, South Kasai province had declared independence and Katanga was fighting for its independence. An unsuccessful attempt was made by Katangese soldiers to take over the airport in Elisabethville. The under-strength Swedish unit of 440 ARs based there were having difficulty containing the situation. They promptly appealed for assistance, an appeal that triggered a major movement of UN troops.

An entire Indian infantry brigade of three battalions was dispatched to Kamina on 1 April 1961 – a move that caused great anger in Katanga. It apparently broke a UN undertaking to the Katanga government not to send Indian nationals into the province on the request of the Katangese. Equally the UN had a problem as it had previously given an undertaking to the Indian government that the brigade would never be split up, and ostensibly by spreading the troops across North Katanga and South Kasai the brigade remained intact with its base in Kamina.

These events raised the stakes for the garrison in Kamina and the frequent alarms and 'turns-out', where we had to man the defences around the airport from dusk until dawn, began to take its toll on tired soldiers. The Indian Brigade began to arrive into Base One in an operation lasting three weeks. The troops arrived with heavy weapons such as jeep-mounted 105mm recoilless rifles, weapons that we could only dream about.

All this time, the situation in Elisabethville was deteriorating and the Swedish battalion repeated their request for re-inforcements. To our delight, 34th Battalion was ordered to move immediately to Elisabethville. B Company was first to move. They returned to Kamina from Luena, making the journey by train. The railway line had been closed for some months and a special train had to be assembled for the journey. It took thirty hours to travel the 200kms and Lieut Jerry Healy found himself sitting up in the cab of the engine for the duration of the trip with two railmen who could not speak any English. B Company plus the Battalion Commander, some staff and elements of HQ Company were then flown to Elisabethville as quickly as possible.

My platoon, with a portion of the support platoon, was designated to be the first element of A Company to fly. Because my platoon was short-handed by now, as I had lost some soldiers to illness and injury, I was given Pte J. Murphy, complete with light machine gun, from HQ Company to strengthen our firepower for the move. Carl Jones from RTÉ arrived and filmed some of our activities.

The main aircraft used in the airlift was the DC4. When a DC4 is parked on the tarmac, a prop is placed under the tail section to ensure that it does not tip back and strike the ground, as might happen in a strong wind. When our aircraft was loaded on the morning of departure, the loadmaster could not remove the prop – it was firmly rooted to the ground. I was still outside the aircraft with a crewman watching with growing anxiety, as I knew just how packed the aircraft was with men, weapons and ammunition. The pilot started up the four engines with the intention of running the aircraft forward. With the help of the crewman and some ground staff, we managed to remove the prop by pushing on the wheels. I was holding my breath as I fully expected the plane to sit back on its tail. But it didn't, and we climbed on board.

I had learned previously that Kamina featured the longest runway in Africa at that time and I was very glad of it on this occasion. The take-off run seemed to last forever, but we finally struggled into the air. The flight to Elisabethville took about an hour, during which time I was talking to my NCOs near the exit door as we had to be the first out when the aircraft came to a halt, in case of any trouble. Our pilot made two passes over the airport before deciding that it was safe to land. It was only when I opened the door, that I saw why he did so – a Swedish guard of honour was drawn up in front of the terminal building waiting to be inspected. I was mightily relieved and made way for Comdt Vaughan to alight and take the guard of honour. While he was busy, I was getting the platoon out and deployed into initial security positions. Shortly afterwards Chalk 2, carrying Ray Roche and his platoon, taxied in and parked nearby. Apparently, somebody on board walked from the front to the rear of the aircraft before the prop could be placed, because it promptly sat down on its tail, nose wheel in the air, to the great amusement of the onlookers.

Fourteen DC4s were used on the airlift, with aircraft arriving into Elisabethville at 15-minute intervals. They transported some 350 men of the rifle companies as well as elements of HQ and HQ Company, all in less than four hours. While this airlift was in progress, the Armoured Car Group was required to travel by road. Under the command of Comdt Joe Foley, they endured a gruelling journey of 650kms over unsurfaced roads in the company of the Swedish APCs.

Using trucks supplied by the Swedes, A Company quickly moved into a temporary camp at the far end of the runway, where the local aero club had a little building. We remained there for several days before moving into some very pleasant houses, known as Sabena Villas, recently vacated by Swedish soldiers to provide us with accommodation. By the time the entire company had arrived the villas were very crowded. Tents were erected and latrines dug in the back gardens of the bungalows to cater for the 'overflow'.

Our company had responsibility for the main road to the airport, and a Swedish 84mm recoilless rifle section was attached to us to provide anti-armour defence. Shortly before we arrived, an agreement between the Force Commander and President Moise Tshombe (known to all in our battalion as 'Mossy' Tshombe), had been reached. As a result of this all tension seemed to have evaporated in the city with the arrival of our battalion and instead of the hostile situation expected, we entered a very relaxed period of duties, with sports and social visits between the Irish and Swedish battalions. The Stade swimming pool was very popular, and it was even possible to go in small groups to the cinema or to a café in the evenings. Our duties mainly consisted of providing security at important sites across the city, including the airport, post office, radio station and fuel depots. The initial refusal of the business people to have anything to do with UN personnel disappeared quickly when they realised that they could profit from our presence.

However, there were a few minor discomforts. Certain foods such as butter and even margarine disappeared for a time and we had to make do with lard and other unsavoury replacements. It was not a good time for the 'bacon and cabbage' men amongst us. It all contributed to the general fatigue, and the wish to return home was growing stronger – we badly needed a break. The nights had become very cold, we were using two blankets by now, and the inner walls of the tents were covered with condensation each night, although they dried out quickly in the morning sun.

While I was initially disappointed by the city, I eventually came to like it very much. I was astonished to learn later that as many as 5,000 American soldiers had been stationed in Elisabethville during the Second World War, to protect the copper and uranium ores for the war effort. It was said that the materials for the first nuclear weapons came from there. Costs were generally much higher in Elisabethville and there was more to do, so soldiers suddenly found that the savings made in Kamina were being eroded quickly. A cinema seat cost 60 Katangese francs, roughly 9 shillings, while at a pavement café, beers cost from 10 to 30 francs each, depending on location, while a cup of coffee and two 'buns' cost 40 francs. By the end of our tour in Katanga, the exchange rate had risen to 140 Katangese francs to the IR£1. Postal arrangements were also severely disrupted at this time and we were informed that workers in Leopoldville, who considered the Katangese traitors, were removing the Katanga stamps or even dumping our letters. New arrangements were quickly put into place to avoid going through the local postal system.

One bright feature was the burgeoning contact with the very many Irish in Northern Rhodesia, who gave any visiting Irish soldiers a warm welcome. A rugby match was played and Gaelic games were planned, but time and events meant these never happened.

At an early stage before our arrival in Elisabethville, the Katangese had acquired three Fouga jet training aircraft and were busy doing evaluation flights at the airport before moving them out to Kolwezi. It was yet another indicator of the determination of the Katangan government to defend their independence from the Republic of Congo by all means including force. These aircraft were used later with unsettling, but fortunately not decisive, effect against the soldiers of the UN when the Gendarmerie made surprise attacks against UN units in Jadotville, Elisabethville and Kamina. In one case, a pilot joked with the control tower in Kamina after an attack, asking them did they think that he was getting any better? The relative success in the use of even a small number of basic training aircraft demonstrated how crucial control of the air is to the success of ground forces.

While the company was on duty at the airport, a man came up to me one day and announced that he was Irish and a member of the Gendarmerie. In a previous existence he had been a gunner in the 1st Field Artillery Regiment in Ballincollig, and when he left the Forces he ended up as a cook with the Gendarmerie. Having met up with some of our soldiers, he decided that he was in the wrong job in the wrong country and he told me he was leaving as soon as it was safe to do so.

By coincidence, around that same time I was approached by a British officer of the Gendarmerie who told me quietly that he also wished to get out. He asked me if I could make arrangements for him to be taken into UN custody. I informed Battalion HQ about this and was instructed to meet him again and arrange a time and place. These two incidents suggested to us that Gendarmerie morale was falling and those who could were getting out while they had a chance.

It was arranged that I should 'lurk' with a small armed escort in a vehicle on the road to the rear of the Gendarmerie Officers' Club at 20.00hrs on a given night. The British officer would come out to us when it was safe. True to his word, he arrived and climbed into my vehicle, handing me his FN rifle, saying that I could keep it as a souvenir. I was delighted and relieved at the lack of bother, and quickly brought him back where he was taken over by battalion staff officers. As for the rifle, I managed to hold on to it for a few days but eventually was ordered to hand it over. This ended my dreams of being the first Irish soldier in Katanga to be armed with an FN rifle.

In May, I was ordered to take a patrol up to Mitwaba to test out the quality of the roads, the condition of the bridges and, more importantly, the mood of the locals along the way. The OC of the 34th Battalion wished to 'test the waters' by sending a patrol as far as Mitwaba, a small town to the east of Kamina, roughly half-way between Kamina and the Rhodesian border, and on the road to Manono. The patrol consisted of myself as patrol commander and with Lieuts Des English and Frank Colclough. Comdt Cyril Joyce, our company Medical Officer, also came along and we were allotted one Swedish interpreter, Lieut Ronald Lindholm.

It was a large patrol of about seventy-five ARs, consisting of my platoon, most of support platoon and a detachment of five Swedish drivers who were needed to supplement our own drivers. We left Socopetrol (a scruffy camp in Elisabethville based on a decrepit regional HQ and depot for that company, which had been distributing oils, diesel and petrol in the area) at 11.30hrs, delayed by the perpetual curse of the mission – inadequate transport. Once under way, we made good time, passing through Jadotville and Bunkeya to reach Kiubo, where we spent the night. The hotel there had been built at the side of the River Lufira beside one of the finest falls in the region, but had been completely stripped of all its furniture and fittings. Apart from a fairly cool reception by a Belgian White Father at his large and beautiful church in Bunkeya, we encountered no problems.

The unpaved roads on our route were in good condition and the bridges were intact, so we arrived at Mitwaba without difficulty, reporting by radio to the Battalion Operations Centre. This was no easy matter, as communications while on the move were out of the question with the C12 radios, so the signallers had to string up an aerial between two trees in order to make contact with Battalion HQ. After a brief rest, we headed back to Kiubo, driving hard to reach it again by nightfall. The drivers were very tired, so I decided that we would spend an extra night at the 'Hotel des Chutes', a pleasant location famous in the previous administration for the excellent crocodile hunting in the river.

We returned via the same route through Jadotville to the company at Socopetrol on Wednesday 31 May without incident, apart from some casual stoning of our last vehicle passing through Bunkeya. We had covered 940kms in four days, the longest patrol undertaken by the battalion during the tour.

Unknown to many of us, a decision had been taken in Dublin to send out a consignment of new weapons for the battalion. In early June a consignment of FN rifles, the new standard weapon of the Defence Forces, as well as a number of 84mm anti-tank weapons was sent out to Elisabethville to facilitate training. This meant that we entered into a brisk period of training in both these weapons, having Swedish instructors for the 84mm anti-tank weapons. Our potential opponents, the Gendarmerie, were of course already equipped with the same Belgian FN rifle. However, as it was close to the end of our tour of duty, the new weapons were passed on to our replacements, the 35th Battalion.

The new rifle was a self-loading weapon and would provide the platoons with a vastly increased firepower, coupled with accuracy up to 200m or more. The 35th, and especially their A Company, were fortunate to have the FN rifles rather than SMGs when they came under siege in Jadotville only three months later, or when the 1st Infantry Group, assisted by Swedish soldiers, mounted a vigorous and successful defence of Kamina air base. An important lesson we had learned from the experiences of the previous battalions was the folly of breaking down the available strength into non-viable packets and scattering them in minor outposts across the landscape. The more cautious policy of keeping the troops together paid off handsomely, as A Company of the 35th Battalion was at full strength, supported by a pair of armoured cars, when they were attacked at Jadotville.

The arrival of the new weapons had another unexpected consequence for me. Lt-Col McKenna, Army Ordnance Corps, who had arrived with the new weapons from Ireland, requested that he be allowed to go and visit a relative in Chikuni Mission Station, located south of Harare, in what was then Northern Rhodesia. His Company Sergeant, Kevin McCourt – later to become a commissioned officer – also wished to visit his brother in Kitwe, just across the border. Thanks to the generosity of the Battalion Commander, Des English and I were given five days leave to escort the Ordnance Corps visitors into Northern Rhodesia, or to give the region its full title, The Federation of Rhodesia and Nyasaland. We drove across into Kitwe in a hired car, staying overnight with Kevin's brother. Leaving Kevin there, we drove south through the capital Harare to Chikuni, calling to a lonely Irish mission priest on the way. We got as far as the Victoria Falls on the Zambesi river between Northern and Southern Rhodesia. We returned via Chikuni and Broken Hill on the way back to Elisabethville.

Back in the battalion all our talk was about preparation for the repatriation to Ireland and nothing else mattered. The personnel of the 12th Swedish Battalion, to which had been added two more infantry companies brought in from UNEF in the Sinai, were beginning to take over our security duties around the city. We began handing in the heavy equipment for crating. Games became the order of the day. A very successful battalion sports day was held with my somewhat portly Cpl Parkes showing a surprising and unsuspected turn of speed to win the 100m sprint. This was followed later by a swimming gala at which A Company did not shine.

Just before we left for home, a medal parade for the battalion staff and senior officers was held at the airport, where speeches were made by Conor Cruise O'Brien, the representative of the UNSG in Katanga, and General Eyassu of Ethiopia, the Deputy

Force Commander, while the company commanders presented medals to their personnel on 21 June, in our case at Socopetrol. Final payouts were made and No. 1 Platoon had a happy breaking-up party that night. Part of my platoon departed the following morning and the balance followed on Chalk 5 on Friday 23 June, becoming guests of the Queen's Own Nigerian Rifles in Base One in Kamina for two nights. (US aircraft were not permitted to land in the public airport at Elisabethville, so we had to be flown to Kamina first by UN aircraft.) The Nigerian battalion was commanded by Lt-Col Cavanagh, who was from Borris-in-Ossory. We were well looked after by the battalion but the CO maintained his distance, more is the pity – I would have liked to have discussed the situation in Kamina with him.

On 25 June, Chalk 1 of the incoming 35th Battalion arrived into Kamina to great cheers and back-slapping. Later that same evening, our flight departed for Leopoldville, where we ended up in the transit camp by 23.00hrs. The following morning, Lieut Jim Motherway, a diving friend of mine and Signals Officer stationed at ONUC HQ, arrived to take me away for a rapid tour of the city. The centre city, what I saw of it, was very impressive, with fine buildings and wide roads.

Soon we were on the move again, bound for Kano, Nigeria, where we landed on three engines in heavy rain, narrowly missing a 707, or so we were told. We left Kano in the early hours and flew directly to Wheelus air base where we were granted the freedom of the base for the day. There a final payment was made to each individual of 42 US dollars as a UN payment in lieu of leave. Most of us had a swim in the Mediterranean, ate as much food as we could and searched for 'mingies' or postcards.

On the final leg of our journey to Dublin, we landed at Evreaux, south of Paris, to drop off the Squadron Commander at his base. We had a meal there before departing again, arriving into Dublin Airport at 11.30hrs on a dull summer day. Customs formalities were swift and painless and we were bused by CIE to Clancy Barracks. There the formalities and the final goodbyes were completed quickly, releasing us to start on our well-earned thirty days' medical leave. It took three weeks for the entire battalion to be repatriated to Ireland.

I remember looking at the street scenes from the top deck of the CIE bus as we drove from the airport to the barracks and thinking just how dull and grey were the buildings and how drably dressed were the people on the streets. I then realised that I was already missing the bright colours, the sunshine, the heat and the excitement of Africa.

The Diary of Capt. Tom Boyle, DSM

Introductory Note: Although it is not part of my personal story, I have decided to include here the important account of the experiences of Capt. Tom Boyle DSM and his heavy mortar troop in Katanga. His troop was part of the 38th Battalion commanded by Lt-Col Delaney. The story is presented as he wrote it, often while under fire, and records for Irish military history the first time that an Irish field artillery unit had been in combat.

Fri 28 Dec 62:
Moved to Golf Club at 10 mins notice (on the outskirts of Elisabethville). Arrived at 11.30 under constant fire and ricochets for the rest of the day. Supported the advance of the Madras Battalion on Keravic, about 5 miles from E/ville. This is a sizeable town and Gendarmerie stronghold. We gave it a terrible pounding, the first rounds landing right in the middle of it. We entered Keravic at 19.30hrs. Everybody was gone except a Belgian priest who stayed through it all in his chapel. Lt Hughes, Lt O'Dwyer and I slept in a Landrover.

Sat 29 Dec 62:

05.30hrs got into position outside Keravic – supported the advance of the Madras Battalion towards Simba Hill, S/W of Keravic (7.5 miles). 09.30hrs moved position and supported the advance of the Ethiopian Battalion on Simba Hill. They advanced from E/ville and took over from the Madras Battalion. This was a very strong position and very well fortified. We hit the defences with a few ranging rounds and then engaged it for five minutes on a fire plan procedure. The Gendarmerie cleared out and the Ethiopians walked up the slopes and took possession, wiping out a few snipers in the process.

14.30hrs we moved up to Simba Hill and supported the advance of our own battalion (38th), from there towards Kipushi. We blasted the road ahead – firing 400–500 yards ahead of our troops.

16.00hrs. Bridge on the main road to Kipushi (three miles from it) was blown up. C Company was left to dominate this bridge and we stayed in a farmhouse for the night, sleeping in our clothes on the floor.

Sun 30 Dec 62:

09.30hrs we took up a position at the broken bridge to support the advance on Kipushi. The Indian engineers had very quickly thrown a bridge across. There was no further firing on that date as Kipushi surrendered to Col Delaney's loud hailer. We entered Kipushi around 15.00hrs but were ordered back to Simba Farm for the night. Black and white turned out to greet the troops to Kipushi, which is about 8 miles S/W of Simba Hill. The Gendarmerie were here in strength but moved out, leaving most of their stores behind them.

Mon 31 Dec 62:

11.30hrs, checked equipment and moved to E/ville, under orders to move to Jadotville. Attended Brigadier's conference at Katanga

Command (E/ville) 18.00hrs – got the detailed plan for the advance of the Madras and the Raj Battalions on Jadotville.

Tue 01 Jan 63:

Reveille 02.00hrs. Mass 02.45hrs, 04.00hrs rendezvous with Indian 121 Heavy Mortar Battery at old airport. Advance commenced 04.45hrs along Jadotville Road. Two types of Indian armoured cars led the column. This is normal SOP for the Brigade here. 07.30hrs I was up with the leading company of the Raj Rifles who had advanced to take the high ground at Lefuni – about 17 miles from E/ville. This company was ambushed around 08.00hrs and suffered casualties (four dead and six injured). The position was well defended with HMGs and 81mm mortars.

I saw the company attack supported by 4.2in mortars (Indian). Our own were deployed but were not required to fire. Saw an Indian soldier in a drain who had earlier got a direct hit from a mortar bomb – a gruesome sight. Indian infantry went into attack and showed in no uncertain way their fighting ability. The position was cleared and the leading armour advanced again. The first car hit a mine – three tyres blown to shreds and the sides and mudwings were like a strainer.

08.45hrs advance continued, no further opposition until 10.15hrs when a bridge about 30 miles from E/ville was blown up. It was about this time that I got my first taste of mortar fire. The Brigadier was up with the leading troops and the OCs of supporting arms had to career up to the front to stay with him. I never saw anybody with such courage and complete disregard for his own safety. He was up behind the leading car when the mortar fire came down and the bullets started to whistle around him. He stood there calm and placid waving his stick and giving out quick orders.

Two platoons moved up very quickly on either side of the road and cleared the high ground across the broken bridge. The engineers came up and in one hour a bulldozer had filled up the site sufficiently to let the transport across. We moved again with the Brigadier up in front and everybody chasing him.

15.30hrs we came to another bridge which was also blown up but the infantry were able to cross and continue the advance. This bridge was about four miles from the Lufira river. Here the range of our mortars proved to be very valuable as we were able to support the infantry right up to the Lufira without having to change position. The engineers improvised a crossing and at about 16.15hrs the transport moved across and the whole column continued. About 17.00hrs our mortars were up again in position on the high ground one mile from the Lufira and firing across the river. We continued firing until night came down. The fire here, as during the whole advance, was mostly directed by Forward Observation Officers. The communications were perfect all through (we were using No. 62 sets). Our C12s were unsatisfactory and the Indians gave us the 62s for the operation.

Our mortars were in position at a native village on the E/ville side of the Lufira. About 150 yards forward from our position, the Gendarmerie had arranged a very clever obstacle. They felled a few pylons carrying HT [high tension] cables with great precision. The cables had fallen across the road and were still taut at varying heights about the road from one to five feet high, so that it was with the greatest difficulty that the Command vehicles could be brought through. Again the engineers came up, the cables were weighted down, charges fixed and each cable cut by explosives.

When the leading infantry arrived at Lufira, the road bridge was blown beyond repair but the railway bridge was only partly demolished and it was possible to send infantry across on foot. OC Madras ordered two companies across immediately to secure a bridgehead. This was executed with great speed considering that the road was heavily mined.

Just as night was falling a troop of Gendarmerie 81mm

mortars got into position and started firing. The Indian Battery Commander spotted the flash and fired our mortars. The first round of gunfire put them out of action. We learned later from a captured mercenary that the Gendarmerie thought they were being bombed from the air. A UN jet had circled overhead some time before. When this engagement was over we bedded down for the night in terrible conditions. We had a lot of trouble with the baseplates as we had no sandbags to support them. We were trying to make do with captured Gendarmerie kitbags but we had not enough of them. Being very tired we were soon asleep.

Wed 02 Jan 63:

At 03.00hrs we were all jolted out of it by a tremendous explosion. Lt Dwyer and myself got out of our bivouac; Lt Hughes emerged from the front of a Landrover. We saw this huge fireball in the sky which lasted for a full five minutes. It was like an atomic explosion.

What happened was that the mercenaries had loaded a wagon full of explosives, set it off down the track through the company area on the left and it crashed into a partially demolished bridge. Here luck played a very important part as the rear platoon, close to the bridge, had been ordered back to collect their entrenching tools. They were well on the E/ville side when the explosion occurred. If they had been in position, casualties would have been extremely heavy. In addition this explosion was intended to set off a chain reaction which would have blown the road as well, but for some reason connections failed.

Shortly our troop went into action engaging defensive targets and kept up the good work until dawn. Night firing equipment was used and worked perfectly. The company commanders told us afterwards that the fire was completely effective.

At 08.00hrs I met OC Madras Battalion and he brought me

forward to show me the effects of the explosion. He is an old experienced soldier with a Military Cross to his credit and very fond of our mortar troop. As we were walking near the bridge he said to me 'I love a good fight, don't you?' At this stage I wasn't so sure whether I did or not, but I said 'yes'. As he was standing near the bridge with a huge staff in his hand his rear companies were moving up. He waved to them all and shouted 'good luck' and to a man they all waved back and shouted 'good luck'.

A raft was already procured and it was interesting watching the Pioneer Platoon and the engineers at work. There were usually nine or ten men in the water swimming strongly in the fast flowing current, securing ropes, etc. They got the raft going in no time and soon the Command vehicles were going across. The ado [*sic*] continued, but the work of crossing the river showed the vigour, training and fitness of the Indian soldier. They took the whole thing in their stride.

Our troop remained in place until 10.00hrs. Before moving position we had an amusing incident. A Gendarmerie soldier came up on our flank and started firing grenades at us from a discharger. The first two exploded behind us and I assumed it was a 2-inch mortar. Thereafter they kept coming over our heads but there were no explosions. We were amazed at this but could not figure it out. A patrol was sent out but in the wrong direction. The Indian Battery sent out another patrol and it was then that we discovered what had happened. Apparently the last grenades he fired, he was so excited that he forgot to prime them first.

Shortly after 10.00hrs I went forward to meet the Battery Commander. At the bridge I met the Brigadier. He asked me if I could get the troop across on the raft. As the Command vehicles had priority, I said it would take some time and on the other side we would then not have any towing vehicles. Eventually, it was decided that the troop would be leapfrogged forward, section by section. As soon as possible the first section (half of the troop) was moved up to the bridge and eventually got across about 13.00hrs. They took twenty rounds of ammunition with them. Lt Hughes was in command of this operation and had a most difficult job. The mortars were manhandled forward two miles together with ammunition and fire control instruments.

Lt Hughes brought the section into action in a banana grove which afterwards proved hazardous. I was left at the bridge to ensure that the other section and the remainder of the ammunition got across. As the day wore on and the advance continued, Lt Hughes was left more and more isolated. When he had occupied the position as per his instructions he was up with the forward troops.

The raft overturned and an armoured jeep went to the bottom of the river. Getting the raft back wasted a lot of time and as night approached I had a section on each side of the river. At this stage I got a written message from Lt Hughes explaining his position. Lt Dwyer and myself were at the bridge and very worried. Snipers were active at the forward section position and a mercenary (later captured) wounded an Indian officer close by. Lt Dwyer then went forward with rations and tents but when he arrived, the section was ordered forward six miles. This time they were towed forward by Indian jeeps. The mortars were laid out in darkness and heavy rain, food was served and the section bedded down. The time was 01.30hrs.

At 21.00hrs Comdt M. Farrell, who had been with me for most of the afternoon, told me that he was likely to stay the night. I met the Brigadier and told him of the proceedings. He then directed that the Irish mortars be given priority on the raft about first light. I returned to the rear section area and Comdt Farrell joined me at about midnight. We lay down in our clothes but could not sleep because of the mosquitos. I had some refreshments but could not get at them as Lt Dwyer had taken the key of the case. We were bitterly disappointed! At 04.45hrs I crossed on the raft with the rear section and at 07.00hrs had succeeded in getting four Landrovers across.

The full mortar troop was in action slightly ahead of the forward infantry troops at 08.00hrs and ready to fire on Jadotville. This move forward showed the troop at its best. All movements were executed at great speed and skill. Drills were perfected. Lt Dwyer and Lt Hughes had devised a modus operandi at the mortars that eliminated all time wasting.

Barring one action on the road and the blowing up of another bridge about two miles from Jadotville, there was little action after Lufira. The rapid crossing of the river took the Gendarmerie by surprise and frightened them out of the town. Brigadier Norhauha and some of his staff entered the town by a side road and were greeted with due civility. We entered Jadotville by the same route at about 19.00hrs. We were now in the Gendarmerie camp in Jadotville resting quietly, all very tired but in high spirits.

The Gendarmerie had left in a hurry, leaving a lot of transport behind. I got three vehicles, a 3-ton truck, a lovely little jeep and a pick-up. (They were partially dismantled but we raided their stores and the vehicles are now on the road with UN markings.) We also spotted some arms captured from Comdt Quinlan's company, which we hope to present to him when we get back.

The troop had done very well and they were highly commended by the Brigadier, OC Madras Battalion and many others.

Mr Bunche, Mr Gardiner and the FC were here the other day and I was introduced to them. They were all fully briefed on our activities and apparently we were highly commended. I think that the Battalion Command will see fit to mention this in his report. We later met Col Ned Shortall, among the VIP group, who was delighted to see the Artillery getting a boost.

The Distinguished Service Medal, 2nd Class, was subsequently awarded to the following members of the mortar troop:

0.7275 Capt. T. Boyle
'For distinguished service and outstanding leadership with the United Nations Force in the Republic of the Congo. The heavy mortar troop commanded by Captain Boyle took part in numerous engagements in Katanga in December 1962 and January 1963 supporting Indian and Ethiopian troops as well as their own. On all occasions the troop performed in a most efficient and praiseworthy manner, due to the example, leadership and devotion to duty of Captain Boyle.'

76595 Sergeant John Quirke
'For distinguished service with the United Nations Force in the Republic of the Congo, for leadership and courage. The heavy mortar troop with the Irish unit in Katanga in December 1962 and January 1963, took part in numerous engagements supporting Indian and Ethiopian troops was well as their own. On all occasions the troop performed in a most efficient manner. Sergeant Quirke, as non-commissioned officer in charge of ammunition, by his initiative and disregard for his own safety, succeeded in maintaining the supply of ammunition to the guns, despite tremendous difficulties. His actions contributed largely to the success of the unit.'

81154 Corporal William Allen
'For distinguished service with the United Nations Force in the Republic of the Congo, for leadership and courage. The heavy mortar troop with the Irish unit in Katanga in December 1962 and January 1963, took part in numerous engagements supporting Indian and Ethiopian troops as well as their own. On all occasions the troop performed in a most efficient manner and Corporal Allen was, by his personal example, leadership and courage, largely responsible for the action of his detachment.'

Chapter 8

THE UNITED NATIONS FORCE IN CYPRUS

When the island of Cyprus was declared a republic in 1960 the two main communities on the island, the Greeks and the Turkish, agreed to share power. The new constitution was designed to reflect the population ratio of 78% Greek Cypriot to 18% Turkish Cypriot (the remaining 4% were minorities). From the beginning this factor alone created serious strains between the communities. Eventually the underlying political tensions between these two communities, covertly supported by the governments in Greece and Turkey, exploded into violence in late 1963. As a result the UN Security Council decided to install a military peacekeeping force in an attempt to restore calm. Ireland accepted an invitation to contribute to that force and the 40th Battalion was raised and dispatched at short notice to Cyprus in June 1964. Another smaller unit, the 3rd Infantry Group was dispatched three months later. The Force Commander of the mission in October 1964 was General K.S. Thimayya, an Indian officer who was a famous soldier in his own country.

While it had never been specified as a principle, it was generally accepted that in the early days of peacekeeping, no permanent member of the Security Council should contribute troops to a UN peacekeeping mission. (UN military observers from the

Soviet Union, the United States and France had been taking part in UNTSO from a very early stage, but they all were officers, no troops were involved.) However, the United Nations Force in Cyprus (UNFICYP) broke that unwritten rule.

In the agreement for the liberation of Cyprus in 1959, Britain had retained two large swathes of territory on the south coast of the island, designated as Sovereign Base Areas. By agreement with the UN, Britain was nominated to supply all logistic support to the new UN mission while the large British garrison on the island also supplied a contingent of troops. This made great common sense, it eased the problem for the UN Field Service in starting up a new mission and it led to a high standard of supply from the beginning.

I was a very late nominee to the 41st Battalion, receiving notification just twelve days before the departure of the first elements of the battalion. I was to be the troop commander of the heavy mortar troop. Recently married, we were not long in our new house in Kilcullen, County Kildare, and while I was naturally very pleased about my call-up, the news was not exactly greeted with delight by my wife, Anne. We were still settling in, there was a lot of work to be done, both inside and outside the house, and we were enjoying the arrival of our firstborn, John. However, like all army wives, Anne accepted the downside of the military life with good grace and we made arrangements for the months in which I would be away.

However, my appointment in the battalion was unsatisfactory from the beginning. Although I was to be the troop commander of the mortar troop, I was also required to operate as the staff captain in the operations section of Battalion HQ, an arrangement that has become the norm for all succeeding battalions. What was different in my case was that the officers, the NCOs and the gunners of my troop were spread across the three infantry companies of the battalion, effectively out of my control.

The Irish involvement in UNFICYP did produce one new and welcome development. Eight AML 60 armoured cars, manufactured by Panhard in France, were purchased. These vehicles, shipped directly from France to Cyprus, were small, fast recce vehicles, equipped with turret-mounted direct-fire 60mm mortars. Our soldiers were delighted to have the use of modern armoured vehicles for this new mission. Four vehicles each were allotted to the two units when they arrived on the island.

On Monday 12 October, the 41st Battalion formed up in Plunkett Barracks, Curragh Camp and paraded for inspection by the Minister for Defence, Gerald Bartley, watched by families and friends. Following this we were quickly shipped out to Cyprus.

Fifteen flights were required to move the complete battalion, together with stores, ammunition and weapons. I was appointed as Chalk commander for Chalk 8, with a total complement of seventy-nine ARs on board, plus a lot of stores.

Chalk 8 took off on Wednesday 14 October, arriving into Rome at 15.00hrs and departing again after a two-hour break. Soon after take-off, the pilot had to climb to 12,000 feet to avoid a large storm over southern Italy. It was my first close-up experience of a spectacular electrical storm and the thunder could be heard much too clearly for comfort inside the aircraft. We landed at Nicosia at 22.30hrs where the warm and efficient reception by personnel of 40th Battalion ensured a swift transfer to Famagusta. The CO directed that the 120mm mortars were to be moved into stores at Battalion HQ in Famagusta under cover of darkness. This was done because such weapons were regarded by some as offensive rather than defensive weapons which should not be in a UN peacekeeping unit. They were transported from the airport in covered trucks, and the ammunition was taken directly to the British Ammunition Depot at Dhekelia. I eventually got to bed by 01.30hrs.

I quickly settled in to my new base and then took the opportunity to look around. We were in a former British Army establishment in what appeared to have been a stores depot situated about two miles north of the city of Famagusta. It had been renamed Wolfe Tone Camp by the 40th Battalion. The area to the west and south-west of Famagusta was relatively flat and heavily farmed, while to the north and on the Panhandle (the nickname for the large spit of land on the upper north-east of the island) the terrain was quite hilly. In good weather, the Turkish mainland could be seen from most of the high points on the north coast.

The UN posts were generally interposed between the Turkish and Greek Cypriot positions. Most of the battalion observation posts were located in a rough circle around the Old City, some of them actually on top of the wide walls overlooking the port, while one particularly memorable one was in an orange grove. This was my favourite location because of the delightful scent of the orange trees. Some of our posts were located beside, or in one or two cases, even in, the same buildings as those of the Greek Cypriot National Guard. Fortunately relationships were generally very good and such strange arrangements rarely gave any trouble.

Famagusta was a small city with magnificent fortified walls surrounding the Old City and overlooking the port where, by coincidence or design, all the Turkish Cypriots remaining in the city were confined. The walls had been built by the Venetians and extended and improved upon by some of the Crusaders. The modern part of the city would not be out of place on any Greek island, reflecting the typical Greek architecture and that nation's way of doing business. This meant that there was a plentiful supply of hotels, restaurants, cinemas, bars and nightclubs to be visited. There was also a choice of fine beaches. This made our soldiers very happy indeed, but our happiness was not destined to last very long.

The sea was a very short distance away from our Battalion HQ and the day following our arrival, with two others, I managed to get my first swim on a beach nearby, enjoying the lukewarm water. The ruins of a major Roman settlement called Salamis lay just to the north, with well-preserved remains that we examined at our leisure.

In the first few days in Famagusta, I was informed that I was to become the Battalion Operations Economic Officer. This was a complete surprise to me, as I thought that my only work would be as the Operations Officer or with the mortar troop. I received a short handover from my predecessor and had to take it from there, abandoning the mortar troop and the operations office for a while. The main task of my new job was to be responsible for the supply of foods, cooking oils and a multitude of other non-warlike goods to the inhabitants of the many Turkish Cypriot villages in our area of operations. These villages were blockaded by the Greek Cypriot National Guard and the inhabitants were suffering as a result. Another of my duties was the supervision of a large warehouse in the Old City, where the supplies were held for distribution across the island to the Turkish people in all the other battalion areas. Approximately 3,000 tons of supplies were held in the warehouse at any time.

I was provided with a small staff – Sergeant Swift from Battalion Signals and a group of Turkish Cypriot workers, while my regular driver was Pte Andy Griffin from the Curragh Camp. The system of distribution was a simple one and operated as follows. Each battalion in UNFICYP had an Ops Econ Officer who would send requests for goods to me. Sgt Swift would then arrange for the Turkish workers to prepare the order in the warehouse. When the goods were ready, I notified the relevant unit and a convoy of vehicles with escort arrived to pick up the order. That battalion then distributed the goods within its own operations area.

Monthly operations economic conferences were held at UN HQ in Nicosia. UN HQ was accommodated in part of a former RAF base at Nicosia airport, closed since the fighting in 1960 between the Greek and Turkish Cypriots. Each Economics Officer had to report on his activities and projected needs, while I also reported on the level of goods held in the warehouse. The various Joint Patrol Officers reported to the conference on potential problems in their areas relating to orange or olive harvesting, or over the level of water to be permitted for irrigation during the growing season.

My new duties also required me to tour the beleaguered villages to the north on a regular basis to assess their needs and to arrange deliveries to them by our battalion. While completely unexpected, this novel task gave me a wonderful insight into the Turkish Cypriot community in our part of Cyprus. I was introduced to the principal Turkish administrator in Famagusta, Mr A. Sami, a large and jovial man who spoke excellent English. I would call to him at least once a week. He would brief us on the problems in a particular village, having to rely on the UN to assist him in dealing with the problems of his fellow countrymen.

Capt. Murphy, the Battalion Joint Patrol Officer who was charged with attempting to settle disputes between the Greek and Turkish inhabitants, usually travelled with a Greek and a Turkish official who acted as interpreters. Most of the problems he was required to investigate concerned disputes over the servicing of water pumps, the unhindered flow of irrigation water, harvesting and access to lands through Greek Cypriot areas. He also dealt with humanitarian problems such as escorting sick people to and from hospital in Famagusta.

On Saturday 22 October, I conducted my first patrol – a day long trek up into the Panhandle, visiting Lefkoniko, Trikomo, Komo Kebir and Boghez. The villages were neat and clean but the villagers clearly lived a lifestyle that owed little to the modern world. In my dealings with the Turkish villagers, our business was conducted at the principal village café. Their problems ranged from the serious to the petty. Some complaints related to access to their fields through the Greek Cypriot fields of neighbours who probably had been on good terms with them prior to the withdrawal of British rule. The village muktars (leaders) were always most courteous and considerate, but the discussions were slow and tortuous, and it was obvious to me that decisions made on the spur of the moment could rebound on us in a very short time. It was imperative that the problems/complaints were brought to the other party to hear their side of the argument before any solution could be arrived at or even proposed.

Although our battalion was barely settled in, we were soon faced with our first major alert. A portion of the Turkish battalion, a unit of the regular Turkish Army, stationed in the Kyrenia region of Northern Cyprus, was to be rotated back to Turkey, starting on Monday 26 October. The number of Turkish soldiers to replace them was set at 330 ARs and they were to be unarmed. This event created great tension across the island as the Greek Cypriots were extremely wary of Turkish intentions, the ceasefire being only a few months old.

The entire UN Force was put on alert for the three days of the operation, codenamed Lollipop. The 41st Battalion was placed in overall operational control, a very early test for Lt-Col Dempsey and his staff. The new Turkish soldiers arrived in a large naval vessel with all on-board weapons fully manned. As our battalion was short on armoured vehicles for escorting the Turkish convoys, a troop of Life Guards – part of the British UN contingent based in Limassol – was placed under the command of our battalion for the operation. The British personnel of the troop were accommodated in Famagusta and the officers dined and socialised with us in the mess each evening. Not an eyebrow was raised, nothing was said by anyone, about what was surely an historic, if very minor, event for the Defence Forces. A sub-unit of one of the premier regiments of the British Army was placed under command to the CO of an Irish battalion. It demonstrated a professional approach by both units to a situation that could not have been conceived of in pre-UN times.

The rotation of the Turkish units went without a hitch, but was marred at the end by a tragic accident. When the Life Guards troop left our location to return to their base in Limassol, one of the Ferret armoured cars left the road and turned over, killing a young officer. He had been standing up in the turret and did not stand a chance. The subsequent funeral ceremony was attended by a large contingent from the 41st Battalion.

On 3 December, another Turkish ship, this time a merchant ship, arrived into Famagusta, but did not arouse the same tensions as the previous naval vessel had. It was carrying a cargo of Red Crescent supplies destined for the beleaguered Turkish Cypriots of the island and required the full attention of my little staff while it was being unloaded. The Greek customs and military were very suspicious and insisted on checking every bag of grain, every tin of cooking oil and every bundle of clothing for possible warlike materials before the Turkish workers were allowed to move anything into the warehouse.

During the early days in Famagusta, I had little contact with anyone in the Greek community, so when I found myself dealing with the Turkish authorities on a daily basis, I decided that I would attempt to learn some Turkish. I began to take notes and to ask questions of our Turkish friends, writing down the words and the phonetic pronunciations as best I could. I was told about Kemel Ataturk and how he coped with the multiple minor languages and the appalling levels of illiteracy that existed in his new country of Turkey. He had introduced the Roman alphabet and a simplified grammar with the intention of making it easier for all to become proficient in the national language.

I was enjoying myself and getting smiles from the villagers in my efforts to speak some words with them, although my best efforts rarely went further than asking for cups of sweet coffee. Unfortunately my attempts to learn Turkish were brought to an abrupt halt within a month, when the battalion was peremptorily dislodged from the comforts of Famagusta and transferred to the mountains of Morphou district in the north-west of the island.

In late November, some Swedish soldiers were accused of attempting to smuggle weapons and ammunition into the Turkish enclave of Kokkina on the north coast, using a Swedish armoured personnel carrier. This event generated a serious problem for the UN and was a major embarrassment for the Swedish military. Archbishop Makarios, President of Cyprus, was outraged and demanded that the entire Swedish contingent be sent home in disgrace. However, after much argument and no doubt pressure from the interested nations, a compromise was reached. The compromise was that the Irish and the Swedish battalions would exchange areas of operation. This was done in the depth of a very cold and wet winter. We went from the relative comfort of our billets in Famagusta to the tented camps in the hills of Morphou district and the Swedes went in the opposite direction.

On the day before we left Famagusta, I went into the Old City to say my goodbyes and Sami gave me a small silken Turkish flag as a souvenir. On 10 December, I travelled with others of the Battalion Staff in the last convoy from Famagusta to our new HQ at Skouriotissa, some 5kms inland from the Greek Cypriot town of Xeros. The Armoured Car Group was stationed there with the Battalion HQ while a portion of the mortar troop was located with C Company in Lefka.

The Battalion HQ and HQ Company camp at Skouriotissa was set up very close to the tip-head of the principal mine of the Cyprus Mining Company, an opencast copper mine where work continued on a twenty-four-hour basis. Copper has been extracted in this area since before the time of the Romans. It was a bleak and muddy location where only the Battalion HQ offices were accommodated in a permanent building.

HQ was set up in a small modern bungalow where there were enough rooms to accommodate, in somewhat crowded conditions, the offices of operations, information, the communications centre and a small briefing room. Communications with Ireland, UNFICYP HQ and the other battalions was conducted by phone and by telex, and communication with the companies was by radio.

The CO, Lt-Col Dempsey, had been offered a house for himself but he rejected it, preferring to share the discomforts of his battalion in conditions that seemed to get worse week by week. The other ranks were accommodated in large twelve-man tents and the officers were across the road in smaller tents in an olive grove. I took over the tent of a Swedish NCO that had a wooden floor and was surrounded by a trench to take away the rainwater.

As a consolation for this abrupt decline in our situation, from my bed in the mornings I could lean out and get a view of the top of Mount Olympus. It was the highest mountain in Cyprus at some 2,000m and was already carrying a layer of snow that lasted until we were heading home in April.

The Morphou district is named after the large bay on the north-west side of the island and it contained a higher proportion of Turkish to Greek Cypriots than any other district on the island. It was also said that the best oranges in Cyprus came from this district. It is easily the most mountainous and the most scenic part of Cyprus, featuring deep valleys and sharp ridgelines. The heavily forested Troodos mountains had been used very effectively as a base and refuge in the recent past by the EOKA led by General Grivas. The few roads were even narrower and more difficult than in the rest of the island.

C Company was stationed in the Turkish Cypriot town of Lefka, a few kilometres to the west of Battalion HQ, a big town overlooked by Greek Cypriot positions on the high ground around it. A Company was located at Limnitis, a very small village on the coastal road running west from Xeros towards Kokkina, and their principal task was to ensure freedom of passage for the Greek communities. B Company was lucky to get what seemed to me to be the best location, although it was also the most remote location in relation to Nicosia. The company was encamped overlooking a beach at Kato Pyrgos, a short distance from the major flashpoint of Kokkina. The Greek Cypriot National Guard had been stopped from overrunning the Turkish positions there only by the intervention of the Turkish Air Force, flying over from the mainland.

While each company had a number of observation posts in the mountains, mostly located between the opposing lines, B Company at Kokkina was the only one required to supervise an actual ceasefire line. This short ceasefire line lay between the opposing forces along the high ground overlooking Kokkina. On the ridge the opposing positions were very close to each other at certain parts of the line. The line was initially marked by whitewashed stones or by marks made on tree trunks or simply by wooden signs hammered into the hard ground. The opposing soldiers could see and hear each other and when a shouting match started it could quickly erupt into something more serious. It was also common practice for both sides to surreptitiously change the markings at night or in bad weather in order to annoy the other side or to confuse the UN soldiers.

It was the uncomfortable duty of members of B Company to patrol along this line between the opposing bunkers and trenches each morning, to check for and to report on any changes or problems observed. As the heavy mortar troop contained a small number of trained artillery surveyors, they were drafted in at an early stage to make a proper record of the entire ceasefire line and to register and mark the various features in an attempt to stabilise the situation and to cut down on arguments.

We quickly settled into our new location, and travelling with Capt. Murphy, I started to familiarise myself with the villages of the area of operations. Later on, I helped to deliver some of the goods arriving from the warehouse in Famagusta. In the New Year, changes in appointments were announced. I was to cease duties as Economics Officer and hand over to Capt. Murphy. He would now combine his own Joint Patrol duties with mine. I was to revert to my original task as the assistant to Comdt Sean Barrett, the Battalion Operations Officer.

Apart from the duties in the operations office, which included all aspects of the day-to-day running of the battalion, I was also the caterer to the officers' mess and did frequent turns as Orderly Officer, on occasion having to pay out the members of HQ. I still had to organise the training for the mortar troop as well as filming for the battalion and for myself. The time flew by, leaving little time for swimming or snorkelling along the coastline. I did, however, manage to organise a Christmas Day swim for a group of officers from the HQ.

Other demands were also made on my time at this stage. With Comdt Gus Mulligan, I became a member of a court of inquiry into the tragic death of a soldier of B Company at Kato Pyrgos during the rotation of the battalions. He had been part of the advance party during the takeover from the Swedish company and was killed in a tragic shooting accident. This required us to be away for a number of days in Famagusta and Nicosia to hear from Swedish soldiers and medical witnesses.

Also in January, I was required to act as the defending officer for two soldiers, one a gunner from the 1st Regiment, a task for which I had little experience. Under the Defence Act, a private soldier has the right, if he did not wish to use a solicitor, to nominate an officer of his choice to act in his defence at a limited court-martial (LCM). It meant that I had to read up on the procedures at such courts, the Defence Act itself and all the evidence relating to the incident and the charges. I did my best and was reasonably satisfied with my efforts for the two miscreants when their relatively lenient sentences were announced. It was worth noting that Superintendent Holland of the Australian Civilian Police, a force that was part of the UN Mission, and some of his policemen who had been invited to sit in on the LCMs were suitably impressed by the procedures. They thought everybody was being very honest!

As if acting as defending officer was not enough, I was appointed with others as a member of yet another LCM to try some soldiers of the 4th Infantry Group in Paphos in the south of the island later that month. At least it gave me the opportunity to visit the south coast of the island, an area that I had not seen before.

In January 1965 the weather was particularly bad, and the soldiers manning the observation posts on the higher mountains in particular, really suffered. In Skouriotissa, probably because of the heavy rain, a very large boulder became dislodged from the face of the tailings dump during the night and rolled to within 2m of a tent housing ten soldiers. During one gale, the church tent was blown down along with part of the officers' mess tent, while my own tent had a narrow escape.

Despite being the fifteenth Irish unit to have served overseas since 1960, Irish soldiers were still not provided with suitable wet weather gear or combat uniforms. The CAO of the mission, Frank Begley, had seen and heard of our predicament and sent a cable to UN HQ. The cable stated baldly that 'the Irish unit was not properly equipped for winter service in Cyprus'. Very quickly, a set of US Marine Corps rainwear was supplied for every man of the battalion. A two-piece suit, it was excellent at repelling water but did not add greatly to the body heat of the wearer. Designed to be worn over other clothing, the trousers came up the armpits of the wearer and were held there by strong shoulder straps, while the hooded jacket came well below the waist. Large numbers of paraffin heaters were also issued to the unit.

It may well have been one of these heaters that caused a fire in the early morning in one of the large tents belonging to C Company. C Company was located outside Lefka, a few kilometres west of the Battalion HQ. I was woken up by the sound of the exploding ammunition and for a moment it seemed to me as if a major battle was under way. Thankfully that wasn't the case, but a quantity of weapons, equipment and personal possessions were lost in the fire. Fortunately there were no injuries.

Despite this incident we were extremely grateful to Mr Begley for getting this equipment supplied. I had met Mr Begley while attending a meeting in Nicosia in December and after talking with him, he informed me that we were probably related. He was from Kerry, as was my family. I was suitably impressed and intended to follow up on this information, assuming that I had plenty of time. Sadly however, Mr Begley became very ill soon afterwards and died in Nicosia shortly after Christmas. I travelled to Nicosia with the CO to attend the requiem mass on 29 January, while another mass was said for him later at our HQ at Skouriotissa.

Because of political tensions, there was a distinct possibility that Turkish forces would invade Cyprus and all battalions were under orders to prepare contingency plans should this happen. Observation posts were ordered to be particularly alert and to report all sightings of Turkish warplanes in Cypriot airspace. One Sunday evening we got an excited report from A Company that a Turkish jet had flown low over the OP at Limnitis heading in a south-westerly direction. However, it later transpired that this was a scheduled BEA flight from London to Larnaca, and the red and white markings on the tail of the aircraft were mistaken for those of a Turkish warplane. This was an understandable mistake, but I was still very impressed when Brigadier Wilson, the acting Force Commander, sent his congratulations to the NCO who had made the report, praising him for being alert.

On 5 February, another OP in Limnitis reported that they could hear (it was after dark) what they thought was a submarine close to the shore. This report, although not confirmed, gave some substance to our long-held suspicions that the Turkish Cypriots were getting surreptitious support from the Turkish mainland. This of course would have been contrary to the agreement between Greece and Turkey, but it was never possible to acquire the necessary evidence. We were not equipped with night-vision binoculars or surveillance radars.

On 12 February, I received some welcome news. The CO informed me that I could organise the mortar troop for serious collective training and that I should withdraw an additional quantity of mortar ammunition from the Sovereign Base Area at Dhekelia. This change in policy came about because of the threat of a Turkish invasion of the island, a threat that fortunately was not realised.

However, as I had expected, centralised training turned out to be a very difficult task. The company commanders were understandably reluctant to release their artillery personnel even for a day's training. In all, I only managed to hold collective training on a very small number of occasions, mainly at C Company camp in Lefka, and never with the full complement.

Under the terms of the ceasefire agreement, those Greeks who needed to pass through the village of Limnitis could do so only under UN escort. A Company, apart from having some of the most remote inland observation posts to man and to operate, were mainly responsible for providing the armed escorts. A Company camp was located in an almond grove in low-lying ground directly under a heavily fortified hill. The Turkish fighters on the hill were well entrenched with an excellent command of the valley beneath, where nothing could move without their knowledge. On one occasion, in response to some perceived grievance, the defenders placed a roadblock on the main road and refused passage to all travellers. This was in contravention of the UN agreement and it created quite a stir. Despite all his efforts, the company commander, Comdt Jack Murphy, failed to make any headway in his negotiations with the Turkish fighters. I was on duty when Lt-Col Dempsey said he would go out there himself to see what he could do. He departed in his Rover with an armed escort saying that he would keep us informed. After a long wait, one of the communications NCOs called me, saying there was a message from the CO in Irish. The message said, 'Chur an cathlán ar airdeall, tá mé chun an constaic bothair a scriosadh le neart' – literally meaning: 'Put the battalion on alert, I am going to destroy the obstacle by force'. This was a serious development and the entire battalion was promptly placed on alert, ready to respond to developments.

As was the protocol, I immediately phoned HQ in Nicosia, asked for an Irish officer and repeated the message in Irish to him. There was what could only be described as a pregnant pause from Nicosia before a message came back to me, also in Irish, 'In ainm Dé, ná dhein' – 'For God's sake, don't'. I passed this on to A Company and the CO. However, by the time the message was received there, it was all over, the obstacle was removed and freedom of movement was restored.

We subsequently learned that the entire UN force across the island had been put on alert just in case the Irish were going to start a war. But the reality on the ground was very different, much more mundane. What happened was that two unarmed, and no doubt nervous, soldiers of A Company left their camp, marched the short distance along the road to the offending obstacle – a simple wooden barrier wrapped in barbed wire – lifted it up and threw it into the ditch after which they retired again to their camp. That was the end of it, no shots were fired and there were no repercussions. We had a good laugh at it, but the CO was not amused. Apparently, he had detailed an officer to send a message saying that he was going to have the obstacle removed physically, not by force!

It was a prime example of the simple misinterpretation of his intentions, further compounded by an inaccurate translation into Irish. The response from HQ in Nicosia was also apparently a direct translation of the words of the acting FC to the message received while at a social event in the capital.

When the weather finally turned warm and dry, I was interested to study the activities of the local Turkish Cypriots and to get some idea of how they lived. In the olive grove in which my tent and others were pitched, an old man arrived one morning to do the spring ploughing. Dressed in the traditional manner of the Turkish male, loose-fitting baggy black trousers, long leather boots, a black headscarf and a heavy pullover, he sported a luxuriant white handlebar moustache and carried a light whip. He was driving a large cow to pull an old wooden plough, encouraging it with words of Turkish as he struggled along, dodging around the olive trees. The 'blade' of the plough was nothing more than a stout wooden post set at an angle to the frame. As the soil was damp, it turned easily under the simple plough.

In the orange groves further west beyond Lefka, entire families were working together, children and all, to pick the oranges from the trees, placing them on sheets in large piles at intervals along the grove. They then went over them again, cleaning and polishing the fruit after which the oranges were taken away in baskets to be boxed and sent to the markets. The children were having great fun, especially when I produced my camera, while the women were laughing and talking amongst themselves in great good humour. The winter was over and they were looking forward to cashing in on the first of their main crop, the oranges. The olive and the grape harvests would follow later in the year.

It was easy to see the deep satisfaction and contentment of those rural people in the slow and steady pace of the lives they led, a lifestyle that had evolved over the centuries and had given them such peace and stability. It is easy to see also why such people should be left to themselves without the interference of those who would wish to change or 'improve' their lives for them, simply to fit in with the latest political 'ism'.

On 17 March, two battalion parades were held at Skouriotissa.

The first parade was held after mass for the presentation of shamrock. Some members of the Australian Civilian Police who were operating in our district attended, as many of them were of Irish descent. Led by Superintendent Holland and Inspector Brewer, they participated in the medal parade later that same day and received their UN service medals from Col Carl O'Sullivan, the Irish Contingent Commander.

Throughout this tour on Cyprus, because I had so many conflicting responsibilities, I was working almost on a twenty-four-hour basis and I found it very tiring. It was more than three months before I had enough time to relax and wear civvies for the first time. While I cannot speak for the personnel of the other companies, I was close enough to C Company to know that all ranks in that company were also exhausted well before the end of their tour – it could not end soon enough for them.

It should be realised by those who have no experience of the military life that simply because we were on a well-known holiday island it did not automatically mean that life was easy. The duties for all ranks were constant and frequent, the tensions and the occasional shooting episodes only adding to the strain. Even being off duty and relaxing in one's tent could all change within minutes in response to a sudden emergency. A six-month tour as a member of a UN battalion has little provision for rest – every member of the battalion is on duty or available for duty on a twenty-four-hour basis.

A suggestion had been made following the completion of the Irish involvement in the Congo that units could easily have served for a full year rather just six months. While attractive from a logistics point of view, I believe it would have placed an intolerable burden on the soldiers concerned. It would have required a much higher level of welfare support than the relatively poor system actually provided, in addition to a working system of home leave for all ranks mid-way through their twelve-month tours of duty.

When we were coming close to the end of our tour in UNFICYP the Greek National Guard staged a surprise attack on the Turkish position at Ambelikou during the night of 11–12 March. They dislodged the Turkish fighters from their protective positions overlooking Lefka. C Company, already feeling the strain, was stretched to the limit by this new development, just when they were starting to pack for home. The company was immediately required to re-position some of their OPs and to establish new ones. Because the company was under such pressure, HQ Company was asked to establish and man a new position on the slope of the Cypriot Mining Company tiphead just behind the battalion medical post. From that location, there was a good view of some of the new Greek positions. Because it was above and behind the battalion medical post, we christened it OP Doc!

Considerable incidents of shooting continued around Ambelikou and Peristeronari. At one point, Capt. Kevin Deeney, with two soldiers of his company, advanced into open ground between the opposing sides trying to obtain a ceasefire. Even though they were carrying a large UN flag, and their intent must have been clear, heavy firing resumed on both sides and they were forced to take cover. Following protracted negotiations, they were extracted after some hours but only with great difficulty.

During the latter half of the tour of duty, members of the battalion, in small groups of about forty, had been going on a week-long break to Beirut and Jerusalem. I had left it towards the end to take my turn and went in a group that included my CO and the Irish Contingent Commander, Col Carl O'Sullivan on 22 February 1965. We spent three days in Jordan and Jerusalem, and four days in Beirut. While in Jerusalem, I met up with two cadet classmates, Capts Frank O'Donovan and Michael McMahon, who were serving with UNTSO. Beirut at that time was called the banking centre of the Middle East and, untouched by war, it radiated prosperity and happiness and appeared to have a cosmopolitan atmosphere. Some of us felt that it was surely the place to retire to when the time came. How wrong we would have been.

After this welcome break in Lebanon and Jerusalem, it was back to the turmoil of the situation at Lefka and for the final weeks of the mission preparations for departure took precedence at all levels. Apart from preparing for the handover of the equipment of the mortar troop and the accounts of the officers' mess, I also started on a last frantic rush to get to some of the OPs in the hills to film them, using the battalion's 16mm camera. By good fortune, when leaving Ireland, I had taken my film editor and splicer with me to use in putting together my own 8mm films. As the splicer could also be used for 16mm film, I was able to put the battalion 16mm footage that I had taken on to a 400 foot reel. I showed the film to the CO and officers in HQ Company, and later on to some of those in C Company, before handing the camera and film over to our quartermaster.

The last few weeks in Cyprus passed in a blur – the details of the rotation were published and the prospect of final release gave a new impetus and energy to everybody to ensure that the handover was as smooth as possible. In a radical departure from previous rotations, this rotation was to take place over just two days. There were to be eight Chalks in all and I was listed for the final one. This was fortunate because Comdt Seán Barrett had to leave early as his father was seriously ill, leaving me as the Operations Officer for the remaining period. The advance party of 42nd Battalion arrived on 31 March and the briefings and handovers started immediately.

Capt. Pat Ghent succeeded me as the mortar troop commander. As a result of my reports, he and the entire mortar troop were now an integral element of HQ Company, located at Skouriotissa. With great relief I handed over the officers' mess accounts to Capt. Dennis Byrne and was finally free to start packing for home. The 41st Battalion handed over responsibilities for the area of operations to the 42th (OC, Lt-Col P.J. Delaney) on 9 April and I found myself on the last Chalk to Dublin the following day.

Chapter 9

THE GOLAN HEIGHTS

No other international issue is more complex and more potentially dangerous for the maintenance of international peace and security than the Arab-Israeli conflict in the Middle East.

No other issue has claimed more of the Organisation's time and attention. It is also the issue out of which the concept of United Nations peacekeeping evolved.

Since 1948, there have been six fully-fledged wars directly connected with the Arab-Israeli conflict, and five United Nations peacekeeping operations have been established in the region, of which three are still active.

Extract from The Blue Helmets, a Review of
United Nations Peacekeeping 1948–1990, 1990

UNTSO was a popular mission with many Irish officers because their families were permitted to live with them in the mission area. Being able to bring one's family was an incentive for some officers, but was a great problem for others, depending on the ages or the schooling needs of the children. At the time of my spell with UNTSO, the tour for Irish officers was for eighteen months. Having already had a taste of UN service in Katanga and in Cyprus, I was particularly anxious to experience the mission in the Middle

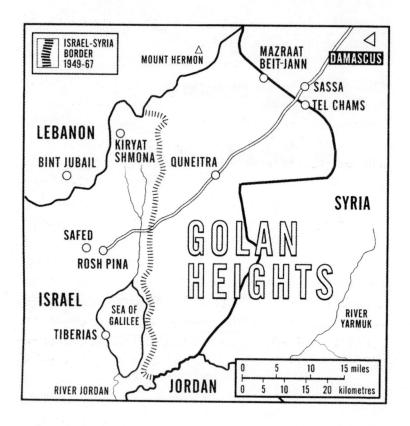

East because of the constant coverage in the newspapers and on radio. Many of my friends and even some of my cadet classmates had already served with UNTSO and spoke in glowing terms about their experiences. The system for volunteering for UN service at that time (1973) was that each officer wrote to his CO saying that he wished to be considered as a volunteer for either UN service in general or for a specific mission. The CO then passed the letter upwards together with his own recommendations. I had expressed my willingness on more than one occasion to be considered for UNTSO service but without success.

At the time I was chosen in 1973, I was a senior captain serving as a troop commander in the 10th Battery, 2nd Field Artillery

Regiment in McKee Barracks, Dublin. Due to the shortage of officers, I was also acting as Training Officer to 14th Field Battery, an FCA unit, then an integral reserve component of the regiment and was also required to act as Barrack Adjutant, McKee Barracks, during the nine-month absence of Capt. Pat McKevitt on a Command and Staff course.

Capt. Jim Mortell and I were chosen for service with UNTSO at the same time and due to travel to the Golan Heights in June to replace two other Irish officers who had come to the end of their tours of duty. However, at that time severe tensions were building up between Israel and its Arab neighbours, and another outbreak of war was a distinct possibility. As a result, the two officers already in the mission, whom we were to replace, were granted extensions of six months. We were naturally very disappointed, as were our families. However, it turned out to be a blessing in disguise as it meant that we missed the Yom Kippur War in October of that year. Who knows what might have happened to rookie observers on the Golan Heights or at the Suez Canal during that period of extreme violence!

On 10 January 1974, Jim Mortell and I finally arrived in Jerusalem via London to take up duty as UN military observers. Capt. Hugh O'Connor, an Irish officer already stationed in Jerusalem, met us at a bustling Ben Gurion airport and after a meal in his house he dropped us to the Italian Hospice nearby where we had been booked in. Next morning he brought us to Government House to begin our formal check-in. This started with a visit to Staff-Sergeant Loibneggar, the Austrian medical assistant, for our medical checks. The next few days saw us being processed through the many offices of the Field Service and the military staff, with whom we would be dealing for the next eighteen months.

Col Dick Bunworth was the acting chief-of-staff (in effect the FC) of UNTSO at the time. On our second day in Jerusalem he and his wife very kindly invited myself and Jim to have lunch with them in the main dining-room at Government House, during which we brought him up-to-date with news from Ireland.

On Monday 14 January, we were picked up by Major Carey and driven to the UN MAC (Mixed Armistice Commission) house in Tiberias via Jericho and the Jordan Valley. After a very interesting drive north along the valley of the Jordan river, we arrived into Tiberias at 17.00hrs in heavy rain. There Comdt Terry McNulty greeted us and brought us first to his house for a meal and then to check into the Scottish Hospice. Major Carey was the Operations Officer and Comdt Terry McNulty was a member of his small staff.

Tiberias, a large town with a population (then) of 24,000, is set in a beautiful location on the steep western bank of what is variously called the Sea of Galilee, Lake Kinneret or Lake Tiberias. The town faces eastwards across the lake to the Golan Heights. It was divided by virtue of the topography into three distinct sections, upper, middle and lower Tiberias. The lowest and oldest part of the town sits right on the edge of the lake at 212m below sea level. A small but beautifully preserved Crusader castle lay there, close to the water, that had been turned into a very nice restaurant. Another Crusader castle, Belvoir, lay a short distance south of Tiberias where the Yarmuk river, coming from Syria, meets the Jordan.

My first surprise related to the Golan Heights, about which I had been reading for many years. The Golan Heights were not really heights at all, as I had expected, but simply the steeply rising ground or, in places, cliffs, replicating the topography of the western side of the lake. Apart from a number of small ridges and isolated low hills, the only mountain to be seen was the ridge and snow-covered peak of Mount Hermon. Militarily, the terrain required that whoever wished to dominate both the Golan Heights and the approaches to Damascus – or to Tiberias – had to have control over the natural strongpoint of that mountain. As a result, it was fought over bitterly on many occasions by Israel and Syria with its Arab allies. One of the Israeli elite units was the Golani Brigade whose soldiers had fought for control of the summit of Hermon in all the wars.

The UN MAC house was situated in a rented house in Upper Tiberias where the air was cooler. The house was referred to in conversation as the MAC House or, if speaking on radio, as 'Tango'. The weather that mid-January was quite cool, with heavy and frequent thunderstorms, and there was snow on the high ground on the Golan Heights. The Israelis informed with us with great glee that the rainfall was very welcome – it would help the crops and fill up the lake, apparently well below its normal level for the time of year.

With the help of Terry and his wife Ann, I quickly settled in, renting a ground-floor apartment in mid-town owned by a Jewish family called Etinger. When my wife Anne arrived soon after, she rejected it out of hand, even though there was a small public park nearby where the children could play. Accommodation is always tricky, but as UNMOs were moved regularly, it was only a matter of time before another option would arise. As it happened, a Danish officer, Capt. Leif Schunk, was leaving for Damascus and we quickly acquired his apartment in upper Tiberias, located on the MAC house road. Our new dwelling was in the basement of a large house and it had a mesmerising view over the lake at the end of the garden, but some 200m below us.

Our new landlords were Iraqi Jews, the Shemishes. The husband was the regional manager for Shechem, the IDF canteen board. The family had fled Iraq about twenty years before. Communication was a problem as the family, apart from Mr Shemish, had very little English, but despite this they were very friendly landlords.

On our arrival Jim and I were given a thorough operational

briefing by Terry McNulty and then assigned to the humdrum tasks of TCC (Tiberias Control Centre). We were briefed on the committees within the TCC community, members of which were both civilian and military. The most important one was considered to be the Recreation and Welfare Committee, who organised 'Happy Hours' in the MAC house – usually to celebrate the national days of the many different nationalities based there. They also organised the more formal functions such as medal parades.

Another committee was the Evacuation Committee, which existed to prepare – in the event of another outbreak of hostilities – an orderly evacuation of dependants from the mission area to Beirut, it being a peaceful city at that time. However, following the increasing instability in Lebanon, the safe refuge was later changed to Cyprus. Each family was required to have $1,500 dollars in travellers cheques and a packed suitcase – only one case permitted per family – ready to move at very short notice. This procedure had been put into effect at the outbreak of the war the previous October. Fortunately, the evacuation plan was never implemented during my time.

Yet another committee was called the Shelter Improvement Committee, born of necessity when the Israeli advance towards Damascus meant that UNMOs found themselves in unprotected locations. Every so often a group of UNMOs and Field Service volunteers would go out to a selected observation post and spend a day improving shelters. The Chief Administrative Officer of the Field Service was Kevin Lavin, one of a small group of Irish working in Tiberias at that point.

We also had to quickly learn many terms that were new to us. The American influence was very obvious in terms such as 'gassing up', i.e. filling up the petrol tank, or references to the 'shithouse', a term freely used in conversation or over the radio without any embarrassment or censure. When I first heard the expression

2nd Medium AA Battery, McKee Barracks, *c.*1939. Sgt Patrick Murray nearest camera.

Clare area competition winning platoon, Ennis Battalion FCA. Capt. Moloney, Lieut McInerney and Capt. O'Neill are seated behind the trophy (*left to right*). Cpl Skerrit and BQMS Maguire are standing on the extreme left and right respectively.

Part of the 25th cadet class after a 'Platoon in Defence' firing practice, Glen Imaal, 1952. Sgt Troy, instructor, on extreme right.

Coolmoney Camp, Glen Imaal – all the comforts of home! Note the trestle beds. Cadets Barney Dobey and Jack Spillane (*right*).

'Ex Youghal', 1956. The Brigade (*extreme left*) forming up for a parade through the town.

Reloading during 8th Battery firing practices, Seskin School, Glen Imaal.

Leitrim gun position, 18pdr firing practices.

Recruiting caravan, Castlecomer. *Left to right:* BS Fahy, Gnr Anderson, Cpl Keyes and Capt. Moriarty.

Shannon floods. Assisting with the removal of animals, Ballinahoun area, 1954.

A detachment under Sgt M. Maher demonstrating the rapid firing ability of the 120mm mortar. Glen Imaal 1960.

Casement Air Station, first lifting of a 120mm mortar. The nets were later replaced with proper lifting cables. Photo: Air Corps

PTI Course, 1954. Vaulting the River Slaney. In the background: on the left, Sgt Hogan, instructor and on the right, Comdt D. McCormack, OC ASPC.

Moise Tshombe, President of Katanga, and his Belgian military adviser Col Weber walking past a Guard of Honour from No. 1 Platoon, B Company, under Platoon Commander Lieut Jerry Healy (saluting). Photo: B Company

No. 1 Platoon A Company just after they received their UN Service medals from Comdt E. Vaughan.

The FC, General Thimmaya and Lt-Col Dempsey, Battalion Commander, leaving the officers' mess tent at Skouriotissa.
Photo: Air Corps

Heavy Mortar Troop, 41st Battalion, UNIFCYP, assembled for training at C Company camp near Lefka, Morphou district. Kneeling at front, fourth from left: Capt. Moriarty, Troop Commander, with Sgt Shanahan and Lieut Dunne on his left. Standing at left rear, Cpl A. Jones.

10th Battery HQ, Brennan's Farm, Glen Imaal. *Left to right:* Capt. E. O'Sullivan, I/G, Lieut A. Maybury, 2/Lieut L. Clancy, Lt-Col T. Ryan, School Commandant, Artillery School, and 2/Lieut C. Fitzsimmons.

Battery Commander, 10th Battery, fined for the illegal parking of a 25pdr in Grafton Street!

10th Battery 105mm guns firing at high angle, Glen Imaal. No. 4 has just fired.

OP 41, Masraat Beit Jinn. Under fire in the shelter. *Left to right:* An Israeli soldier, Israeli Capt. Avni Shlomo and Capt. Asteljoki. Photo: Capt. Asteljoki, 1974

The Golan Heights. OP 4 badly damaged in the Syrian assault during the Yom Kippur War 1973.

OP 42, Tel Chams. Capt. Kalevi Hukkanen, Finnish Army, at the living caravan, Mount Hermon in the background. Photo: Capt. Hukkanen

11th Battery Heavy Mortar, the 'Greyhound Battery', Magee Barracks, Kildare. The Battery Commander, Comdt Pat Buckley, is standing in the second row from the rear, sixth from the left.

Christmas dinner, 46th Irishbatt, at the 'Tramshed'. *Left to right*: Capt. K. Heery, CQMS, B. Moore, CQMS, J. Chester and Capt. A. Fogarty (*bottom right*).

HQ Company pistol, rifle and SMG teams for the battalion shooting competitions at As Sultaniyeh. Standing, second from left, Sgt Nolan and beside him, Capt. John Byrne, team captain.

THIS IS HOW the 46" EARNED THEIR WAGES

Near miss, C Company building, At Tiri.

Further damage at Naqoura. Capts G. Kerton and D. Hyland inspecting the damage.

HQ UNIFIL, Naqoura. The Swedish Medical Company (nearest camera), followed by Italair and Camp Tara. The road south to Israel can be seen in the distance.

Medal Parade, Camp Command, 1985.

The funeral of Lieut Aengus Murphy, killed by a roadside bomb in 1986.

Norbatt Ops Conference. In the centre is Col Backer, Chief Operations Officer, UNIFIL, standing with his arms folded. At extreme left, Lt-Col Purcell, Force Signals Officer.

At Luanda, preparing to depart for Lubango in an Antonov 26 (at rear). *Left to right*: Comdt Ryan, Col Moriarty, Majs Kimani and Jakoube.

Lubango UN Complex. *Left to right:* Snr Mungo, Deputy Foreign Minister, Col Moriarty, Marrack Goulding, Lt-Gen. Francisco dos Santos Ndalu, Brig.-Gen. Opande and Mr Hisham Omyad.

Distributing some metal badges, bearing the message 'UNTAG Free and Fair Elections', with Maj. Rodrigues.

Sharing a joke at a PLAN camp north of Lubango. PLAN fighters become civilians and prepare their belongings to bring to Namibia. Maj. Arias, Maj. de Los Rios and Maj. Jakoube, with Comrade Juan (*centre*), PLAN leader.

At a former SWAPO prison – an abandoned field cooking trailer. Maj. Kimani on the left with Irishman Inspector P.J. McGowan.

Medal Parade, Lubango, December 1989. DFC Opande taking the
parade.

Former members of the 7th Field Artillery Regiment marching in the
stand-down parade at McKee Barracks, September 2005.
Photo: Comdt Joe Kelly

'chinese mortar' I couldn't even guess what it meant – I had to see one to understand. It is quite simply a urinal and its construction could not be more basic. A hole of about a metre square is dug to a depth of one metre into which is sunk a length of piping. A small amount of canvas encloses the urinal to provide a little privacy. The 'shithouse', however, needs little explanation. It was a small hut made out of galvanised sheeting and timber positioned over a deep hole in the ground. Such structures were known to Irish soldiers for years as 'the long drop'. A big surprise for us was the use of first names by all UNMOs, regardless of rank.

During my first months there, all was quiet on the Golan Heights, partly because of the severe weather, but also probably as a result of exhaustion following the end of the Yom Kippur War. Both sides were no doubt busy training new soldiers, repairing or replacing armoured vehicles and aircraft, and racing to be ready for a possible round two. The guns had fallen silent, but not for very long, as even then the UN was attempting to put in place yet another peacekeeping mission, this time on the Golan Heights.

When on duty, UNMOs travelled in clearly marked white painted vehicles, flying UN flags. The observation posts themselves were made as visible as possible – they were painted white, with 'UN' in large letters on every surface and on the roofs, while the UN flag was flown on a twenty-four-hour basis.

Painting every possible external surface on the OP was regarded as recreational therapy for the observers. I often smiled to myself and wondered what the gunners of 2nd Field Artillery Regiment would have said had they seen me, one of their battery commanders, with a bucket and brush in hand, spending hours painting rocks!

In the aftermath of the Yom Kippur War, some of the observation posts on the Israeli side had become redundant as the ceasefire line had been moved eastwards. New temporary posts had to be put in place in a hurry to maintain observation over the ceasefire line in the Saasa salient. These were designated as patrol bases and had been hastily built. The unprotected living caravans were usually above ground in full view of both sides, and the bomb shelters provided were temporary and inadequate. The observers in these patrol bases, in addition to the normal observation and reporting tasks, were required to conduct limited mobile patrols on designated routes in their localities. Such patrolling was only with the prior agreement of their Israeli LOs. On the Golan Heights, the LO was accommodated at the Israeli military post nearest to the UN observation post. He would be driven to and from the UN post in his own IDF vehicle, accompanied by a radio operator. The LOs were usually reservists beyond the age for active service, and most of them were pleasant, chatty types, full of curiosity about us and our countries.

While the patrolling was a welcome break from the general routine, it was also fairly hazardous. For me, a sobering indication of the hazards of the job came when, on arrival at my first patrol base, I discovered that the floor of the jeep was covered by a layer of sandbags while each UNMO wore his flak jacket and sat on another. Movement outside the base area after dark was strictly prohibited by the Israelis. They regarded any movement during the hours of darkness as hostile and their post commanders were under strict orders to open fire immediately.

Unlike some of my earlier missions, communications were excellent right across the entire mission area. Every UN vehicle – trucks included – was equipped with a VHF radio, and drivers were required to report on their movements at all times. Good communications were very important from a safety point of view. It enabled the control centres, or even drivers, to warn all listeners of firing or other hazards in sufficient time to take evading action or to seek shelter at the nearest UN post.

The primary function of the UN observation posts was to

maintain a continuous observation of the entire ceasefire zone and to report immediately on all incidents within those zones. The chain of reporting from the observation post went directly to Tiberias from where it was passed to Jerusalem, ending up swiftly at the United Nations in New York. On the surface it might appear to be a useless or innocuous way to contain the many violations of the ceasefire in 1973 between Syria and Israel. However, all sides on the dispute were aware that every action would be reported promptly and accurately, and this fact proved to be a surprisingly effective deterrent. The pressure that could be brought on Syria or Israel by the nations of the Security Council was considerable and none of the countries in dispute were willing or able to resist it for very long. The simplicity of the plan was its very success – on most occasions.

After about seven days of briefings and discussions, my name appeared on the duty roster and I found that I was to spend four days in OP 2 with a Norwegian, Capt. Thorsen Ronvaal. However, the rain in Tiberias turned into heavy snow as we crossed the Jordan on an army girder bridge, climbed up onto the Golan Heights and drove with difficulty to the UN post at Quneitra. A forward sub-HQ had been established there, the principal reason being to maintain a UN presence in that uninhabited and devastated town. At Quneitra we were informed that the Israelis were unable to declare that the road to our observation post had been cleared, so we had no option but to return to Tiberias.

On the morning of the second attempt, Major George Mayes of Australia replaced Capt. Ronvaal and we set off again from Tiberias. George, formerly an NCO and now a Transport Officer at home, asked me to drive, saying that I was probably more used to snow conditions than he! Naturally I was delighted to oblige, and I was even more pleased when he quickly said that he could tell that I was army trained by the way I held the steering wheel. At times there could be quite a bit of tension over who should drive and usually an agreement would be worked out in advance for taking turns at the wheel. Such attitudes might appear to be childish, but in fact the standards of driving varied greatly and the circumstances sometimes were such that speed and skill were essential. Few of the roads had either a fence or ditch and to drive off the road accidentally could mean driving into a minefield.

On this occasion we were forced to spend a cold and uncomfortable night at Quneitra. Late on the third day, the roads were declared open and we finally made it through to replace the two besieged UNMOs. By now the occupants of OP 2 were quite annoyed as they were two days over their relief day and were living on pack rations, having run out of fresh food.

The snow was lying nearly 25cm deep and deeper in drifts. On the first morning I had to dig my way from the living caravan into the OP before I could have a look at the landscape. Digging snow was not what I had expected to be doing on my first duty, but it was a great way of keeping warm. Having been tardy with the relief, we only spent two days at the OP before being relieved. I was a bit disappointed at this but at least it ensured that the duty roster did not need to be adjusted.

My second duty was at OP 7, the most southerly of the posts, situated in a dramatic location overlooking a deep wadi where the borders of Syria, Jordan and Israel met. OP 7 traditionally had been the quietest of the OPs and many novice observers were sent there first to learn the ropes. I enjoyed the simple routine, and even managed to produce reasonable meals to the satisfaction of my companion, Mario Verreschi, a marine captain from Venice. On OP the officers took turns, usually every second day, at preparing the meals. There was an onus on each officer to prepare the best from the national cuisine to impress the other. This did not really apply to some like myself, never having learned to cook! I simply followed the instructions on the packets or tins, ensuring that first my companion had a large aperitif of Irish whiskey. The dinners generally were very enjoyable and the discussions ranged far and wide.

The weather on one of the days was very wet and we didn't leave the caravan, but the sky cleared after dark. I spent a lot of time outside looking at the wonderful night sky, trying to identify my favourite stars and constellations. Looking east towards the Syrian lines, the only lights to be seen were a few weak yellow lights in one or two small villages. These lights appeared to be from candles or paraffin lamps and there were no street lights to be seen. The contrast could not have been greater when looking west. While Tiberias was well below our line of sight, it was possible to see four or five kibbutzim to our rear because they were lit up with thousands of bright lights in the windows of the houses, on the streets and also on the defensive perimeter fences that surrounded each settlement. In between the kibbutzim, the countryside was in total darkness. In that moonless night, the kibbutzim looked like glittering galaxies in deepest space, shimmering and twinkling. It struck me that the presence or absence of public lighting epitomised the gulf between the western and eastern worlds.

The sole operational report we had to make during our four days at OP 7 was to report an over-flight by two Israeli Skyhawks, flying low from south to north along the line. I never even saw them as I was filling the tank of the generator, but I was very impressed by the reaction of Mario. He dashed to the radio and reported their passing to Tango. I learned from him that it was a matter of pride to get in one's report before the next OP up the line, as we could have later been accused of inattention or incompetence. On our relief day, we returned to Tiberias via the southern route, a spectacular drive, arriving down at the southern tip of the lake and then driving north into Tiberias.

With discussions under way in New York to arrange for

the installation of a new UN peacekeeping force on the Golan Heights, tensions started to rise again, as both sides wished to negotiate from a position of strength. In February and March exchanges of artillery fire were frequent, although no heavy weapons were fired during the hours of darkness. As the negotiations leading up to the formation of UNDOF accelerated, each side intensified their efforts to put pressure on the other. Heavy artillery, rocket and mortar exchanges, in some cases using white phosphorous, became frequent. This made life very busy and at times uncomfortable for the observers. Yet despite all this effort, the enormous expense and the probable loss of life, it was significant that no movements of ground troops or armour by either side took place during the lead up to the establishment of the new mission.

If either side had really wanted to improve on their dispositions in order to have a bargaining chip at the negotiation table, it would surely have been logical to attempt to take or re-take some important hill or road junction. Could all that noise, expense and risky behaviour have been for bravado, for internal consumption in Israel and Syria, or simply to impress the international community? To me the whole exercise did not make any sense.

The agreement on disengagement between Syria and Israel was finally signed in Geneva on 31 May 1974, bringing UNDOF into being on the Golan Heights. Thus commenced a remarkably stable situation in this critical region that has continued to this day. To have been involved in the events of this period was a wonderful education for an artillery officer like myself coming from a country that has never fought in a modern war. In the following stories I will try to give an account of some of my experiences with apologies to those other Irish officers whose experiences, I know, were considerably more exciting and stressful than mine.

My next duty, on 7 February 1974, was to PB 43 with Swedish Capt. Sven Sundin, a reservist on a one-year tour. He was a schoolteacher at home. The base was set on the forward slope of a low hill facing almost due south into Syria towards a large solitary hill called Tel El Charrar. There were very few attractions to this particular PB. The living caravan had no protection whatever, standing out in full view of anyone on the plain to our front. The entire area was muddy and the floor of the shelter, close to the steps of the caravan – an old Syrian bunker – was covered in about 30cm of water. The weather was terrible, the generator refused to start and the gas-powered fridge went out on our first evening. Not a good start to this particular duty.

Each day, we conducted some interesting patrols, getting a vivid picture of the concentrated violence of the fighting that had raged in the vicinity only a short time before. The patrols could be undertaken only with the permission of the IDF, and our LO, a pleasant man called Samuel, always accompanied us in his IDF vehicle. The entire landscape was littered with the debris of war, vehicles, weapons and even a crashed helicopter, while small items of equipment and discarded ammunition lay everywhere.

I had seen a very sobering sight just to the east of Quneitra as we travelled to the patrol base. A Syrian Air Defence battery of 37mm towed guns had been caught on the move and totally destroyed. They lay in line just off the road, one behind the other, guns, towing vehicles, ammunition vehicles, the generator and the radar vehicles and, pathetically, bringing up the rear, a civilian fire brigade vehicle. It clearly illustrated the folly of travelling in a textbook peacetime convoy when the opposing forces had complete command of the air over the area.

The first three days at PB 43 were quiet and we were undisturbed at night. On the fourth day, I was busy preparing the dinner, when there was a sudden outbreak of heavy firing that literally shook the caravan. It appeared to be on all sides of us and my first impression was that we were in the middle of an attack. We both rushed outside and headed for the shelter. Then I remembered that I had soup on the gas and that we were supposed to be recording the shooting for Tango. So I asked Sven to count the detonations and to try to give me an indication of the details. The detonations were rapid and the fog both exaggerated the sound and made it very difficult to decide on direction.

I have to confess that my legs were shaking as I climbed back into the caravan where I spent a very busy half hour. I had to write down the details as shouted by Sven, then call the information in to Tango, while at the same time stirring the soup on the gas stove. I had to laugh at myself afterwards because it never even occurred to me that I should abandon the dinner and switch off the gas! Calm was restored by about 18.00hrs, after which we sat down for a thoughtful dinner.

The night was peaceful, but at about 11.30hrs on our final day, it all started up again, just as heavy as previously. Again we could see nothing because of thick fog. We were delighted and very impressed therefore when our relief crew arrived, one of whom was Irish Capt. Dave Taylor. Because of the firing, Tango would not give us permission to depart for some hours. When the fog lifted, we were able to detect Syrian artillery batteries firing from around Tel el Charrar at targets to our right rear towards Quneitra. Some of the engagements were heavy, but because we could now see, it was quite obvious that we had not been in any danger, apart from the possibility of breaking a leg in dashing to the shelter!

My next duty was with US Marine Capt. John Ready to OP 4, overlooking the Rafid Junction, roughly halfway down the line of OPs. John was a veteran of Vietnam and was suffering from a bad back due to injuries received there. OP 4 had been badly knocked about in the fighting as it lay in the path of the most southerly of the three Syrian armoured thrusts aimed at cutting the IDF line to the south of Lake Galilee. A large anti-tank ditch, dug by the Israelis, passed across the front of the OP, extending for some distance in both directions. A Syrian armoured bridge-carrying vehicle had been driven into the ditch and unfolded to cross the gap. On the temporary bridge were two knocked out tanks and the immediate area was littered with wrecked or abandoned vehicles of all types.

We were told later that the Israel Air Force may have saved the day for Israel by preventing a major Syrian breakthrough towards the southern end of the Sea of Galilee. Despite the desperate Israeli situation at that time on the Sinai, a difficult but correct decision was made to divert aircraft and armour resources from the Sinai front to the Golan Heights. Even so, a Syrian column managed to reach the Heights overlooking the lake. They came to a halt only because they had run out of fuel. A monument to this very close call – from an Israeli point of view – can be seen there in the form of a Syrian tank mounted on a concrete platform.

The four-day duty passed without incident, apart from a visit by Lt-Cols Dunne and Gal. The sun was strong, we read a lot and my principal claim to fame was that I tasted my first St Peter's fish, beautifully cooked by John Ready. By now I had the support of my wife Anne, who had arrived from Ireland with our three children. She would prepare the main meals in advance for me, which I could store in the fridge and then merely had to heat up. Because of the cold wet weather at that time, her shepherd's pie was particularly popular!

By a quirk of the duty roster, I found myself back once more at OP 4, this time in the company of US Capt. Al Sarno. He was an Air Defence officer and we had long discussions about air defence and other artillery matters. Our LO was a Capt. Cohen, who knew Dublin quite well and had met Adrian Hardiman at RTÉ. In civilian life he was a legal adviser working for Israeli TV. At the end of the second day, he gave us extra eggs, tomatoes and oranges, which I added to the pork chops for dinner that evening.

It was the custom for the Israelis to fly a photo-reconnaissance mission along the ceasefire line every morning when the sky was clear enough. They used two aircraft and flew at a great height. One aircraft clearly did the photography, flying in an arrow-straight line as the other weaved and dodged around, presumably as a decoy in case missiles were fired. On one of the days, I spotted the aircraft and reported 'two Mirages, high, from south to north'. The aircraft were Phantoms!

After the usual break for off-days and standby days, I found myself heading for my next duty at PB 42 in the company of Finnish Capt. Kalevi Hukkanen, known to us all as Charlie. He was a recent arrival in UNTSO and this time I was the 'experienced' UNMO. Our LO was a Capt. Amiel Brosh, whose real job was as a professor at Jerusalem University. During one of our many enjoyable discussions, he issued an invitation to my wife and I to visit him if we were ever in Jerusalem. I thanked him, not really expecting to take him up on his offer. However, subsequent events ensured that we were able to do so sooner than I expected.

PB 42 was located on the forward slope of a low ridge called Tel Chams, controlled by the Israelis, just south of the main road leading from Quneitra to Damascus. Damascus was only about 40kms away to the east and while it could not be seen from our location, it was possible to see the glow of the city's lights after dark. We were at the most easterly point of the Saasa salient, just forward of the Israeli positions.

The stony terrain stretching away to the east and south was flat and featureless, with low rolling ridges and the occasional small hill. Our PB was placed on a small byroad that gave access to what had been an important Syrian ammunition depot, stored in a large number of concrete bunkers that were tucked into the eastern side of the ridge. Many of the concrete ammunition bunkers were destroyed and the ground around them was littered with dangerous debris, ranging from live fuses to hand grenades to 120mm tank and 122mm artillery rounds.

During our first night we had little sleep as there appeared to be a sizeable small arms battle going on to the north of us that lasted most of the night. Kalevi dashed outside with his tape recorder, but being the seasoned UNMO by now, I stayed in bed, as I had decided that the Israeli posts were simply conducting a night firing exercise.

Both the Israeli and Syrian gunners used to play 'cat and mouse' games with each other in a manner that was very educational to officers from peaceful armies like mine. On the afternoon of the second day, we watched while a Syrian battery, located somewhere north-east of Saasa, opened fire on an Israeli strongpoint about 4kms north of our location. The Syrians were only using one gun, probably a Soviet D30 (122mm), firing a single round in a desultory way. After about fifteen minutes of this, the entire battery (of six guns), suddenly fired three or four rounds each at the Israeli position next to the one that had been getting the single rounds' treatment. This presumably was done with the expectation of catching Israeli soldiers outside their bunkers watching their comrades next door being shelled.

During our last night at PB 42, we were woken by the sound of heavy tracked vehicles clanking forward on the main road. I said 'get up quickly, we're in big trouble'. I was certain that I was hearing tanks on the main road, approximately 500m from us, and that it was only a matter of time before the Syrians opened up. We pulled on combats over our pyjamas and went outside, Kalevi clutching his tape recorder. It was quite dark and even with the binoculars we could only see vague shapes and strange sounds. In any case, we reported what we could hear to Tango.

Thankfully, the Syrians, who must have been aware of what was going on, remained quiet, even when the Israeli vehicles withdrew some three hours later. It was only with the arrival of daylight that we could see that the Israelis had dug a deep trench across the road out in the middle of the plain.

The next morning was our return day, but first we were ordered to go down to inspect the trenched road. So Kalevi and I drove as far as was advisable into no man's land and then we got out of our jeep. I told Kalevi to carry the UN flag as high as he could and we walked the last 200m with a certain amount of anxiety, keeping a sharp eye out for mines. It is not a comfortable place to be in, a demilitarised zone – one was aware of the hundreds of eyes on both sides watching our movements intently. The trench was deep and extended beyond the edge of the road, with barbed wire and mines around it. I described the scene as best I could for Tango. We returned to our PB without incident. Our return to Tiberias later on was delayed for some hours by heavy shelling to our rear, but eventually we got through for a welcome break.

A week later I was back on duty with Finnish Capt. Ilka Asteljoki at PB 41, located on the eastern outskirts of the Druze village of Mazraat Beit-Jann. Ilka was a veteran of the Yom Kippur War, as he had been in the Sinai when the Egyptians attacked across the Suez Canal. He had moved to Tiberias half way through his tour, no doubt expecting to have a quieter time on the Golan Heights before going home.

PB 41 was the most northerly post on the Israeli side of the line, situated on the lower slopes of Mount Hermon. The village, directly behind our caravan, appeared to be abandoned but we were able to see that there were possibly as many as six Israeli tanks hidden in and around the houses. The living caravan was above ground on the eastern side of the village with a four-foot high bank of earth on three sides, while the makeshift and seriously inadequate shelter was close by and above ground. Our observation post caravan was about 1,000 metres further to the east, on the top of a small, bare, rounded hill. The only protection there for the UNMOs was a small shallow slit trench. The IDF occupied a strongpoint only about 100 metres away.

The morning of 22 March 1974 was sunny and cool, and the front was quiet so we drove up to the OP accompanied by Capt. Avni Shlomo, our Israeli LO. He travelled in his own vehicle together with his driver and radio operator. While we were admiring the scenery and having a relaxed chat, we were interrupted by some shelling of Israeli positions well to our south and west.

I was sitting down to do the writing up and Ilka was passing the shooting reports (shootreps) over the radio to Tango. I then heard a strange noise behind us, quickly getting louder and nearer. I looked behind me and saw a Saggar anti-tank missile (of Soviet manufacture) passing close behind us, about two metres above the ground. It was so close that to this day I have a clear mental picture of the missile with its red and white lettering on the nose. It detonated within the barbed wire of the Israeli position about fifteen metres away from us, severely injuring the Israeli soldier who was sitting beside me.

I have no memory of hearing the explosion or of diving into the small and inadequate foxhole. Ilka quickly, and with great presence of mind, moved the jeep to a position almost straddling the foxhole. He dropped the mike into the foxhole so that we could hear from and transmit to Tango. When I looked out I saw Capt. Shlomo kneeling over the soldier who had received a severe wound to his stomach.

What followed next was a great example of comradeship and bravery. The uninjured soldier ran at speed into the Israeli post and returned with a folding stretcher. Capt. Shlomo and he then carried their injured comrade into the strongpoint. I risked peeping out and saw them running into the shelter of the Israeli compound, miraculously escaping the rounds that were beginning to fall thick and fast. The wounded man was later evacuated by

APC to a waiting helicopter, to be flown to hospital at Porryia near Tiberias.

By this time, in our general area, about six or eight separate targets were being fired on at the same time, to which the IDF replied with gusto. The bombardment lasted for well over an hour and we dared not move from where we were. The foxhole was very shallow as bedrock had been struck at only about one metre. This meant that we had to sit or kneel in order to keep our heads below ground level.

After some time, we were informed by Tango that the cease-fire was set for 14.15hrs, more than seventy-five minutes after firing began. After 14.00hrs the firing appeared to be abating, but at 14.14, we both heard the sound that we did not want to hear – the distant and very distinctive sound of a Syrian mortar platoon firing six rounds in our direction. We looked at each other and held our breath for thirty seconds. The rounds impacted around us and a blissful silence ensued. We had survived. After a short pause, we emerged cautiously to examine the jeep and our position.

While the OP caravan appeared to be undamaged, our jeep was in tatters. The radiator and the tyres were punctured, but the battery and radio had survived. Fortunately it had not gone on fire or we would have been compelled to run for cover into the IDF position. We looked around our foxhole and found two impact craters: one was six metres and the other only three metres away from our foxhole. As nearly always in the case of mortars, the tail fins of the 82mm projectiles were lying in or near the shallow craters. We each claimed one as a souvenir. We never used the OP again as two more days of heavy shelling prevented us from going near it.

That evening, over stiff whiskeys, Ilka apologised to me for not calling out a warning. He had recognised the sound of the approaching missile, having heard many on the Suez Canal, but he could not think of the English word in time to shout out a warning. The Field Service Transport Officer, Tom O'Neill, told me afterwards that he had counted 132 holes in the body of the jeep when it was returned to Tiberias.

At this stage it is worth describing the process by which any breach of the UN agreement by either side was brought to a halt. As soon as an exchange of firing commences, the operations officers in Tiberias and in Damascus will put pressure on their respective senior LOs to bring the firing to a halt. However, in the case of a major outbreak as I have just described and during a time of clearly rising tension across the zone, the UN pressure to halt the firing moved to New York. Sustained pressure was put on the ambassadors of Israel and Syria to get their governments to halt the firing before it got out of hand. A time would be agreed for a cessation and then each side had to ensure that that decision was communicated down through all the military levels and firing units involved. It was always a slow process.

Over the next two days we spent much of our time in, or close to, the shelter. After one long engagement we discovered that an artillery round had impacted some twenty-five metres to the front of our caravan while a house in the village about sixty metres behind us was in flames. Emerging from the shelter following a long barrage, we found two more Saggar missiles had passed over our shelter during the bombardment. In the general hubbub, we did not even hear them passing overhead. They had been fired by the Syrians attempting to hit some of the Israeli tanks near our location.

As a result of our experiences, and because of the unsuitable slit trench shelter, that UN position was never manned again. About three weeks later, a new location for the post was established some 2.5kms to the west of the village, making use of an old Syrian bunker. Although not a typical occurrence, the post was fired on by the Syrians shortly after it had been occupied by Irish Capt. Noel Donagh and US Colonel Dashiel. One round actually impacted on the roof of the bunker.

I had definitely qualified for my 'cooking medal' by the time I found myself back on duty in PB 2 with Capt. John Ready. The cooking medal was the UN service medal awarded to those who had spent six months on the mission. Its name was a reference to calm days when the biggest chore was the preparation of the evening meal.

Things were really warming up on the Golan Heights by now (March 1975). On the way to our PB, we were delayed for some hours at the now unused OP 6 by Syrian shelling beyond Quneitra. By the end of that first day, we had reported no less than fourteen shootreps from our location.

Later on the first day at PB 42, we had an unusual experience. About 09.00hrs an Israeli battery, somewhere far to the rear, opened up, firing just one round at about twenty minute intervals. The time of flight (from discharge to impact) of each round was very long and it took us some time to discover what the target was – a crossroads behind the village of Saasa. Standard operating procedures required that an observer must report each shooting event in a shootrep format. Once opened, a shootrep could not be closed again until thirty minutes had passed following the firing of the last round. This particular shootrep continued for a total of five hours, and always at the same target. We soon became fed up with this and so did Tango.

The second day of the duty was peaceful with an overcast winter sky casting a chill over the bleak landscape. We were going about our normal jobs when suddenly the morning peace was shattered by a loud explosion approximately 500 metres away and below us near the Israeli customs hut. Located on the Quneitra–Damascus road, it had been abandoned by officials some weeks earlier when tensions had started to rise on the Golan Heights.

It was a mysterious explosion. Normally, an observer would get some indication of the weapon and from where it had been fired. A second detonation had us putting on our flak jackets and helmets, but by the third and fourth rounds, we relaxed because it was now clear that the customs hut was the target. The fifth round destroyed the hut completely. In reporting this to Tango, we were unable to report from where the rounds were coming and we debated the problem for quite some time.

It was John Ready, the Vietnam veteran, who eventually solved the mystery. He said that it had to be tank fire and that the tank had to be somewhere along a line extending from our location through what remained of the hut and across into the Syrian lines. Looking along this line, we could see a large white-painted building, possibly a school, surrounded by a high concrete wall. John decided that because of the very high velocity of the tank shell, the detonation of the round at the hut was concealing the sound of the discharge of the weapon, so we reported accordingly.

Within ten minutes of our report, an Israeli battery from our rear opened fire using both high explosives and white phosphorus on the school, many rounds impacting near or within the compound. Initially, we were disturbed that our report to Tango might have given the Israelis the location of the offending weapon. Later we relaxed when we realised that the Israelis had several positions to our north, considerably closer than we were to the Syrian position at the school.

The next morning proved to be very interesting. For two days we had been puzzled by hearing a very distant Syrian battery firing single rounds at up to twenty-minute intervals, but we could not hear or see any impacts. It had to have some connection with what had been going on the night before (a distant sound of heavy small arms firing away to our north) so I started watching Mount Hermon through the binoculars every time we heard a discharge.

At this time, there was no UN OP between our position and the summit of Mount Hermon, so we had to maintain a watch over a much larger zone than normal. PB 41, at Mazraat Beit Jann, had been abandoned and its replacement had not yet been established. The summit of the mountain was 14kms away and it was with great delight that I eventually noticed tiny black smudges in the snow near the summit of the mountain. From this we realised that the sound of firing was connected to the impacts seen near the summit of the mountain. 'Tango from PB 42, shootrep – from NE 10km to NNW 16km, 1 round, impact seen, continuing.' At the debrief afterwards at TCC, we were credited with the most distant shootrep ever reported on the Golan Heights.

Earlier that same morning, we had noticed that PB 44 had missed First Call, and was still not answering the radio by Second Call at noon. It was sometimes possible that an OP would miss a call, because of radio or other problems, but to miss two in a row was a cause for alarm. The two officers at that post were Irish Capt. Jim Mortell and US Marine Capt. Jack Holly. The Israeli position overlooking the PB was able to confirm that all appeared to be normal except that there was no movement to be seen. However, because of heavy shelling in the area, they were unable to investigate for some time. In the early afternoon an Israeli patrol was able to report that the PB was empty.

There was great anxiety about their situation. But shortly after Capt. Ready and I returned to Tiberias, Damascus Control Centre reported that the two UNMOs were in hospital there and were being treated for foot injuries. It transpired that they had been taken prisoner during the night by a Saudi Arabian soldier who thought they were Israelis. He forced them to march barefoot and in their underwear across the stony ground, they were beaten several times and had shots fired around them as they lay on the ground. However, once in Syrian custody, they were very well treated and brought to a hospital in Damascus. Both UNMOs eventually made a full recovery from their injuries. I was detailed to bring the good news to Jennifer, Jim's wife, who received it with great relief.

The following day, while Anne and I looked after their children, Jennifer was taken across the line to Damascus, placed in a hotel, gifts were bought for her and she was taken to see Jim each day in hospital. After some weeks, they both returned to Tiberias, where the IDF continued to provide Jim with medical treatment right to the end of his tour.

During the period of my service with UNTSO, the mission comprised just under 300 observers, with about the same number of Field Service civilians. Over the span of more than fifty years, the small number of UN casualties was surely a reflection on the effectiveness of the observation system, the secure construction of most of the OPs, and the communications and the care with which operations were conducted. Sadly the mission, up to 1990, cost the lives of twenty-four individuals killed in action or in accidents, of which two were Irish. Comdt Tommy Wickham was shot dead in June 1967 on the Golan Heights while on his way from Damascus to take up duty at his OP. Comdt Michael Nestor died near Beirut when his vehicle ran over a landmine in September 1982.

On Friday 5 April 1974, I was informed that I had been transferred to Jerusalem with immediate effect. This came as a shock to me. I had not applied for it and was fully expecting to spend another six months in Tiberias before becoming due for rotation. When I met Col Bunworth later, he admitted that he had ordered my transfer, even apologising for the short notice. The Shemishes, our landlords, were very sorry to hear the news too, even though I was able to arrange for an immediate replacement – Capt. Noel Donagh – who had arrived some time after Jim Mortell and myself. There was a 'happy hour' at the MAC house that evening but I was too distracted to be able to enjoy it.

I drove up to Jerusalem on the Sunday night to report for work as a staff officer in Government House. I had to leave my family in Tiberias for nearly a month until I could find suitable accommodation for them, returning to Tiberias only for the weekends. Thus began a new and very different work experience in what for any Christian was the most attractive and important city in the world.

Chapter 10

GOVERNMENT HOUSE, JERUSALEM

Government House had been the residence of the British governor-general in Palestine and was taken over by the UN soon after UNTSO was established in 1948. It is a very beautiful building standing in its own large grounds on a prominent ridge on the south side of Jerusalem with an excellent view over the Jewish Quarter of the Old City. The grounds contained fine sunken gardens, a tennis court and restful plantings of trees and shrubs. It proved to be a delightful place in which to work.

On Monday 8 April 1974, I reported to the Military Personnel Office on the first floor in Government House. One of the first things I noticed was that the tiled floor in what was to be my office bore the marks of where an Israeli grenade had exploded. This happened when the Jordanian troops were unceremoniously ejected by the IDF during the 1967 war. Dutch Marine Capt. Paul Horsting, the man I was to replace, introduced me to the Military Personnel Officer and to the rest of the staff before showing me around the building.

My new post was to be that of assistant to the Military Personnel Officer, Major Colin Douglas of New Zealand. His office dealt with all matters relating to the military observers in the mission. Capt. Horsting brought me to see Colonel P.D. Hogan, the senior staff officer (effectively the second-in-command of the mission), and to meet Australian Lt-Col Keith Howard who had been at Government House for some years and who filled the role of military advisor to the General. I was informed that in addition to my UN duties I was also to act as an unofficial deputy to Col Hogan. He required me to assist him in dealing with Defence Forces HQ in Dublin in all administrative matters relating to the twenty Irish officers serving in UNTSO at that time.

Government House had been converted into a UN base with extensive car parks where I was allotted my own parking space close to the building. The large reception room on the ground floor was now a dining-room where all members of the mission, and even their families, could have meals. The dining-room was run by a gentle and efficient man called Joseph from the village of Hal-Hula near Hebron.

A PX facility was provided in the grounds, open to both military and civilian UN, offering a wide selection of attractive foods, cameras, perfumes and electronic goods. The PX was run at that time by Pat Kennedy, an Irish member of the UN Field Service. Other parts of the grounds featured large workshops, a petrol station and a servicing garage large enough to maintain the extensive fleet of UN vehicles. To the rear lay a large storage area for both new and old wrecked vehicles, caravans, generators, radio antennae and all the usual bric-a-brac of materials required to support a long-lasting and widespread mission.

During the early days I was hunting for a house for the family. The market was good, there was always a movement of both UNMOs and Field Service in and out of Jerusalem, but while I saw many houses, none fitted the bill. The UN community was scattered all over the city, mostly in the Palestinian areas because of the lower rents. As is often the case in UNTSO, the man I was replacing, Capt. Paul Horsting, suggested that I might like his house in Beit Hanina when he was ready to leave.

Beit Hanina was originally a little village a few kilometres north of Jerusalem, on the main road leading to Ramallah and the airport at Kalandia. By this time it had become a suburb of greater Jerusalem. When he brought me out to see the house I said yes on the spot. It was an attractive bungalow with three bedrooms, a small kitchen and a large conservatory. To the front of the house lay a fine orchard, a separate garage and a basketball court. The house was owned by the Sisters of Zion of the Mount Zion convent in the Old City and had been bought by them years before as the site for a new school. However, the Six Day War ensured that they were not able to go ahead with their plans. Having had another look at the house, I closed the deal at 700 Israeli lirot per month and signed the contract with the Mother Superior, Sister Joachim, an Englishwoman. When I brought Anne and the children up from Tiberias in May to see the house they took to it immediately, delighted with the space, the orchard and the basketball court.

We became friendly with the nuns over the following fourteen months and we had regular social visits from Sister Joachim, presumably also to check up on the state of the nuns' property. They were very quick to provide a gardener or a repairman whenever I requested assistance. When we were departing for Ireland in July 1975, Sister Joachim presented us with a copy of the Jerusalem Bible, beautifully bound in olive wood and soft white leather. (In 2008, I was informed that the school has finally been constructed and that 'our' house had been demolished in the process.)

Further to the north from us lay a huge Israeli settlement of ultra modern, mainly high-rise buildings, called Nevi Yacov. It appeared to have been built under specifications designed to make it easy to convert into a strong defensible location. It was one of the earliest of a series of such settlements built in strategic locations under the programme entitled 'Fortress Jerusalem'. It was an indication of the determination of the

Israeli government to retain Jerusalem whatever the future might hold for the State.

In Government House I shared my office with an American Sgt-Major, Bob Avena, a jovial and efficient NCO who was on a two-year tour prior to his retirement to Florida. We became close friends and he told me that he had come to UNTSO from the most senior NCO appointment in the US Army. He had been based in Washington, where he and his staff had wide responsibilities over the career structures for all senior NCOs of the US Army.

Two UN Field Service men worked in the general office, Hans Hobisch, an Austrian, and Mattie van Oijen from Holland. They did all the typing, filing and the preparations for the weekly pouch to New York. They were both excellent typists, skilled at the intricacies of the office and were of great help to me in the early days. By a strange quirk, another young Field Service officer arrived into the MPO office only a few weeks after me. His name was Mick Moriarty, a former Garda from Pearse Street Station in Dublin. We were not related but his arrival caused a confusion in postal arrangements that lasted for many years. We frequently received each other's post, often accidentally opening letters destined for the other. This continued even after we had gone our separate ways from UNTSO. More than thirty years later I received a letter from his bank in New York while serving in Southern Angola (all UN employees were required to open an account in a particular New York bank into which their salaries were paid). I put it back into the UN postal system and eventually received a nice note from him from Damascus!

The office of the MPO was responsible for the military processing of all UNMOs into and out of the mission, and for all matters relating to them while members of UNTSO. This covered the details of their arrivals and departures, the balance of numbers and nationalities between the outstations, their postings and transfers within the mission, promotions, staff appointments, qualification for the UN service medal, the production of certificates of award and liaison with the outstations for the awards ceremonies.

The arrival and departure of UNMOs was a demanding but pleasant aspect of the office, and Bob Avena and I shared the task of collecting or delivering the officers to Lod Airport, or as it became known later on, Ben Gurion Airport. I also had responsibility for the production of a monthly document called Special Orders, a report for UN New York. This document was like the daily document produced in all Irish units, at home or abroad, known to us as Routine Orders. It was effectively a summary of all the activities of our office for the preceding month. It gave all the intricate details needed by UNNY to keep track of, and to finalise, the passage of the UNMOs through the UN accountancy system.

I was some months into my new job when I found out that I also had responsibility for the Efficiency Reports. The Efficiency Reports were those sent via New York to the home HQs of the officers who had served in the mission. Such reports were usually sent within a few weeks of the departure of the officers concerned. My predecessor was long gone before Hans Hobisch called me in one day and opened a press. He pointed to a pile of blank forms and quietly told me that there was a backlog of nearly 300 Efficiency Reports to be completed and forwarded to New York. I remember he stood back as if waiting for me to explode in anger, but I think I must have disappointed him. It was a backlog that had been allowed to creep up, probably for a few years, well before my predecessor's time. It did not seem like a huge problem to me though, all it required was a bit of application.

The typical Efficiency Report was fairly harmless and the format was simple. Most officers had no problems either with their duties or with their fellow UNMOs – it being a mission where most were more than happy with their lot. I decided to tackle the problem in a methodical way, ensuring that I completed at least one report every day, office circumstances permitting. I quickly developed a formula for the reports to speed up the process and found that the three clerks in the general office were only too happy to keep up with my output.

I was, of course, reporting on officers, including Soviet officers, I had never even heard of, much less had met. Even those COs who had commanded the officers I was reporting on were long gone from the mission, so I had to be careful that each report was as anodyne as possible. Equally, I was determined that no injustice would be done. As I approached the end of the pile I found that I was now dealing with officers that I had actually met, and this helped me to be more realistic. I managed to clear the backlog completely within about five months.

It is interesting to note here a peculiarity of the mission that concerned Soviet officers. Israel had refused, from the very beginning, to permit UNMOs from the Soviet Union to enter Israel on the basis that their governments had not exchanged ambassadors. This created a problem for the MPO, as the twenty Soviet officers, one of whom was a full colonel, could only serve in Cairo or Damascus. As they typically served for two years, Soviet UNMOs slowly graduated into many of the staff appointments at both locations, an imbalance that gave rise to some complaints from the other nationalities. A pleasant aspect of this anomaly though was that the MPO or the Assistant MPO was required to travel to Cairo or Damascus from time to time to carry out the military processing of the Soviet officers. (The chief administrative officer in those stations took care of the civilian matters.)

A much-appreciated perk for staff officers like myself was that if I was travelling on duty, I could bring my family with me. Switzerland was not a member of the UN, but in a magnanimous gesture in support of peace, the Swiss government paid all the substantial costs of maintaining an F27 aircraft, crew and ground staff at Jerusalem Airport for use by the mission. While the aircraft was primarily intended for use by the general and his staff, observers and their families were also permitted to use the aircraft. They had to book their flights well in advance, but were liable to be bumped off if the seats were required by anyone travelling on official business.

As a result of this concession, I was able to bring Anne and our three children to Cairo on a number of occasions. Because both Egypt and Israel maintained significant air defence systems, the F27 had to take a roundabout route via Beirut and Cyprus when travelling to Cairo. On the return journey via Ismailia, the Israelis permitted the UN aircraft to fly along the Sinai coast into Jerusalem.

Jerusalem lay about 1,200m above sea-level and had a very pleasant micro-climate where it rarely became too hot in mid-summer. However, the winter weather was harsh and quite cold, with snow, heavy rain and gales from time to time – fortunately the winter was short. Occasionally we experienced the very strong winds of the sharraf (Hebrew) or hamseen (Arabic) that blew very humid, dusty air from the south, making life uncomfortable for everybody. As the year warmed up, we went to Gaza frequently to sample the UN Beach Club there.

Gaza at that time was quieter than it is today, mainly because the population was lower, but also because it had only recently been designated as an area for Palestinians. While there was a MAC house there with a small staff, it was rarely used except for humanitarian purposes. However, the UN had rented another premises down on the beach for use by UNMOs and Field Service members. This club provided limited accommodation, basic meals and of course access to the beach and the warm Mediterranean. The beach was patrolled regularly by the Israeli Army. I also joined an Israeli Country Club at Abu Gosh. I was charged IL 350 for the season, but it was great value and we went there most Sundays.

As I have described earlier, I had received an invitation from an Israeli LO, Capt. Amiel Brosh, to call on him when we were in Jerusalem. When life had settled down sufficiently, Anne and I took up his invitation and went to his apartment in Beit Hakerem. There we had cold drinks and finger food and met his children. He was a lovely man and very pleasant company, but his wife was typical of many Israeli families. She was very sceptical of the UN and what it was or was not doing for Israel.

At an early stage we also made friends with our nearest neighbours, living across the road from us: the Abdallahs, Rose and George, and their two little girls. George worked in Birzeit University and Rose worked for the local office of UNRWA. They were unusual in that they were Palestinian Catholics, or Latinis as they were known locally, and were a great help to us especially in the local markets. We are still in contact with them today.

On 17 May, we heard on the BBC about the bombings in Dublin and Monaghan, when thirty-three people had died. This incident had an unfortunate after-shock for all the Irish military in the Middle East. It was announced that the government had decided to withdraw the 25th Infantry Group from UNEF 2. This unit had only just taken over duties in Sinai and had not quite settled in when ordered home to Ireland. This was a severe blow to all 400 members of the unit. Moreover, the sudden withdrawal of the Irish soldiers without prior notice created major problems for the UN and the Irish name was mud for a few years afterwards in New York.

The withdrawal order also included the small number of Irish staff officers and ORs at both Cairo and Jerusalem. To the relief of the UNTSO officers only those staff officers and NCOs associated with UNEF 2 were to be recalled. I took time to go down to Ben Gurion to see off one of the flights. I found them sitting in dejected groups in the shade of the wings of the Aer Lingus jumbo, waiting for the crew to arrive. They were a most dejected lot, reluctant even to talk to me, even though I knew quite a few of them.

For me, life continued in Jerusalem. The peacekeeping mission for the Golan Heights – UNDOF – required, among many other factors, the transfer of ninety officers from UNTSO to UNDOF on 5 June to assist in setting up the mission. It was only a temporary transfer and they reverted to UNTSO prior to departure from the mission. Col P.D. Hogan, who had already performed wonders in Egypt for about three months when appointed as the chief-of-staff for UNEF 2, was now detailed to move to Damascus to perform the same job for UNDOF.

In June, Comdt Frank Dunne arrived out from the office of the Adjutant-General in Dublin carrying ballot papers for the Irish UNMOs in UNEF 2 and UNTSO. A cable from Ireland a few days later announced the good news that Terry McNulty and myself had been promoted to the rank of commandant with effect from 12 June. Frank, who stayed in our house with the all-important votes the night before his return to Ireland, very kindly gave me his rank markings before I drove him to the airport. In July, Major Colin Douglas set off on the long journey back to New Zealand and was replaced by Danish Major Chris Christensen. He had excellent English and turned out to be another relaxed individual, very easy to work with.

Things started to settle down after the establishment of UNDOF and I was able to take in more of the attractions of the area, travelling with family to Beirut, Damascus and Amman, on a number of occasions, partly on MPO business but also to pick up or deliver various relatives who came out to see us and the Holy Land. On one trip, we exchanged our house in Jerusalem for the apartment of Comdt Tony McCourt in Beirut for a few days. On another trip, the McNultys and ourselves went to Eilat for a few days camping, using our chalet tent. I set it up literally within feet of the sea, and we kept our cool-boxes in the sea water, weighed down with stones. I introduced Terry and Ann to the delights of snorkelling in the warm clear water, while taking my first ever aqualung dive in the Red Sea.

On 1 November Anne sang at a Hallow'een party at Government House (she had been one of the leading sopranos in Ireland on both stage and TV when I first met her). On 16 November, President Childers died suddenly while in office in Ireland and a special mass was organised in his honour at the École Biblique on the Nablus Road on 22 November. Anne sang a number of hymns in both Irish and English at the mass. Fr Murphy-O'Connor was the principal celebrant. What appeared to have been the entire Irish community, as well as a number of non-Irish UN military and civilians, attended the service.

In early December I was ordered to travel to Cairo to conduct the in-processing of four new Soviet observers. I had been told of this at very short notice at the Saturday morning briefing, so I phoned Anne and asked her would she like to go to Cairo and to bring the three children. She thought I was joking but I said 'you have to decide right now, as I have to apply for seats for you on the F27 and to book my own crossing by car'. Later that day, Anne and the three delighted children flew via Beirut and Akrotiri (in Cyprus) to Cairo. I drove across the Sinai, via the coastal road through Gaza and Khan Unis. On the drive I experienced for the first time the border arrangements on the Sinai and saw for myself some of the military positions of both the Israelis and the Egyptians. I crossed the Suez Canal on a floating Soviet bridge outside Ismailia. It was dusk when I got lost in the outskirts of Cairo and had to ask by radio for a guide from the MAC house.

We stayed four days as guests of cadet classmate Capt. Seán MacNiocaill, his wife Caitlin and their children in Heliopolis, a large suburb of Cairo where most of the UN personnel lived. The in-processing for the new Russians was straightforward and did not take up a lot of my time, so we took the opportunity of seeing the Pyramids, the Egyptian Museum, and to do some shopping in Khan Khalili, the principal bazaar in central Cairo. On the return journey to Jerusalem, I brought the family with me by road.

Christmas was a very low-key affair in Jerusalem. In the lead up to the day, it was rarely mentioned on television or in the *Jerusalem Post* – the English language newspaper. The Christian population of Jerusalem was very small, so the festival of Christmas had very little impact on the city generally. However, because of the children, we tried to follow the usual customs as closely as possible.

It had been the habit for many years that the mayor of Jerusalem would provide Christmas trees to the members of UNTSO. The mayor in 1974 was the famous and long-time holder of the office, Teddy Kollek, who invited all those who wished to have one, to bring a Christmas tree back to their homes. I collected a tree, much scrawnier than those we were used to at home, and Anne and the children decorated it in the traditional way. A few days before Christmas, some Jewish friends from Tiberias, Rina Hochfeld and some of her children, arrived unexpectedly. Apparently their eldest, Segal, had asked to see a Christmas tree. Their visit was all the more surprising as we were living in a Palestinian area of Jerusalem, but we were delighted to see them.

Christmas 1974 was as usual a very big event for the residents of Bethlehem, but Israel was concerned that it might be the excuse for a terrorism act against the State or against the worshippers. They cordoned off the town of Bethlehem so tickets were necessary for all those wishing to enter the town for the services, services that were traditionally broadcast to the world by radio and television. Good American Navy friends of ours, Lieut John Major and his family, who were Episcopalians, attended the service, but were bored stiff as it was all in Latin and the Patriarch apparently could not stop talking!

I did not even attempt to get tickets and we opted instead for the alternative ceremony to be conducted by a friend of ours, Fr

Isaac Jacob. We had come to know this Roman Catholic priest as he said mass frequently in our parish church for the Catholics of the area. He was a remarkable and compelling preacher who could hold his audience spellbound, walking up and down the aisle of the church as he spoke. Born in Pittsburgh to a Jewish father and an Irish mother from Cork, and raised as a Catholic, he had been ordained in the Benedictine Order in 1955.

Because of his unusual background, he was given permission to go to Israel to follow his dream, to establish a special kind of kibbutz – a Christian kibbutz. With the help of many friends he was given access to an old house and some land at Beit Jamal, near the Shimshon Junction, some 20kms west of Jerusalem. Here he intended to set up his kibbutz, a place where Christians of any denomination could come and spend time with him and his followers.

In December he invited all his supporters and their friends to join with him in a Christmas Eve mass. It was a beautiful occasion, much more in keeping with the original spirit of Christmas, surrounded as we were by the empty rural landscape with only some small clusters of lights in the distance. We put our children to bed early, woke them about 10 p.m., dressed them warmly and drove out to Beit Jamal. There, about eighteen adults and children experienced a very unique celebration in a simple and dignified manner. After the mass, we sat around a huge bonfire under the stars for a small barbecue, singing to the sound of a guitar played by a man from Liverpool. We arrived back to our house in Beit Hanina by 02.30hrs on Christmas morning. It was a truly memorable event.

In mid-February 1975, I was again sent to Cairo, this time to check out a Soviet Col Belik, who was being sent home from the mission. This time I took the family by road. Col Belik was clearly very unhappy about his early departure. I had met a number of Soviet officers by this time and had always found them to be pleasant and efficient. While we were in Cairo an explosion occurred near Kantara Control Centre in Jerusalem, on the road I traversed every day on my way to and from work. Two people died in this attack.

In March Anne sang again at a mass at the École Biblique in Jerusalem to start the celebrations for St Patrick's Day, after which we all retired to the Palace Hotel to continue for the rest of the day. It is remarkable just how highly regarded this particular national day is in the UN community – people are always eager to get invitations. My diary states that St Patrick did not let us down – on our way to dinner later at Government House, the rain, thunder and lightning were very impressive.

It was also in March that I availed of an invitation from a diving friend from Belfast, Conor Craig, to travel to Aqaba for a week's diving. He was employed in the Royal Jordanian School of Diving, where he had trained members of the Royal family to dive. On the way through Amman, we spent a night with Mick Mulcahy, an old friend from my days in Listowel. He had served in the army but was ahead of me by two years and was commissioned in the Cavalry Corps. He left the army early to join the UN Development Programme and had been stationed in Amman for two years.

In Aqaba, we set up our tent at a very unsuitable site and the heat in the tent, even early in the morning, was such that I felt that I could not keep the children there for the full week. Fortunately, Conor allowed us to move our tent into his back garden where we had full access to the toilets, showers, the kitchen and the fridge. Aqaba was at that time small and quite undeveloped, but the water and the scenery were fascinating. During this week, I took time off from diving to bring the family to see Petra – about an hour north of the seaport – the ancient rose-red city built into solid rock.

Later in March, we hired little stools to sit and watch the traditional Easter parade around and into the Old City. Shortly afterwards, on 28 March, a bomb exploded on a bus at Bethany, near the tomb of Lazarus, injuring thirteen tourists. Pressure and tensions were starting to build up in Jerusalem, and security became much more evident everywhere in the city. Off-duty military personnel, male and female, started to carry weapons and as the tension rose, even schoolteachers and public officials began to carry arms.

By June the family was in full withdrawal mode as my final day in the mission was to be on 10 July. Our daughter Niamh received her first communion from Fr Jacob in the local church across the road from our house. A few days later we brought John to receive his confirmation from the apostolic delegate to the Holy Land, Archbishop Carew, a Canadian.

An elderly Dutch couple had expressed an interest in taking over our house and with the approval of Sister Joachim, our landlady, we agreed. Part of the deal was that the couple would take over our little dog, Sídheóg (meaning Little Fairy). We had acquired her as a puppy from Bill Mulcahy, a member of the Field Service soon after my transfer to Government House. We had become very attached to her but of course could not bring her back to Ireland, so we were glad she would have a good home. Seven large wooden crates soon arrived from Household Stores to enable us to start the considerable chore of packing our possessions and in particular, making up the manifests for each crate.

Capt. Leo Brownen took over from me as Assistant MPO on 2 July, leaving me free to complete the many remaining tasks. I had planned to drive all the way to Dublin using our new Citroen GS Estate, a left-hand-drive car purchased in Jerusalem. As we had our chalet tent with us, I intended to make full use of it on the journey home. I had already arranged for twenty-five days annual leave and had booked the ferry crossing from Rosslare with Irish Continental Lines.

Due to rising tensions in Lebanon, and particularly Beirut, we were not permitted to follow the traditional route along the coast north through Beirut, so we had to take the longer way around via Damascus. We said goodbye to the Abdallahs and our many friends and left Jerusalem with heavy hearts on 9 July. Driving to Tiberias, we said goodbye to the Hochfelds and our many other friends. The Mortells, who were also leaving, were to have travelled with us, but Jim had bad luck on the very morning of his departure when he collided with a milk truck near his apartment in Bethany. He was forced to remain two extra days in Jerusalem to attend to the repairs and insurance matters. I promised to travel slowly on the journey to give them time to catch up with us.

We left Tiberias that evening and crossed the Golan Heights to Damascus where I booked us in for two nights in the White Sisters Hostel near the Street Called Straight. The Mortells did catch up with us eventually but not before we had reached a pleasant, crowded MOCAMP campsite on the European side of the Bosporus at Istanbul. MOCAMP was one of a series of camping sites in Turkey run by Karvansaray, a subsidiary of BP. We remained there for four days to enjoy one of the world's great cities. The journey home across Europe was a hugely enjoyable holiday in itself. We parted company with the Mortells at Katlanova, near Skopje in Yugoslavia on 18 July. Jim had taken less leave than I and needed to hurry home, calling on German relations on the way.

The UNTSO mission was, for me, easily the most enjoyable of my UN experiences, principally because I had my family with me throughout. The level of interaction with the officers of the many nationalities with whom we were involved was excellent and I believe it helped me to see the military world in a different and more relaxed light.

Many members of our extended family had taken advantage of our situation to visit us and to see the Holy Land. From a religious point of view, I believe that it altered and strengthened the manner in which I perceived my own faith in a practical way that I had not expected. We all have many pleasant memories of these places and experiences, while the values we acquired in the region remain with us to this day.

Chapter 11

UNITED NATIONS INTERIM FORCE IN LEBANON

On 23 March 1978, the first soldiers of the United Nations Interim Force in Lebanon (UNIFIL) arrived in Lebanon with the aim of confirming the withdrawal of Israeli troops from the area, restoring peace and assisting the Lebanese government to restore its authority in the area. The Defence Forces were involved in this mission from the outset.

The tour of duty in South Lebanon of the 46th Battalion, the fourth Irish unit to serve in Lebanon, was a tour of remarkable tension and harassment. The battalion was subjected to deliberate attempts to subvert the morale and determination of the Irish soldiers in the carrying out their duties. Particularly from December to March, when the weather was very wet and cold with strong winds and some snow falls, a lesser CO and a unit composed of less experienced men might not have stood up to the attempts to destabilise the battalion. These included frequent shelling and harassment attacks, accompanied by misleading propaganda. For HQ Company, it cost the lives of two soldiers, one a member of the engineer platoon and the other a HQ Operations driver. These were soldiers who could not, in the normal course of events on a peacekeeping mission, expect to find themselves in the firing line.

It also meant that some soldiers from my HQ Company, most of them technicians and specialists, spent nearly one week at At Tiri performing as infantry soldiers, something that few of them could have anticipated. Yet they performed bravely and effectively, as one would expect of professional and experienced Irish soldiers. In recognition of the exceptional difficulties experienced and the remarkable conduct of all involved at At Tiri, no less than four Military Medals for Gallantry and one Distinguished Service Medal were awarded to members of the battalion (see Appendix C).

An excellent Unit history is available for reading at the Military Archives, and because of this I will confine this chapter to relating the story of my own experiences and observations as OC of HQ Company.

My nomination to the 46th Battalion for service in Lebanon was made at short notice and this meant that I had missed out on much of the valuable preparation time. The job was that of OC HQ Company. HQ Company in any given unit is a hotchpotch of all the specialists – engineers, signals, transport, MP, ordnance and medical – six platoons in all, each of which had its own officers. It is a job usually loathed by most officers, as it provides all the headaches and problems with none of the satisfaction that goes with command of a line unit.

I went for my UN medical in St Bricin's Hospital on 11 September and received my first injections, following which I met Capt. Tony Gilleran, my second-in-command, who briefed me on the preparations of the company. Matters passed at breakneck speed after this and the battalion was assembled at Gormanston on Monday 15 October. The CO, Lt-Col Jack Kissane, the Quartermaster and the Operations Officer left on 17 October, followed a week later by Chalk 1, carrying all the company commanders and their advance parties. We travelled in great comfort aboard an Aer Lingus 747, the *St Patrick*.

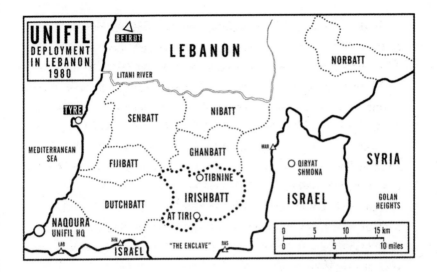

Landing at Beirut Airport, we were swiftly transported through a very battered Beirut to Tibnine. I ended up staying in a room in the local hospital for a week until space became available elsewhere. The battalion medical platoon was based at the hospital for the duration of the tour, during which they provided normal medical support to the members of the battalion as well as a wide range of medical support to the local population. From time to time they also had to deal with those injured in the many shelling and firing incidents in the area of operations. This gave them the experience of dealing with the kinds of injuries they would never experience in the army at home.

Tibnine was overlooked by a high ridge to the south lying between the town and some of our battalion positions. Part of this ridge was controlled by the DFF led by Major Saad Haddad, a former Lebanese Army major. The DFF was a force paid for, trained, equipped and controlled (poorly) by the IDF. The road network in the area meant that Tibnine was a crucial 'crossroads' and therefore a location of military importance. The roads were narrow, with steep gradients. They were reasonably well surfaced, but they looped and swung around to climb and descend the successive wadis of the region and as such were quite dangerous, while the speeds, especially convoy speeds, were always very low.

Irishbatt was located in a vital sector of the UNIFIL line. Effectively it was the keystone in an arc of UN battalions facing Israel, flanked as it was by Dutchbatt and Ghanbatt. The writ of the Lebanese government was very weak in the UNIFIL area, with just a handful of small army posts, one of which lay within the Irishbatt AO. It was high on a ridge close to Gallows Green, the quaintly named post of the battalion military police platoon. The Lebanese did little enough patrolling but at least they provided a government presence in the area.

During the two-week takeover from my predecessor, Comdt Bill Ó Riain, I discovered that HQ Company was scattered over no less than twelve locations in Tibnine and Haddathah – up to 4kms apart. There were even Signals personnel stationed at UN HQ at Naqoura, down at the coast.

Our battalion, at 625 ARs, was composed of a large percentage of individuals who had already served in either the Congo or in Cyprus and only the more junior officers and the more recently enlisted men were new to UN service. This gave the unit a very strong backbone of experienced soldiers which perhaps the DFF – and Israel – might not have fully appreciated.

Significantly, the 46th Battalion had a different organisation to all previous Irish units in Lebanon. In addition to the usual HQ Company and three infantry companies, a new company called the Recce Company was included. This company comprised three elements, the recce platoon, the heavy mortar troop and the anti-tank platoon. The combination of mobility, armour, heavy weapons, good communications and swift reaction time made the Recce Company a formidable rapid reaction force immediately available to the CO and under his own control. Because such a company did not exist in the previous battalion, it was necessary to transfer all the stores, equipment, ammunition, vehicles, bedding, chairs, tables, etc. from HQ Company to the new company. While the creation of this new company within the battalion was a most sensible move, it also meant that my company Quartermaster Sergeant Brian Moore, spent most of the six months with the CQMS of Recce Company and the Battalion Quartermaster Sergeant of Battalion HQ, Ned Freeman, battling with the paperwork.

A Cypriot company had been contracted by the UN to build the main elements of the new Camp Shamrock in Tibnine and to provide most of the general workers. Our own engineer platoon under Capt. Eddie Fitzgerald provided much of the specialist work and of course the technical supervision. By the time our battalion had handed over to the 47th, a fine cookhouse, additional accommodation huts and an administrative block had been completed.

The rotation arrangement – three flights one week apart – for our battalion was by far the most efficient system employed to date, superior to the rotations in the Congo or to Cyprus, admittedly facilitated by larger aircraft and shorter flights. However, it had its problems too. The DFF attempted on two occasions to take advantage of the rotation of the 45th and the 46th Battalions. In one case, an unusually strong foot patrol of DFF soldiers was seen advancing on Brashit. As our B Company had not yet taken over in the village, the remnants of 45th Battalion personnel were forced to withdraw their weapons and equipment from stores. They then advanced to confront the DFF. They were very angry at having their departure preparations disrupted in this manner and were not in a kindly mood for a confrontation.

It was a very tense situation, weapons were pointed at each other from close range. A stand-off ensued until one DFF man made a bad mistake. He attempted to knock down the Irish captain by striking him with the butt of his rifle. The captain, a large and powerful man, and an All-Army boxer, promptly lashed out and floored his attacker. One can well appreciate his satisfaction in smashing his fist into one of those who had been tormenting his unit for the last six months. While all present took a deep breath, expecting the worst, the DFF leader backed down and called his men to return to Bayt Yahoun from whence they had come.

In the second case, a lone half-track armoured vehicle advanced from a DFF position known as the Cuckoo's Nest at Rshaf, in an attempt to get into Haddathah, an important Irish location overlooking Tibnine. In the scramble to counter this, A Company placed obstacles in front of and around the vehicle. An AML 90 and two 84mm Rcls rifle teams took up position also, ready to destroy the vehicle. By now the DFF personnel manning the half-track were thoroughly frightened and when offered the chance to retreat to their position, they did so with alacrity.

The high number of 'old sweats' (experienced soldiers) in both units who had served previously in Africa and Cyprus ensured that they knew exactly what was required and had simply refused to be browbeaten.

As a result of these attempted incursions I decided to do something about the situation on my own initiative. I had not been asked to do so, but it struck me that if one of the incursions, say that from Rshaf, had succeeded in getting into Haddathah, the battalion position would have been seriously compromised. I felt that yet another reserve was required, a reserve to the reserve, as it were. So, in consultation with Capt. Tony Gilleran and Company Sergeant Peter Barry, I drew up an infantry platoon of over forty soldiers and appointed Capt. Gilleran as the platoon commander. The platoon included members of the pipe band, ordnance artificers, cooks, mechanics, drivers, some signallers, engineer soldiers and some of the staff from the messes. When we had completed the task, I informed the CO, Lt-Col Jack Kissane, of what I had done. He was grateful and we then forgot about it for nearly five months.

In arranging this, I never in my wildest dreams imagined that the platoon would actually be called upon. But, right at the end of the tour, when all the soldiers were already starting to pack for going home, the HQ reserve platoon was called upon to form up at Haddathah. The crisis at At Tiri, which arose close to the end of the tour, meant that this group of individuals was thrown into a hot and dangerous situation just when their minds were on going home, not on fighting a very difficult battle. However, they rose to the occasion in a most professional manner. I even discovered later that one NCO from HQ Company, not a nominated member, turned up in At Tiri. He had not wanted to miss out on the excitement.

On the departure of the 45th Battalion, I moved into Tibnine House, located close to the Lebanese Hospital, with the CO and the rest of the senior staff. Our routine became well established very quickly. We rose at 06.30hrs, usually having breakfast together in Tibnine House, and would then walk the 400m to the Battalion HQ. The staff and duty officers met every morning for a briefing at the HQ at 07.30hrs.

Early one morning the CO, generally among the first to rise, was heard to shout 'fire'. It seems a small fire had broken out in the kitchen but he calmly directed operations to have it extinguished before some of us were even fully awake. That the entire senior battalion staff might have been wiped out in this incident gave rise to much humorous comment across the battalion for some time afterwards.

A month and a half into our tour, two incidents gave us all a very bad feeling about the circumstances of our situation. On Saturday 1 December, a local man from Tibnine killed a man from Blida (within the DFF enclave and therefore one of

Haddad's 'subjects') at Total in full view of a number of soldiers of the transport platoon. After an argument, he had chased this unfortunate around his car and shot him dead. As a result Haddad had threatened to 'Boom Boom' Tibnine. To add to the jitters, later that evening a shootrep was reported from Tibnine House. An individual in the turret of an APC parked across the road at Caltex, the garage in use by Recce Company, accidentally fired a small burst from the turret machine gun. Thankfully no one was injured.

The bulk of my company lived and worked in Haddathah school, so after a few weeks I moved my office there to be closer to the action. The large three-storey former schoolhouse was in a deplorable condition, having been damaged in all the battles and skirmishes that took place since the Israelis had invaded Lebanon in 1978. It boasted one important feature – it had a large basement into which had been crammed much of the ammunition and stores of the battalion. It also happened to provide a good shelter for the personnel in times of shelling. For all that, in the bad weather of February 1980, it became flooded to a depth of several inches. The building was known as the Tramshed to all the unfortunates who were forced to live and work in the place.

Shortly before I moved my office into the Tramshed, the battalion tailor, Gnr O'Connell, had a lucky escape when a 12.5mm HMG round crashed through the south-facing wall beside him. After this I tried to get as many as possible of those who were working above ground into safer locations. The cookhouse for HQ Company was also inside the south-facing wall, but at least it was on the ground floor and had some protection from a number of low mounds on the rising ground outside. Sgt Daly and his staff worked there under deplorable conditions for some months until they were able to move to the brand-new and well-equipped cookhouse in Camp Shamrock, opened just in time for the St Patrick's Day celebrations.

On another cold and wet day, I was on the top floor of the school working on administrative matters, when the DFF position at the Cuckoo's Nest opened fire, using the 75mm main weapon of their Super Sherman tank. They were shelling Dutchbatt and we could clearly see the detonation of the shells from our third-floor location. It was a desultory sort of engagement, but then the DFF suddenly changed targets and a shell passed very close to our building and detonated in the wadi behind us. It landed close to the Total garage where the transport platoon lived and worked, fortunately causing no casualties or damage.

When the battalion had arrived it had taken over (unofficial) responsibility for the small orphanage in Tibnine where the children were supported by successive Irish units. The chaplains visited regularly even though the children were Muslim. The battalion was facilitated by the small sums sent to us by Foreign Affairs to assist in the upkeep of the orphanage. This aspect of the part played by Foreign Affairs in helping the Lebanese inhabitants via the orphanage, and indeed similar assistance in other UN missions, is generally under-reported in Ireland, but it was hugely appreciated by the people of the area.

In early December, LÉ *Emer* (the captain was Lt-Comdr Eamonn Doyle) arrived into Beirut port after a winter passage across the Mediterranean carrying stores and replacement equipment for the battalion. This was the first time that the Irish navy had been used to support the army in a UN mission, a practice that has since been repeated on a number of occasions in other missions. While in Beirut port, the LÉ *Emer* flew the flag of the United Nations, another first for the navy. Our battalion sent a convoy, escorted by Recce Company, up to Beirut to collect the stores. Unfortunately, because of the very precarious situation in the city, where outbreaks of firing were frequent, LÉ *Emer* had to depart again as soon as the unloading and loading was completed.

As a member of the operations duty panel, I spent a lot of time in the operations room. On one occasion, when on duty during yet another of the many episodes of the shelling of Tibnine and its environs, an UNTSO two-vehicle patrol from OGL braked to a sliding halt outside our building. Four officers, two of them American, came rushing in for shelter. I well remember one of the Americans pacing up and down the floor in a towering rage. He was complaining bitterly that he paid his taxes to his government so that they could send artillery ammunition to Israel to attempt to kill American officers serving with the UN.

I was duty officer on a different occasion during another episode of the shelling of Tibnine. One young local woman was killed and a number of injured were rushed to the hospital to be treated by our doctors. Both the CO and second-in-command were outside the building at the sandbag wall 'rubbernecking' when a shell struck a building beside ours. The detonation was followed by a shower of flying objects and both officers came rushing inside, closely followed by a spray of small stones that rattled around on the tiled floors. I was busy recording the details for transmission to HQ UNIFIL and as they rushed past me I asked: 'Are you all right?' Both said they were fine, so I replied: 'Damn, there goes my chance of a battlefield promotion!

The battalion, like our predecessors, used a code word 'ground-hog' to warn ARs to either take cover or be prepared to do so. It worked very well, being sent to all locations in the battalion by landline or by radio, as well as to Naqoura, where the HQ of UNIFIL was based. In the course of my daily strolls in Tibnine, like most other members of the battalion, I was continuously selecting a suitable bolt-hole or a convenient wall to hide behind in the event of suddenly coming under fire. As I walked along, I was constantly on 'listening watch', trying to assess the many distant, and not so distant, bumps and bangs that were part of our daily lives. Having lived with this constant tension for a period of six months, for some time after returning to Ireland I would jump at any unexpected loud noise. Even a door slamming shut was enough to trigger the 'groundhog' instinct.

By December, weather conditions were deteriorating rapidly and there was an urgent need to make the hilltop OPs more comfortable for their occupants. We experienced severe winds, thunderstorms and even a heavy fall of snow that lay on the ground for a few days. The activities of the DFF and the AEs were fortunately at a low ebb and this allowed us an opportunity to work on the necessary improvements. We all knew that as soon as the weather improved and conditions on the ground changed for the better, we would be back in the thick of the action again.

Christmas was cold and lonely, even though it marked a turning point of sorts in our six-month tour. Despite the dreadful conditions, Sgt Mick Daly and his staff produced a lavish Christmas dinner for 146 diners in the Tramshed. It was attended by the Battalion Commander, Lt-Col Kissane, who was invited to cut a huge cake.

One of the most popular sporting activities at that time was the 10km race, held over the road network between Tibnine, Harris and Haddathah, most of the course being within the battalion area. Often an entire platoon would undertake the race, attempting to return a new record time for the course. Many individuals or small groups set out to improve on their fitness levels or even simply to be warm for a while.

Every two months, the three infantry companies were rotated within the area of operations to permit a change of scene to soldiers, but also to ensure that they would remain more alert in their new locations. The greatest pressure always came on those soldiers who were required to man the check-points on the roads leading into our battalion area. The typical check-point, usually set up at a crossroads or on the outskirts of a village, consisted of obstacles placed in such a way as to prevent a driver charging through at speed. The obstacles were overlooked by sentries in heavily sandbagged positions, at least one of whom would have his rifle trained on any vehicle entering the chicane.

The tricky part came when one of the soldiers or the NCO in charge had to leave his shelter to question the driver and occupants and to search the vehicle. For perhaps ninety eight per cent of the time, the occupants were well-known locals only going about their daily business. However, where weapons, explosives or military-style radios were found during the searches they had to be confiscated and the individuals forced to turn around and to go back to where they came from. Known 'subversives' were also turned back when identified. Check-point duty was very stressful for soldiers as there was never any certainty that on the next occasion a soldier would not be met with a hail of gunfire from the occupants of a car.

The road leading from Tibnine to HQ at Naqoura on the coast had been named the Burma Road by one of the previous battalions. This road passed through Dutchbatt first and then through Fijibatt. The Fijian soldiers generally were possessed of a delightful sense of humour. For some reason they had started to shout out, as our vehicles passed through their check-points – 'On the ball, Irish'. Our soldiers were then expected to reply with 'On the big ball'. This response had the effect of making all Fijians in the vicinity burst out laughing.

On most Sundays, a group of these Fijians (Anglicans) would come to mass in the school at Haddathah, during which they sang haunting hymns in their own language. Throughout the tour of duty, it could be observed that the attendance at Sunday mass was always noticeably larger following a night of shelling or firing-close events. Our two hard-working chaplains, Frs Conlon and Dempsey, circulated constantly bringing mass and other services to all the battalion locations.

The chaplains were not the only ones constantly on the go. While Tibnine today has a piped water supply, water for all the battalion posts in 1979–80 was a major problem. During our tour, it was necessary to have one or more water trucks on the road every day travelling to a water supply point near Qana, about two hours away. The drivers of the water trucks had a never-ending task in bringing water not just to the company HQs (where water was then moved out to the various company posts in jerrycans), but also to individual houses. It was an onerous task, the driver's day was very long and the road was slow and difficult. As much as 250,000 gallons of drinking water per month was being brought into the battalion area.

There were few chances for relaxation on this mission. However, at the officers' mess in Tibnine, where bar hours were strictly curtailed, Saturday night was designated as the let-your-hair-down time where all available officers of HQ would congregate for drinks and a sing-song. Our CO was quite a shy man who did not take alcohol, but he manfully stayed with us each Saturday night to sing his only party piece – 'The German Clockwinder'. Capt. Eddy Fitzgerald, the engineer platoon commander, by popular acclaim, would give us his rendition of a man from the Aran Islands visiting Galway. Comdt Johnny Vize, the Battalion Operations Officer, was a skilled player of the guitar and he always played and sang 'Young Willie McBride'. This sad and haunting song relating to the First World War era was quite appropriate to our difficult and tense situation and I felt that it created a great sense of introspection in his audience. It was Comdt Martin Gibson, the Battalion Transport Officer, who introduced his own favourite song to us – 'A Bunch of Thyme', made popular at home by Foster and Allen. This song became the unofficial song of the officers of Battalion HQ, and was sung with some considerable nostalgia every Saturday night.

In the dark and cold nights of the winter months, a series

of darts competitions, bingo, sing-alongs and inter-company talent competitions were also organised and proved to be hugely successful. It is very heartening to see how soldiers turned with gusto to such simple projects, considering the daily dangers they faced. In HQ Company, where we possibly had a greater pool of talent to draw on, Pte Derek Smallhorne turned out to be one of the leading lights. Possessed of a sunny disposition, a quick Dublin wit and a can-do attitude, he was a great hit at all the concerts telling stories, singing songs and introducing acts.

As the weather started to improve in February, extensive firing practices for HQ and Recce Companies were carried out in a deep wadi to the north-west of Tibnine, where all the personal weapons on issue were fired, including the APCs and the main weapon of the AML 90s – the 90mm cannon. These exercises went on for several days at a time, with different soldiers, until all had been put through their paces. At the conclusion of practices a complaint was made by some local herders that we had killed seven goats. We were very sceptical of this claim, as great care was always taken to ensure that no persons or animals were in the target areas before firing commenced. The military police section carried out an inquiry, but when they asked the herders to show them the carcasses, they could not produce them or even point out where the goats had been killed.

In March, battalion shooting competitions were held at the range near As Sultaniyeh, a village to the north of Tibnine. It was not a firing range in the manner of those at home, but merely a very deep and narrow valley with steeply rising unoccupied ground behind the target area. It was now that we came to appreciate the spring in Lebanon. The weather had finally turned and the entire barren stony ground was covered with thousands of beautiful wild flowers. They sprang up through the green grass, showing us a more attractive side to this landscape. Unfortunately this display did not last very long.

In all missions, danger could come from unexpected situations. On 11 March, my driver, Pte Robbie Norton, had a narrow escape. He had been changing a wheel on the Landrover in front of the guard-room at the Tramshed in Haddathah. The jack suddenly slipped and he was pinned underneath the vehicle. Fortunately there were plenty of friends around and they lifted the vehicle bodily to free him. He suffered no after-effects.

Throughout early March, there was pressure to have the new cookhouse ready for St Patrick's Day, and it was. It became the focal point for the celebrations at Tibnine where the guests from UNIFIL HQ, the other battalions, the Muktar of Tibnine and as many as possible of the locals, were entertained to a lavish meal and to music from the pipe band. Earlier, we had mass and the presentation of shamrock at a parade for all available personnel. UN service medals were presented by the FC, General Erskine, to a representative group from the battalion. The day was a great success and Sgt Daly and his staff produced yet another wonderful meal. On top of this Geraldine Brannigan and a backing group had arrived to provide entertainment for the troops. Her musicians were the very first entertainers to visit the Irish soldiers since the Lebanon mission started. Accompanied by a group of journalists, she was given a huge reception everywhere she went. Not only did she perform for all the companies of Irishbatt but also for the French and the Ghanaians, ending with a concert in Naqoura.

For some time, I had been worried that a shell could strike the new cookhouse – a large and very visible white prefabricated structure – during mealtime, when the maximum number of soldiers might be present. We had been struggling to develop a large shelter close to the dining-hall and were badly in need of assistance to move the large boulders and to dig down into the stony soil. I was at the dining-hall some time after Patrick's Day when I was informed that a French engineering unit had called in for a meal. Using my fractured French, I persuaded the chef (the NCO in charge of the group) to use their heavy equipment to give us a 'dig out'.

While it was not on his schedule of work, he was kind enough to provide a bulldozer and a digger for a few hours and we made significant progress on the project. Unfortunately, he had to continue back to Naqoura later that evening. We didn't get the job finished in the few weeks that were left to us, but at least the heavy work was done and both the floor and the steel frame (to support the overhead cover) were in position.

On 6 April the battalion sports day was held, and HQ Company, who do not normally feature prominently in such matters (the soldiers tend to be older), were actually on the point of winning the tug-o'-war event when the general alarm was sounded. The competitions were abandoned and all ranks hastened to take up their posts. The DFF had staged a surprise incursion, charging into At Tiri village in an attempt to take it over. C Company reserve was deployed and Comdt Taylor asked for further reinforcements. Recce Company deployed promptly and the Force Mobile Reserve was called out and sent to Tibnine.

I did not have a direct role in this affair but nearly all platoons of HQ Company were involved, principally in the supply of food, water and medical assistance. As it was very close to rotation, I was preoccupied in the company office with the completion of the large amount of personal reports to be made out for the members of my company. Later, when I was up in Haddathah school, I received a call to say that the HQ reserve platoon was being called upon to go into At Tiri.

The platoon was collected at Haddathah and sent directly to At Tiri where they were deployed by Comdt Dave Taylor. Soon after, Pte Stephen Griffin, a member of the platoon, who had been manning a light machine gun on the roof of an outhouse in At Tiri was seriously injured. He was evacuated to Rambam

Hospital in Haifa where he died on the night of 16–17 April. Many other soldiers had very lucky escapes during that week while a small number of Irish soldiers were captured and held for a day by the DFF, mainly to provide propaganda for the Israelis by demonstrating the effectiveness of their soldiers.

During the week, others from HQ and Recce Companies were admitted to hospital suffering from shock, including the driver of the AML 90 overlooking the incursion site. A tank round fired from a location in the enclave known to us as the Brown Mound, smashed into the house used as a billet by one of the platoons of C Company. The solid shot passed through no less than three walls of the building before burying itself in the floor of a room at the rear of the house. It impacted close to a small group of soldiers, the reserve section of the platoon, who were resting there. Nobody was injured.

On 12 April, widespread aimless shelling of Tibnine meant that I ordered all in Camp Shamrock to take cover, including two soldiers who were in their beds following an all-night duty. There was only one shelter available in the camp and by the time everyone had been rounded up, it was so full that myself and my Company Sergeant, Peter Barry, had to stand outside in the sloping approach to the entrance. It was also on this day that, having put up with the most outrageous attacks and provocations by the DFF for nearly a week, the 46th finally went on the offensive. A major assault started and very quickly the entire village of At Tiri was cleared of all DFF personnel and restored to UN control. Sadly a Fijian soldier, Private Savaloina, a member of the Force Reserve, fighting beside our own soldiers, was killed in action. During this assault, the DFF half-track in At Tiri was destroyed by Lt Molloy and his crew in their AML 90. In the over-crowded shelter at Camp Shamrock, a huge cheer went up when informed of this highly satisfying event.

During the events at At Tiri, the battalion posts within the DFF enclave, known to the UN as the enclave posts, and to us as the hostage posts, were also attacked and some prisoners taken. They were quickly released unharmed. Others made a remarkable and very dangerous evacuation after dark by walking through the wadis to reach the safety of B Company at Brashit. These posts, situated well within the DFF enclave, had been the bane of our own and previous battalions because they served no useful military purpose, only being retained for political purposes on direct instructions from UNNY.

On 14 April, Major Haddad came on Radio Free Lebanon, located at Marjayoun, and made a speech verbally attacking the members of the 46th Battalion for their actions. The speech accused the Irish soldiers and other UN forces of attacking At Tiri without provocation.

From the beginning of the mission, some battalions in UNIFIL had a policy of permitting their soldiers to return fire when fired upon. If twenty rounds of light machine gun fire were directed towards one of their posts by the DFF, a soldier in the post concerned was permitted to respond by firing the same number of rounds and from a similar weapon in the general direction of the attacker. This policy was intended to assist the morale of the soldiers concerned while serving as a reminder to the attacker not to take things for granted.

However, from the beginning of the mission, Irish battalions never operated this policy, a matter of some debate from time to time. The restraint shown by the Irish soldiers was seen by most others as the behaviour of a disciplined and confident group of soldiers. However, it is likely that the DFF, and possibly the Israeli Defence Forces, could well have assumed that this policy of not firing back was an indication of weakness. 46th Battalion was only the fourth Irish battalion in Tibnine and I believe that Major Haddad and his Israeli handlers may well have made the mistake of thinking that the Irish were a pushover – that if sufficient pressure was put on them they might not resist.

The locals were delighted at the result in At Tiri, and when Hassan from Ayta az Zutt, the local representative of the Lebanese Electricity Company, met the CO, he congratulated him and uttered the immortal words, in his own stuttering way, 'Haddad; you f—ed him good!' Soon afterwards a threat was issued to every Irish soldier by the DFF who promised revenge for their humiliation and expulsion from At Tiri and for the death of some of their comrades. As a result of warnings received, all ranks were ordered to be vigilant and to carry weapons with them at all times. This upset our friends in Tibnine, as they were not used to seeing us in this mode and it made them very uneasy.

The euphoria of having given Haddad a bloody nose did not last long. Three Irish drivers in a small UN convoy, on a re-supply mission to the enclave posts, were dragged from their vehicles after they had crossed into the enclave. They were taken away and two were brutally killed; the third, although wounded, was very lucky to escape with his life. For a period of some hours the bodies could not be found. The shock and anger was palpable right across the battalion. I am certain that if the CO had ordered an attack on all DFF positions to kill or to take as many prisoners as possible, the battalion would have responded with vigour.

Later that night, I went to Camp Shamrock to break the news of the discovery of body of one of the men, Pte Smallhorne, to his friends in his billet. They were deeply shocked and angered, and I had to disarm one man who swore that he was going out right away to kill the first Arab that he met. I was certain that he would not have carried out his threat, but it was an indication of his shock and anger.

I found it interesting to notice the difference in the reaction of the company to the death in action at At Tiri of Pte Griffin and the cowardly killing of the other two. Soldiers can accept with sadness the loss of a comrade in action – it is after all, one of the hazards of the profession. But their reaction to murder is entirely different – it generates a huge anger and a strong desire for revenge. However, being the disciplined professionals that they were, the soldiers of the battalion restrained their natural instincts and carried on as before. The body of Pte Griffin was seen off for home from Beirut Airport on 24 April by the CO, myself, Comdt P. Nowlan, Chaplain Seán Conlon and Comdt S. Hurley, OC B Company.

While the battalion was heavily engaged at At Tiri, UNIFIL HQ at Naqoura was also attacked. Firing commenced on 11 April and continued sporadically until 14 April. Some ninety rounds of mortar, as well as possibly thousands of rounds of small arms fire, struck the HQ area, damaging four helicopters and putting three of them out of action. The orderly room and the PX of Camp Command were badly damaged, a workshop was destroyed and a total of twenty-one prefabs were struck by small arms fire. The UN Field Service personnel, all residents of Nahariya in Israel, were prevented from coming in to work at the HQ for nearly a full week.

The personnel of Camp Command, the Irish-led administrative unit supporting the HQ, as well as the members of the other units such as the military police, were in 'groundhog' or manning defensive positions for some days. Even as the clean-up of the initial damage began, small arms fire continued from the 14–18 April from the area of the Arab village overlooking the camp. Fortunately, only one individual was injured during the attacks.

A typical example of the bizarre conditions under which the UN was required to operate occurred on Friday 17 April. A temporary pause – not arranged by the UN – occurred during which the local Arab workers came down, collected their pay and returned to their village. The shooting then resumed!

46th Battalion had come through a sustained and calculated attempt to break or weaken its determination to resist yet another of the many DFF attempts to push UNIFIL northwards from the initially agreed positions in an attempt to gain ground and make an attack on Israel more difficult. In demonstrating that a UN force can be pushed only so far, a strong marker was laid down by this action for successive units in UNIFIL and perhaps for all other missions. As General Siilasvuo stated: 'The incident at check-point Gamma near Suez in 1956, taught us another lesson, if a UN force never strikes back, it cannot gain the respect of the parties.'

On 23 April 1980, following the arrival on Chalk 1 of our replacement battalion, I started the handover to my successor, Comdt Eoin Maloney. After two weeks of intensive briefings, on 3 May 1980, control of the area of operations was handed over the CO of the 47th Battalion, Lt-Col Frank Stewart.

At Beirut Airport, at the side of a large hangar, the 200 plus soldiers on Return Chalk 3, the final Chalk, began to change from their green uniforms into khaki for the journey home. In the middle of this, a great cheer went up as a very welcome sight greeted us. A green Aer Lingus jumbo was just then coming into land. We were eager to go and little time was lost between the unloading and the loading. We were soon on our way home.

Chapter 12

HQ UNIFIL, NAQOURA

24 April 1985 to 6 November 1986

In early 1985 I was happily serving as CO of the 2nd Field Artillery Regiment in McKee Barracks in Dublin and enjoying life as always in my favourite unit. However, I had continued to declare that I was available for UN service, a policy I maintained right to the end of my service. One morning in February, I received a call from Brigadier-General Savino. He told me that I was nominated to become the next Camp Commandant and Officer Commanding the 12th and 13th Irish Components, HQ UNIFIL at Naqoura, South Lebanon.

On 24 April, the members of the component were assembled at four locations for final training and processing at Kilworth Camp, County Cork, Columb Barracks, Mullingar, the Curragh Camp with the 3rd Battalion and at Clancy Barracks in Dublin. I was delighted to find that an old friend, Sgt Mick Daly from the 27th Battalion, who had been the Cook Sgt in the 46th in Tibnine some years before, was now to be the Cook Sgt at Camp Tara, Naqoura.

The component was activated on Monday 15 April in Clancy Barracks for final processing and baggage preparations. Our flight departed Dublin at 01.35hrs on 24 April and arrived into Ben Gurion Airport where we were met by a reception party from Irishbatt. The following morning I went to a mission briefing for all officers, and then went to meet Lt-Col Jim Condon from whom I was to take over as Camp Commandant.

My new appointment was a most unusual one. Firstly, it was for a tour of duty of twelve months, during which time I would have command of the 12th Component for six months and then the 13th Component for the other six months. Whatever about having a chance to assess the personnel of the 12th Component, I had no input into that of the 13th. The appointment was different in another way too. My command was of a composite unit comprising the Irish personnel, plus two Ghanaian platoons – one of engineers, the other of infantry. Both platoons were commanded by Major Francis Adjerlolo, who effectively became the Deputy Camp Commandant. The infantry platoon was later replaced by a Fijian defence platoon.

The Irish Component, composed of just over eighty ARs, was intended, in the main, to support the administration of UNIFIL HQ. I had two Irish staff officers, Capt. Michael Brown, the adjutant, and Capt. David Whelan, the QM, both excellent and hard-working young officers. BSM Patrick O'Boyle and BQMS Tom Browne were the senior NCOs.

The nearest Israeli town to Naqoura was Nahariya, while Tyre (pronounced 'Teer') was further north along the Lebanese coast. Originally Naqoura had simply been a border and customs post between Lebanon and Israel. When UNTSO was established, an out-station had been set up there for OGL. That part of UNTSO assigned to supervise the Lebanon-Israel border had its HQ at Beirut with a sub-HQ at Naqoura. Five outposts were manned and controlled from there.

By 1985, UNIFIL HQ at Naqoura had grown to be an impressively large and complex base, composed in the main of prefabricated buildings, while the original stone-built Lebanese custom post buildings had become the principal offices for the FC and his senior civilian and military staff. Several hundred civilian UN Field Service personnel were working in the camp, crossing and re-crossing the border from Israel on a daily basis. The heavily fortified Israeli post on the border crossing at Rosh Haniqra was about 4kms away to the south of the UN HQ.

The UNMOs, having freedom of movement within the DFF zone, provided a valuable additional asset in the operation of the UNIFIL mission. In 1985, the FC of UNIFIL was Lt-Gen. William Callaghan, Capt. Gerry Breen was his hardworking ADC, while the DFC was Brig.-Gen. Jean Pons of France.

Probably because of the long association between Lebanon and France, the French were providing a substantial portion of the UN force at this time. A logistics battalion and an engineer battalion were both located at Naqoura, with an infantry battalion in the north-west part of the mission area. Sweden provided a medical hospital and Italy provided a small Italian helicopter unit known as Italair. Camp Martin was the base for the UNIFIL Military Police Company, another multi-national unit containing military police drawn from each of the units.

Across the main road from UNIFIL HQ a line of shacks had sprung up over the years, built by local Lebanese who sold a wide assortment of goods to the soldiers. This stretch of road – known to all as 'Mingi Street' – was some 400m long. They sold such goods as cassette tapes, video tapes, records, clothing, cigarettes or alcohol while a few were developed as small cafés or restaurants.

An important aspect of UN forces is that the FC has no direct disciplinary powers over any member of the force. Within a given unit, the CO can deal with most matters of this kind in the normal way under the regulations of his own country. When a 'higher authority' is needed for more serious matters, the UN allows for a contingent commander from each nationality in the force. In

UNIFIL in 1985 and 1986, the Irish contingent commander was Col Walter McNicholas.

The talks that preceded the Israeli withdrawal from Lebanon had taken place at Naqoura and the special walled security compound, constructed within the camp area for the talks, had only recently become redundant. I was able to recover the walled-off area, eventually moving into a hut there. My new accommodation had the advantage of being close to the operations room and to the tennis courts, while I had an excellent view of the nearby sea each morning as I rose. I used the now redundant concrete 'T-walls' to add to the security around the FC's building, the entrances and at other vulnerable locations in the camp. ('T-walls' are built of reinforced concrete, each about 2m wide by 3m high with a heavy base, forming an upside-down 'T'.)

As in all military units, sports were regarded as a prime source of that essential development of a common purpose within a multi-national force. Highly developed at this stage, UNIFIL competitions covered all the sports that the minimal facilities permitted or that the ingenuity of those involved could conjure up. For a military force, shooting competitions came high up on the list and were always popular. The infantry battalions naturally enough claimed superiority over the other lower-life entities such as the logistics elements or Camp Command!

Throughout my time at the HQ, whenever I had some free time, I played a lot of tennis, as there were four beautiful hard courts with floodlighting a short distance from my hut. I quickly found that there was an international supply of players with whom to share the courts and later on I developed a great rivalry with Company Sergeant O'Shea from the MP Company, a fine player. Because the natural lagoon – used by all as a safe swimming pool – was almost under my window, I also spent a lot of time swimming and snorkelling.

My family arrived for a six-week stint in July. I was lucky enough to rent a house in Nahariya from a member of the Field Service, Tim Norris, an Englishman who was going home on two months' leave. It was a fine detached two-storey house with four bedrooms and a good-sized garden. The cost of the rent was less than the going rate for Nahariya because Tim had asked me to mind their dog, Bethy, a large and placid sheepdog who dragged me out after dark each evening for walks on the beach. The family integrated easily into the extensive international community living in Nahariya, courtesy of the OGL club near the beach.

It was during August that the FC sent for me and asked me would I be willing to extend in the mission in order to take over the job of Senior Operations Officer. The incumbent, Lt-Col Pat Condron was due to depart the mission in November. Gen O'Callaghan asked me to discuss it with my wife first before giving him an answer, but I knew immediately that Anne would agree. This re-positioning for me amounted to an extension in the mission until November 1986. The family was delighted and the following day I assured the General that I was only too happy to take up his offer. In the meantime, business at Camp Command continued as usual.

On 19 August, having heard that DFHQ in Dublin was preparing to celebrate twenty-five years of Irish participation in UN missions, I organised a special dinner for all Congo veterans in Camp Tara. The FC himself was one of those veterans and so became the chief guest. Most of the older Irish officers and some NCOs had also served in the Congo, and when I discovered that my deputy, Maj. Adjerlolo, and two of his NCOs had also served in the Congo, I included them. It so happened that Lt-Col Tom Furlong, a retired Artillery officer, himself a Congo veteran, was visiting the FC at the time and I was delighted to invite him as well. I sent to Ireland for a large number of First Day covers of the special set of postage stamps issued by An Post to commemorate the occasion and sent a First Day cover to each commanding officer in UNIFIL and to members of the senior staff. I also designed special certificates, based on the UN medal certificate, and presented them at the dinner.

Shortly after this a high-level group arrived out from Ireland to visit the troops. It comprised the Minister for Defence, Mr Patrick Cooney, the secretary of the Department of Defence, Dr Michael Somers, and the Chief-of-Staff, Lt-Gen. Gerry O'Sullivan. I arranged a dinner where they could meet with the entire Irish component of Camp Command at Camp Tara. It proved to be a very successful and enjoyable event and the meal itself was of a very high standard, produced by Cook Sgt Mick Daly and his staff.

In September 1985, my attention turned to the medal parade for the personnel of Camp Command and for the Ghanaian complement. After some discussion, I had decided to hold a joint parade and that, because our words of command were in Irish, it would be easier for both groups if the commands were given in English. After the first rehearsal I was quite happy that this would work although I was concerned how the FC might react. For the occasion I had borrowed the pipe band from Irishbatt and the brass band of Ghanbatt and the parade, which included all those Irish staff officers who had not previously served in UNIFIL, was held on 24 September.

That night, a party was held at the Blue Beret Club in Camp Tara to which an open invitation was issued to all units in Naqoura. Camp Tara was looking its best, recently repainted and improved. Located as it was within metres of the placid Mediterranean, conditions could not have been better for such a large open-air party. The sea was calm, the sky was clear and star-studded, and the air was warm. At an early stage in the party, a sound of singing was heard in the distance, getting louder by the minute. It was coming from a platoon of French soldiers moving at the double along Mingi Street from their own base in Frenchlogs (French Logistics Battalion). A talented group of musicians from within the Irish pipe band entertained the party with pop songs and some rousing Irish ballads.

I had arranged for a 'COs Table' at the centre rear of the patio. At an early stage in the proceedings, BSM O'Boyle tapped me on the shoulder and said that a Swedish colonel would like to join our group. When he was seated beside me, he told me that he had just arrived from Sweden to carry out an inspection of the Swedish Medical Company. After some time in our company, clearly enjoying himself, he said that he wished his fellow Swedes could learn to enjoy a party in such a relaxed and exuberant manner as the Irish. The party was a memorable occasion attended by about 300 happy peacekeepers. Some days later, I received a very nice note from the first secretary to the ambassador to Lebanon, John Rowan, one of our guests. He said that hearing the Ghanaian brass band (a very small one) play 'A Nation Once Again' (an Irish patriotic song) had made his night.

A few days after this, the Fijian officers held a special party at Fiji House to which I and other Irish were invited. This was where I tasted for the first time the national tipple of Fiji – the kava root drink. It was fascinating to watch the care and attention given to the pounding of the kava root in a special bowl to which was added water from time to time.

Dutchbatt had been in occupation of an AO to the west of Irishbatt and to the south of Fijibatt, but was withdrawn in 1983 and replaced by a much smaller Dutch company of about 160 soldiers. The company controlled an important part of the mission zone that included the main road from Naqoura to Beirut, part of which was much used by all UN traffic between HQ and the 'inland' battalions. At this time a struggle for supremacy had developed between the two main Lebanese organisations, Amal and Hizbullah, in South Lebanon. Both were out to prove their mettle by trying to be more daring and more ruthless than the other.

This aggressive attitude also developed into a more anti-UN attitude, where the AEs would refuse to give up their weapons at check-points or would threaten individuals or even entire posts. They began to put severe pressure on the Dutch company in particular, making life very difficult. The Dutch soldiers, who were mainly national servicemen, began to complain about the severe restrictions laid down by their government under which they were required to operate. It seemed that they were not permitted to resist harassment or even to return fire when fired upon, surely an intolerable situation for any group of soldiers.

Once the local AEs, many of whom were little more than armed criminal gangs, realised the predicament of the Dutch soldiers, they became progressively more daring. In one incident, they even entered a Dutchcoy position, disarming and robbing a number of soldiers at gunpoint and taking some of their possessions. Not surprisingly, the soldiers themselves were very embarrassed. They started to make demands that their orders be changed or that they be withdrawn from the mission. The Dutch armed forces apparently were highly unionised and eventually a demand was made to have a vote on whether the soldiers should stay or withdraw from UNIFIL.

Within a few weeks, a Dutch general and assistants arrived to distribute the ballot papers to the Dutch soldiers. This very novel situation was being watched with incredulity by the other contingents, especially by the soldiers of Irishbatt, all of whom were professional volunteer soldiers. The Dutch soldiers voted overwhelmingly to go home and in October 1985 the unit was withdrawn from UNIFIL, as were all the staff officers and NCOs at UNIFIL HQ. A Nepalese battalion then occupied the former Dutch area of operations.

The long planned replacement of the Ghanaian defence platoon by a Fijian platoon also took place in the middle of October and after that all my efforts were devoted to the preparation for the rotation of the 12th and the 13th Irish Components. Final reports on all officers and NCOs had to be completed and many speeches and presentations made in the last few days before they departed. The rotation proceeded without difficulty over a three week period starting on 23 October, during which time I took the opportunity of a week's leave at home, missing the celebrations for UN Day on 24 October.

In November I was launched into a series of interviews with the individuals of the 13th Component, while at the same time I was planning and working for the takeover of the job of SOO. In preparation for this I accompanied Lt-Col Condron to some of the units to familiarise myself with the situations in the area. In Finbatt, our briefing was given by a young lieutenant, the son of General Ensio Siilasvuo, a renowned former UN FC.

I conducted my last inspection of Camp Command on 18 December and from then on I spent more and more time in Operations with Tony Condron and travelling to meetings and conferences around the AO. I collected my replacement, Lt-Col Mick Harrington at Ben Gurion on 4 January 1986 and after an intensive handover to him, I finally took over the appointment of SOO on the 7th.

Senior Operations Officer, HQ Unifil
07 Jan 1986 to 05 Nov 1986

Once I had assumed responsibility for my new task, I moved into an entirely different world, where my horizon expanded far beyond that of a camp commandant. My new boss, the COO, was Col Zacharya Backer from Norway, a tall, efficient and very pleasant individual with excellent English who had been a paratrooper in his earlier years. We got on very well from the beginning, remaining in contact for many years afterwards. I was responsible to him for all aspects of the running of the operations room and its staff. One officer, usually of captain or major rank, drawn from each of the contingents, formed a duty panel to staff the office on a twenty-four-hour basis. While the official language of the mission was English, having an officer from each contingent ensured that an interpreter was quickly to hand to deal with language problems should such a need arise.

A Scottish Field Service secretary, Marion Summers, the official operations office secretary, would normally type up all the reports and cables to be sent to New York. She worked the normal office hours and the duty radio operators in the ops room did any typing after hours. Having been in that job for quite a while, she was the 'guru' in preparing cables to UNNY and she gave me valuable advice and direction in the difficult early days. The radio operators were Irish Signal Corps personnel from Camp Command under the direct control of Sgt R. Walsh. They were supervised by the mission's Chief Signals Officer, Lt-Col Patrick Purcell, who had responsibility for all communications in the mission. We worked very closely together and he often stood in for me in my absence.

Just after taking over, I was plunged into a welter of activity created by incidents in Kunin and another incident in At Tiri in Irishbatt. The difference in time between New York and Lebanon was the cause of much hassle. Where an urgent query came from New York relating to one of our cables, it arrived during the night, while if I needed to talk to an individual in New York, I could only call during the early hours, local time. At times it made for lack of sleep and even some terse conversations. Gen. Dibuama was the military adviser in UNNY and while we had numerous discussions over the phone, I never met him until the final days of the UNTAG mission in Windhoek in 1990.

One of the 'perks' of being a staff officer at the HQ was that I was allotted my own UN vehicle, initially a VW Combi and later a more upmarket VW Passat Combi staff car. Now that I had moved into a more demanding position in ops, I had fewer opportunities to use the vehicle. It was often the case that officers from the Irish battalion going on leave into Israel would borrow the vehicle of a friend. I was able to accommodate some, especially when my family had returned to Ireland.

Fr Mark Coyle, a Franciscan chaplain to Irishbatt, approached me on one occasion for the use of my car. He had never been in the Holy Land before and it was very moving to witness his excitement. As he always wore the full-length brown habit of his order, and not a uniform, I went with him to the border post at Rosh Haniqra to introduce him to Maj. Khammai, the Israeli LO at the post, to make sure that he had no difficulty in crossing the border. To my relief, the Israelis had no problems with this unusual soldier in their midst.

In February a UN helicopter on its way south from Beirut, was forced inland by a severe thunderstorm (for safety reasons the UN helicopters normally travelled over sea parallel to the coast). It was shot at by AEs in the hills and crash-landed, fortunately without casualties. The Swedish postmaster suffered bruising when the Finnish chaplain fell on him as the aircraft rolled onto its side! All six crew and passengers were captured, but quickly released to OGL and brought to Frenchbatt at Marakah. The helicopter was a write-off and was destroyed in situ. One week later, a man that I was to meet years later in another UN mission, arrived at Naqoura for a three-day briefing. He was Englishman Marrack Goulding, the new USGS.

In April, we heard that our FC was being replaced and would become the Chief-of-Staff of UNTSO in Jerusalem. A stand-down parade for Gen. Callaghan was held at the French Logistics Battalion base on 30 April, with representative groups from all the contingents on parade. Maj.-Gen. Gustave Hagglund, the new Finnish FC, arrived on 3 June to take up his appointment, the same day that my mother died at a nursing home in Ireland. While arrangements were being made for my flight home, I gave the new FC a briefing on the current operational situation in the AO.

At an early stage during my takeover of the new job, I had expressed surprise at the unsatisfactory conditions under which the duty officers were working. The room was small, without air conditioning and it was poorly fitted out. As a result I went to the DFC at an early stage and showed him a sketch of a plan I had made to modernise and generally improve the conditions for duty officers. To my delight he agreed, saying that my design looked like a much smaller version of his own division operations room in the south of France.

I had designed two consoles, one for the ops duty officers, big enough to permit up to four persons to work side by side, and the other for the radio operators. The consoles, faced in melamine, were slightly curved and placed back to back with space between them for the easy movement of personnel. The operations console faced the wall where the new map of the AO was to be placed. All electrical cables, telephone lines and radio cables were sunk in ducts below floor level and all the telephone and radio units themselves were recessed into the sloping faces of the consoles. The second console, the communications console, manned by Irish signalmen, also had space for four operators. It faced the rear wall where various clocks were mounted showing the various international times crucial to the mission.

Work commenced quickly with the full co-operation of the Field Service maintenance section led by an enormous, efficient and jovial Fijian charge hand. Not only was he just excellent at his job, but he made his own practical contributions to the work as the project went on. Sgt R. Walsh added his own welcome suggestions, based on his experience of the needs of the duty signallers. During the construction, the duty officers were moved to another room nearby.

The maps we were using were 1/50,000 and were too small to be mounted on the wall as the detail would not be easily visible to the duty officer at the console. When discussing this with Col Backer, he promptly arranged to send a copy of the map of the AO to Norway where the scale was changed to 1/25,000 by the mapping section at his HQ. I then asked the Fijian if he could mount the maps on a sheet-metal backing so that magnetised symbols could be placed on the map. He had no problem with this, it required only two large metal sheets to which the map was successfully glued.

Brig.-Gen. Pons, the DFC, arranged for a French officer going on home leave to buy a set of small magnets and coloured plastic symbols in France. They were delivered to the office in just over two weeks. I then got the staff to glue the symbols onto the magnets which were then placed on the map display.

The newly rebuilt, re-decorated and air-conditioned operations room was occupied in July and opened officially by the FC, Maj.-Gen. Hagglund, on 26 September. The project was a good example of the ability of a multi-national group of individuals to work together to achieve a common end in a relatively short time, the sort of co-operation at which the UN can excel.

My family arrived out again in July for a second visit and I placed them in a rented apartment in Herzel Street in Nahariya. The following week, the Israeli border post at the Rosh Haniqra crossing was attacked. All the attackers were killed, while Israel also suffered casualties, including an officer.

The family returned to Ireland in August, having had an exciting flight. Their BA Tristar pilot had to shut down one of the three engines over Cyprus. If that was not enough, soon afterwards, a

3–4m-long flap on the starboard wing fell off, an event witnessed by many on board. The pilot was forced to make an emergency landing in Athens. British Airways gave all the passengers a fine meal in one of the city's best hotels and a conducted tour of the tourist spots. For Anne and the children, they were given an overnight stay in a hotel at Heathrow before travelling on to Dublin.

Frenchbatt occupied the north-west part of the AO covering the crucial coast road. In August, an incident occurred at a Frenchbatt checkpoint where two local members of Amal were shot dead by a sentry. An eruption of assaults on all Frenchbatt positions and on individual French soldiers followed immediately, causing a number of deaths and many injuries. At the same time the French Logistics Base at Tyre Barracks was attacked and kept under siege for four days. The French soldiers there had to be evacuated and were later replaced by a Norwegian group.

To add to the pressure, a young French officer was shot and injured on Mingi Street after which all French personnel in Naqoura were confined to their bases. The new Nepalese battalion, the unit that had replaced Dutchcoy, was also coming under increasing pressure, with soldiers killed and wounded. These events almost overwhelmed the abilities of the duty staff at Naqoura to cope with both their frequency and the language problems that arose and could not be dealt with by one translator. To overcome the problems of language between the French battalion and UNIFIL HQ, it was quickly arranged to hand over the large room adjoining the operations room to form a temporary second and parallel operations room, to be staffed by officers and signallers drawn from Frenchlogs. I spent a lot of time in this room, listening to the events as they unfolded. On one occasion I could hear the soldiers in one post telling HQ that the Amal attackers were on the roof of their bunker, attempting to roll grenades inside.

Diplomatic pressure eventually succeeded in calming things down and a plan was drawn up for the withdrawal of the French battalion from the AO to Naqoura and distributed to all units. On the day before implementation, it was noticed that a number of French drivers from the French logistics battalion had been nominated to drive some of the vehicles. This was a mistake. Their lives could be in danger if they were spotted, so they had to be replaced by additional drivers from other battalions. The Operations Order, already in the hands of the battalions, had to be amended and time was very short. The alterations were achieved by having each staff officer at operations talk to his own battalion in his own language, outlining the changes to be made. This provided some short-term security. (While we always accepted that by this time the Israelis had interpreters for all the languages of UNIFIL, it was reasonable to assume that the Amal were not so well equipped.)

I spoke to OC Irishbatt, Lt-Col John O'Shea, myself, giving him the changes to the Operations Order. We must have spoken over the radio in Irish for about ten minutes or more. When I had finished, I looked up to see Brig.-Gen. Pons leaning over the console, watching me in amazement. He clearly had never heard me speaking in Irish up to this and presumably had never before heard Irish spoken in a military context and at such length. I felt very good about that.

Time was running out for me, but the activities of the AO never let up, a seemingly endless list of firings-close (where a projectile landed within 50m of a UN post, vehicle or person), threats and attempted kidnappings, including yet another incursion by Israeli forces.

I learned who my successor would be, Lt-Col Jim Harold, and started to prepare for his arrival and my own departure from the mission. In the UN system, it is necessary for staff officers, when preparing to depart the mission, to complete a checking-out form.

This required the individual to go to the heads of all departments, military and civilian, to get a signature of clearance. The clearance document stated that this person has handed back all UN items on location to him, and that he did not owe any monies to the UN. My final port of call for clearance was to Brig.-Gen. Pons, the DFC. When I presented him with the check-out sheet, I received an unexpected and much-appreciated compliment. He looked up in surprise. 'You are leaving?'

'Yes,' I replied, 'I will be gone within a week.'

'Well then, I am glad that I am leaving too,' he said and signed my check-out sheet with a flourish. He was due to leave in about four weeks.

Jim Harold replaced me as SOO in November 1986 and I departed for Dublin with Chalk 3 of the 59th Battalion on 5 November. It had been a great experience, working at the coalface of a major international UN force, dealing with very difficult and fractious adversaries under an inadequate mandate, where the UN forces were only allowed to use force in self-defence, as well as having no clearly defined area of operations.

Chapter 13

'JACK OF ALL TRADES'

Ireland 1961–1989

While UN missions were an important part of my career, the vast majority of my time in the army was spent on Irish soil. I will now try to give a glimpse into some of the varied roles that I was expected to fill across the span of my years in the Defence Forces.

THE GUNNERS OF MCKEE BARRACKS, DUBLIN

While I had served in, and enjoyed hugely, my years with the 4th Regiment, the Artillery School and the 6th Regiment FCA, my time in the 2nd Regiment, based in McKee Barracks, was the most influential role in my military career. I arrived there from the Artillery School on promotion to captain in December 1961 and apart from a considerable number of breaks, including overseas service, I remained in that unit in many capacities, ending up as the Commanding Officer in April 1984.

With the 1959 PR1 re-organisation of the forces the three regular regiments, 1st, 2nd and 4th, became larger and more effective, combining the very best of the regular and reserve personnel. In the case of the 'integrated' 2nd Regiment, it now consisted of HQ, HQ Battery and 10th Field Battery, all of which were regular elements, plus two reserve batteries, the 14th and 19th Batteries, FCA. When the 2nd Regiment went on exercises, the FCA elements were able to participate in, and to profit from, all aspects of the training. The division between the regular and FCA elements within the regiment became almost seamless.

While integration worked very well for the Artillery, it did not find favour with other corps. The entire plan was abandoned in 1969 and replaced by yet another re-organisation plan. Under this new reorganisation plan (jokingly referred to in Artillery circles as 'Disintegration'), all the FCA field batteries were removed from their comfortable relationships and were formed into new regiments of their own. One artillery unit only was not affected. The Air Defence Regiment became the only line unit in the army to retain its FCA components – the Air Defence Batteries.

I found the pace of life in the 2nd Regiment to be much faster than that of the school in Kildare where the number of courses and visits from other corps dictated the level of activity. As a line unit, the regiment was subject to the demands of both 2nd Brigade and Command HQ, Eastern Command – demands that became progressively more onerous as the troubled situation in Northern Ireland developed. Boredom was certainly not an issue.

One of the aspects of service life in those early years was the frequent call for assistance to the public in the case of bus or bin collection strikes, fire brigade disputes and so on. Being stationed in the capital city, demands on the services of the regiment's soldiers were frequent and varied. As always, such jobs were carried out with the best of good humour and understanding of the problems of the public.

When the annual Command inspections were being held in McKee Barracks, I always requested that the Band of the Eastern

Command play a particular tune. It was a piece of music that I felt epitomised the manner in which the gunners of the regiment reacted to the never-ending demands on their skills. The tune is called 'Jack of All Trades'. It has a vaguely traditional Irish music tempo, suggesting the skirl of the pipes and the swirl of kilts, and was played with great panache by our band. I regarded this piece of music as the unofficial regimental marching tune.

When I first arrived from Kildare, I was struck by the lack of a proper gymnasium for the garrison and decided to do something about it. First I ensured that we were granted swimming time in the nearest pool, which belonged to St Joseph's School for Deaf Children. While swimming was a popular exercise with many, mainly the younger soldiers, I felt that it was not enough. I had a series of discussions with a good friend of mine, Capt. Des Travers, an infantry officer who was working with cadets in the Military College. We wanted to do something about the concept of adventure training like that already introduced in the British forces. We agreed that the provision of activities such as orienteering, mountain walking and canoeing would be very acceptable to young soldiers while at the same time teaching them additional skills not directly covered by existing military training schedules. Des Travers arranged to have a number of fibreglass canoes made in Clancy Barracks. These were divided between the 2nd Regiment and the Cadet School.

Later, in 1972, with the enthusiastic support of the NCOs and young officers, I formed an organisation called The Warriors Adventure Club. Membership was open to all ranks and units in McKee Barracks. On one of our early trips, I brought a group of soldiers to Sandycove, County Dublin, for canoe training in the sea. When I left the regiment to become the senior staff officer to the Director of Artillery in 1977, Lieut Shane Gray took over the running of it. He maintained the momentum, eventually taking a large group on a week-long safari down the River Barrow by canoe. They ended up in Fort Duncannon, the old Coast Defence fort situated on the estuary of the three rivers, the Suir, the Nore and the Barrow.

Very soon afterwards The Warriors Club became redundant when a new organisation was launched at DFHQ to take over all forms of adventure training. It was called the Defence Forces Council for Adventure Training – DFCAT. All existing activities were included, while newer activities such as scuba diving, parachuting and rock climbing were quickly included. Selected personnel were sent abroad for specialist training with other armies and organisations to train as instructors. DFCAT has been a great success and the participation of soldiers in its varied activities has grown and developed in a way that just could not have been imagined back in the days of The Warriors.

The 1960s and 1970s saw the start of an era of film-making in Ireland, where many soldiers were officially drafted in as film extras. Quite a number of films were made employing large numbers of regular soldiers and members of the FCA, films such as the *Blue Max*, *Viking Queen* and *Zeppelin*. The demand for extras became so frequent a practice that some individuals actually joined Actors Equity to ensure that they could claim the actor's rates of pay! I was present in the Glen of Imaal when the 10th Battery provided 18pdrs to represent First World War anti-aircraft guns firing at raiding dirigibles for *Zeppelin*. Because the 18pdrs could not be elevated enough, a deep hole had to be dug under the trail of each weapon to get the necessary elevation. It was a night shoot and blanks were fired to a background of searchlights and drifting smoke. I saw the film afterwards and was satisfied that no gunner could have been fooled for a moment into thinking that he was seeing actual anti-aircraft guns in action.

When I returned from service with UNTSO in 1975, I was fired up with enthusiasm for some new approaches to training as a result of what I had seen and experienced on the Golan Heights. I was Battery Commander, 10th Field Battery and I had a large, well-trained and experienced battery of some 130 ARs, a hugely efficient and hard-working young Battery Sergeant called John Moore, as well as a platoon of about fifty recruits in training.

I believe that soldiers react well to innovation and so I attempted to introduce as much change as possible to raise the level of interest in training. We made great use of Glen Imaal and Fort Duncannon, both very popular with the members of the regiment. I also made use of the lands and facilities at Kilbride, Kilpeddar and Gormanston for tactical training activities whenever possible. My CO, Lt-Col Johnny White, was always keen to spend time at Fort Duncannon. He had a sentimental attachment to this fort, as an ancestor of his had served there as Commanding Officer in the previous century.

Weapons training was particularly important for the battery. All members of the Defence Forces were required to fire the weapons – rifle, SMG or pistol – with which they would normally be armed, at least once a year and more often if possible. The problem was that it was becoming more and more difficult to book a rifle range due to the increased demands created by overseas service and an expanding army. After some frustrating booking failures, I introduced a new policy for the battery. We would use the range when nobody else wanted it – after hours. I decided that we would camp out behind the 600 yard firing point on the range in Gormanston – in the spring and summer months only, when the weather and the long evenings would be more amenable – until all available soldiers of the regiment had completed their annual practice. We were thus free to conduct our firing practices after the other units had gone home. During the day, while other units were using the range, we would play football on the beach (tide permitting), volleyball, or else do whatever essential training could be done in the limited space available to us.

Starting the system of going under canvas for the conduct of range practices, I gradually expanded it to include tactical training in Kilpeddar and the Glen of Imaal, where the emphasis was on training after dark. These two- or three-day exercises were highly enjoyable and successful for all involved. I finally graduated to a five-day exercise, running from Monday to Friday, that I called 'Rollerball' after the film of the same name. The first two nights of this were spent under canvas in the deer field high up in the Slieve Bloom mountains overlooking Kinnitty. From the Slieve Blooms, we conducted a series of artillery tactical moves and occupations of positions across the countryside including the Heath at Portlaoise and the Curragh Plains. Finally, we occupied the planned firing position in the southern end of Glen Imaal, arriving in at midnight. The following morning we fired our howitzers to a small-fire plan under the supervision of the Artillery School Commandant, Lt-Col Tom Ryan and his staff.

All military units must maintain high levels of training to be able to respond to unexpected circumstances. In response to the alarming situation in Northern Ireland certain first line reservists and a number of FCA personnel were called up in 1979. Some temporary military posts were established on the border and for a time the 2nd Regiment was stretched to provide large numbers of personnel on rotation to these temporary border units. This situation finally eased with the establishment of three new battalions and a cavalry squadron along the border.

In the Dublin area, the regiment was regularly required to provide armed escorts for the movement of important prisoners, for the transport of large sums of cash or for explosives to be used in mining or in quarries. All the more important buildings and vulnerable points such as Government Buildings, electricity generating stations, broadcasting masts and so on had to be protected on a twenty-four-hour basis, all tasks shared with the other units of the command.

Units providing cash or explosives escorts were often tasked to provide personnel to operate air cover also. This was one of the tasks that I enjoyed, where we escorted the convoy in an aircraft from the Army Co-operation Squadron based in Gormanston. If the convoy was attacked we would report on what we were seeing and track the attackers as far as possible. Gnr Browne was my usual signaller and to be fair to him, while he did not particularly like flying, he never actually turned down the task. I met up with one particular pilot on more than one occasion who eventually persuaded me to take the wheel. While I was very reluctant at first, I came to enjoy it, remembering his basic rule, 'keep her nose on the horizon'. I eventually clocked up a total of four and a half hours of gentle banking and cross-country flying. To be fair, for a young pilot aspiring to more exciting challenges, flying such a slow-moving aircraft must have been terribly boring. Our pilot even offered to let me land the Cessna on one occasion, but I had no hesitation in declining that one, no doubt to the relief of my signaller!

All the above demands on a soldier's time, while placing a strain on military units, were at least predictable, as most of them were scheduled events. It was the sudden weekend call-out of bodies of troops, usually of platoon size, that imposed the greatest strain on the soldiers of all units. Usually occurring on Friday afternoons, just when soldiers were preparing to go home, it meant that up to forty soldiers were required to stay in barracks for the night, sometimes even for the weekend, usually as a response to threats of IRA attacks on cash or explosives escorts. I was always filled with admiration at how well the soldiers of the regiment responded to these frequent and irritating demands on their free time and how cheerfully they performed their additional and unexpected duties.

CEREMONIAL GUN SALUTES

All artillery regiments are required from time to time to engage in the firing of ceremonial gun salutes for formal occasions. These occasions can range from State ceremonials in honour of visiting heads of State, to events like the 50th anniversary of the 1916 Rising. In March 1962, the regiment fired a 21-gun salute at Dublin Airport for President de Valera, who was going to the US on a State visit. The weather was very cold, heavy rain was threatening to turn to snow, and while the gun salute went without a hitch, three members of the guard of honour collapsed, as they had been standing for forty-five minutes in the cold – they were not wearing greatcoats. A second salute was fired to mark the occasion of his return on 24 March.

Gun salutes for visiting vessels tend to be the most frequent type. The firing of a gun salute by a shore battery is a very old and traditional form of greeting to a visiting naval vessel and is practised in all countries. The gun salute bears all the importance and formality of an exchange of compliments between the two nations involved and no slip-up can be tolerated. Two Saluting Batteries, each equipped with four 12pdr naval guns, are maintained at present, one at the end of the East Pier in Dún Laoghaire harbour and one in Fort Davis overlooking the entrance to Cork harbour. Because of its location in the capital city, 2nd Regiment tends to get the bulk of the diplomatic duties in Dublin. As a result, the NCOs in particular have built up a great lore of knowledge and experience of these ceremonies.

A gun salute sounds like a simple enough task, as generally the officer in charge has a good view of the bay and the approaching vessel and there are few safety concerns. I have had experience of a number of these salutes, and while there were no problems with most of them, a tricky situation did arise on the occasion of the visit of a Swedish vessel in the early 1970s. At 06.00hrs that morning, the weather was bad, there was a heavy fog and we could only see for about 300m. As the time arrived for the Swedish salute, I commanded absolute silence and asked everyone to listen. We could hear nothing and the sweat began to dampen my brow. Just when I was on the point of despair, one of the most experienced NCOs in the regiment, Sergeant Ollie Denis, shouted to me that he could hear some detonations and we were able to count about four or possibly five muffled sounds. My next problem was – were these the first four or the last four Swedish rounds, or worse, could it even be possible that the Swedes had some misfires and were stuck in the middle of their salute? I had to make a decision.

Could I possibly be heading for a diplomatic *faux pas* like a very famous incident many years before? In that case, a visiting Argentine sail-training vessel arrived with an admiral on board. It so happened that the return salute could not be completed because all four guns had misfired. The Argentine vessel docked in Dublin port, but the admiral refused to allow any Irish official to board or any of his complement to go ashore, until the salute was completed. In great haste, a battery of field guns was rushed to the waterfront, where the salute was fired to the satisfaction of the admiral.

So I waited for what seemed like an eternity of about one minute before ordering our return salute to begin. As the salute continued – it only takes 100 seconds to complete – the Swedish vessel appeared out of the fog heading straight towards our location on the pier. It was a small minesweeper-sized vessel, equipped with 40mm Bofor guns with which they had fired their salute. This would account for our failure to hear them; the detonation of a 40mm Bofors was quite light compared to the normal naval guns used for this purpose and the thick fog helped to muffle the sound.

There were no repercussions, however – our salute must have been 'on target'. I wrote a strong complaint afterwards requesting that in future the Irish naval officer designated as the liaison officer for the duration of the visit should be sent out to board the incoming vessel, equipped with a radio with which to keep in touch with the officer at the saluting battery. This could obviate problems such as that described above.

In July 1971, the Chief-of-Staff, Lt-Gen. P.J. Delaney died suddenly, after only a few months in the position. The death of a serving Chief-of-Staff was a most unusual event in the short history of the Defence Forces and a major ceremonial funeral was prepared. Defence Forces Regulation (DFR) A11 specifies that a Chief-of-Staff who is serving at the time of his death merits a full battalion of marching soldiers and a gun salute, amongst other things. I was appointed as officer in charge of the Salute Battery, and went into training immediately with the men of 10th Battery. The Defence Forces regulations describe the gun salute as a 'Minute Gun'. Eleven rounds are fired at intervals of one minute – hence the name. The burial was to take place at Glasnevin Cemetery and 10th Battery was placed in the extension graveyard across the road from the entrance to the cemetery.

I placed two signallers down at the far corner of the graveyard with instructions to let me know exactly when the cortège commenced the final slow march to the graveside. All the mourners, the pall bearers, the senior officer escort, members of the family and others had to leave their vehicles and move forward to take up their positions in the cortège for the final brief march into the cemetery. Only when they were ready did the MP officer in charge give the order 'Paráid, go mall mársáil' ('Parade, slow march').

I had ordered the signaller to repeat the words of command over the air to me as they were called out by the MP officer. I ordered 'No. 1 fire' exactly in time with the order 'mársáil'. As we were surrounded by high walls and many buildings, the detonation made a most satisfying boom, echoing from all the hard surfaces. The salute, and the funeral, went without a hitch and the brigade commander was kind enough to phone me later that evening to congratulate me and to say that the eleventh round was fired just as the coffin approached the grave itself – he said that the timing was perfect.

Government Buildings

One of the security duties that arose for all junior officers at McKee Barracks was that of Orderly Officer at Government Buildings. It was a fairly relaxed affair – the officer went on duty in the afternoon to spend the night in the buildings, although he was permitted to retire after midnight. A standard guard of one NCO and three privates was installed on a full twenty-four-hour basis and a cook was also provided in the guard-room to prepare and serve meals for all ranks. The guard-room was located on a narrow laneway to one side of the main buildings, with a large and heavy gate about 30m away on the public road. This gate was used by most of the government ministers and the Taoiseach when entering and leaving Dáil Éireann. It was a most unsatisfactory position from a military point of view.

On the afternoon of 2 February 1972, I had taken up duty and was looking forward to the usual quiet evening. However, this was the night that the British embassy was attacked and burned down. On that day a huge demonstration had taken place outside the embassy, in protest at the events of 30 January 1972 in Derry where a civil rights protest had been fired on by British paratroopers, killing thirteen people. The British embassy in Dublin was on Merrion Square, which was only around the corner from our location at Government Buildings, and during the afternoon we could hear the commotion as the crowds built up.

I had seen some of the early scenes on TV, but as darkness fell a crowd of people started to gather on the street outside our location. Some appeared to be staring in through the gates and I formed the idea that they might be planning to attack Dáil Éireann when they had finished with the British embassy. I phoned the command duty officer, a senior officer in HQ Eastern Command and told him of my unease. While a small band of MPs was present elsewhere in the buildings, I requested further reinforcements. He assured me that a company was already assembling in Cathal Brugha Barracks as we spoke.

The orders for the Orderly Officer laid down exactly what was expected of me during this twenty-four-hour security duty, and the orders for any sentry on post are very clear. He was permitted to use live ammunition 'in the defence of his own life, the defence of his comrade's lives and in the defence of Government property'. So, as my military training required me to do all within my power to defend my post, I gave certain instructions to the guard in case of an attempted break-in. If some of the rioters were shot, even in the act of saving the Dáil from destruction, my career was probably finished. Equally if Dáil Éireann was burned down by a mob, I would have clearly failed in my duty. Fortunately, no attack was made on the buildings and the need for such drastic action did not arise. Still, I spent a most uncomfortable night – during which I heard the explosions at the embassy – and early morning, while the promised reinforcements never arrived. Although I asked a number of times for them to be sent, I was told they were being held for immediate deployment but only if needed!

Other Postings

In 1977, I was posted to the Directorate of Artillery. I was to work as the senior staff officer to Col Tom McDunphy and would continue to do so for the next two years. The Directorate was a part of DFHQ, but located in McKee Barracks. I became deeply involved in the planning and acquisition of all forms of new equipment for the corps, as well as the supervision of training and career development for gunners of all ranks. The Artillery Corps was in great need of modernisation by now, having finally cast off the remnants of the Emergency period and the equipment that had served the corps so well, but was by now out-of-date.

The corps had already commenced re-equipping all of its units and had recently acquired the first of its new field guns, the British 105mm light gun, along with an initial stock of ammunition. Other acquisitions during my time there included the Air Defence low-level missile system, laser range finders, Field Artillery Computer Equipment (FACE) and many other electronic devices, as well as new gun-towing vehicles. It was an exciting time to be in this appointment and I enjoyed what was to be my only excursion into DFHQ.

An indication of just how rapidly the IT age was moving, even then, can be judged from the development of fire control instruments for field artillery. When FACE arrived in the corps, it was the latest and most up-to-date equipment and in regular use in the British Army. However, it was big and heavy, and it needed its own Landrover for mobility. This vehicle provided the necessary batteries and charging facilities for the computer, but very little room was available to the operators within the vehicle. Much of the limited space was taken up by the a large and cumbersome telex machine and the radios, to the extent that the vehicle was on the borderline of being overloaded. Today, practically all the functions provided by the cumbersome FACE can be carried out by a small hand-held computer, thus providing a great saving on space, on battery power, training time and vehicles.

The 7th Field Artillery Regiment, Fca, 1979 to 1981

If there was any one posting, of the very many I experienced over my career, that gave me a real sense of pleasure, it must surely have been that of Officer Commanding, 7th Field Artillery Regiment, FCA. (The original 7th Regiment, part of the 7th Brigade Group, had previously existed during the Emergency as a regular unit in the Limerick area more than thirty years before.) I have already mentioned the re-organisation of the Defence Forces in 1969 by Planning and Research. As a result of this the 14th and 19th FCA batteries now surfaced as a new regiment based in McKee Barracks, Dublin – the 7th Field Artillery Regiment.

These FCA Batteries had travelled a long road from the pre-war years where they were attached as independent sub-units to the North Dublin Area FCA HQ. At the end of the Emergency years they were left to exist in a curiously semi-detached situation in Collins Barracks. That they survived in the era of relative indifference after the Emergency years was due solely to the very fine officers and NCOs who sustained them for so long in their unswerving dedication to the spirit and ethos of the corps to which they looked for guidance and support.

The members of these batteries had finally received the status and recognition that their loyal and faithful service deserved. The new FCA regiment was organised very closely on the lines of the regular regiments. It had an HQ Battery, complete with all the usual administrative personnel, and two field batteries, the 14th Field and the 19th Heavy Mortar Battery. I had the privilege of being their first Commanding Officer.

However, I spent less than three weeks in my new appointment before I was appointed as OC HQ Company of the 46th Battalion for service with UNIFIL. This meant that I found myself struggling to establish a new unit, to meet and greet staff, to take charge of weapons, equipment, premises (former married quarters in McKee Barracks) and barrack services, while at the same time attempting to prepare myself for service in a new overseas unit. This complicated life hugely for me, but the officers and NCOs of the new regiment rose to the challenge and carried on, as I knew that they could and would. For years they had endured the constant chopping and changing of the regular training personnel, both officers and NCOs, who were assigned to them. They had become hardened to it all and had demonstrated that they were very capable of carrying on without help. The new Regimental Sergeant Major was Micky Proctor, a superb NCO of the old school who was delighted to have arrived at the well deserved pinnacle of his career; equally so our Regimental Quartermaster Sergeant Paul Magee. However, the posting did mean that I could reasonably expect to resume the appointment of OC 7th Regt, FCA on my return – an important consolation for the initial short time I spent there.

I had the good fortune to have known most of the officers previously, having met them on many occasions in Glen Imaal during their annual camps. Later, I had been Training Officer to the 14th Battery when it was an integral reserve element of the 2nd Regiment and I felt that we were already firm friends.

The regiment's enthusiasm was almost overwhelming – they had an insatiable thirst for new and challenging training activities. I quickly found that I had to be careful with what I said to them about new ideas for training. A suggestion of possibly conducting some new types of training exercises in the Wicklow mountains, on the Curragh Plains or in the Glen area, only served to start them planning and preparing. Because they were part-time soldiers, they had only limited training opportunities in barracks – meeting on Thursdays and Sunday mornings for a few hours, and having only a two weeks' full-time training camp each summer. Even that inadequate time was reduced to one week's training later on as a cost-saving exercise. They did have one great advantage over the regulars, however. They did not have to suffer the endless demands for guards of honour, inspections, security duties or even overseas service that could interfere with their training and their plans.

Early in the winter of 1980, I proposed at a conference that they should go to a very different location for their next Annual Training Camp. I said it would be different to anything that most of them had ever experienced before. It would not be an artillery camp but primarily an exercise in movement to, and administration in, a distant location never seen by them before, while the training would be solely infantry tactics and range practices. I proposed that next year's camp be held in Bere Island in West Cork. I was not disappointed at the reaction – nobody was shocked or horrified, rather they received the proposal with great excitement and immediately started on their preparations. Before putting this suggestion to them, I had checked with the operations section of both the Eastern and Southern Commands to seek their support, and while it was unusual to have an artillery unit travelling from Dublin to West Cork for a two-week long camp, there were no objections. I also went to the Department of Defence, Lands Branch, where I was given every support by Mr Michaele Wade. He had responsibility for all Defence lands across the country. He was very helpful and gave me a copy of a map defining the departmental lands that were scattered in pockets across Bere Island. He even asked me to ensure that during our camp we would enter every part of the Defence property in the area and make some use of it. I was only too delighted to get this support and promised to do as he had requested.

I informed a staff meeting that the OC HQ Battery, the unit adjutant, the quartermaster and their respective staffs needed to read up on their responsibilities and to prepare as far as possible to do what would be required of them. I told them that they had to plan ahead and to work out for themselves what they needed before coming to me. I would then arrange to have the necessary support provided. I deliberately left them to their own devices as much as possible during the long run up to the annual camp. We were very fortunate to have the willing co-operation of the 2nd Regiment throughout. In fact many of their drivers and cooks actually volunteered to be part of the exercise.

I knew Bere Island well from time spent there with the Army Sub-Aqua Group. It was of course an old Coast Artillery station and had been manned by gunners up to 1958, although they had been there more in a care-taking role than any other. I was also aware that the Southern Command had initiated a programme of modernisation of the old quarters at Rerrin. I quickly found out that OC Southern Command, my old cadet Training Officer, Jack Gallagher who was now a brigadier general, was delighted to have the location used, even by troops from the Eastern Command!

In January 1981, I led a reconnaissance group of officers, including the RSM and the RQMS, to Bere Island for a hurried weekend to see for themselves what they were up against. In our brand-new minibus, just recently allotted to the unit, we set off in good spirits for the island. When we arrived at the ferry crossing point, I announced that we would have to do a lot of walking when we crossed over, as the vehicle would have to be left on the mainland. The ferryman, Patrick Murphy, was surprised and said that he could take the minibus over on the ferry without difficulty, that he did it all the time for similar vehicles. It should be noted that the ferry was not a car ferry, but more like a trawler with space for foot passengers. I was therefore loath to agree, thinking of what would happen if we lost our minibus overboard in rough seas. I knew only too well how difficult it would be to justify a replacement if we lost our brand-new vehicle in the sea off Bere Island. After some consideration I eventually agreed to put my faith in the ferry operator. However, I realised that I was in for a very tense half or hour or so.

Two long and very heavy planks were stretched across the thwarts to the vessel and the driver, no less than the regimental Transport Sergeant, Sergeant Fitzpatrick, was invited to drive carefully onto the boat over these planks, guided by Patrick Murphy. Once we were all on board, the ferry moved off and headed for the port at Rerrin village about twenty minutes away by sea. I watched very anxiously as every little wave rocked the boat and the minibus. I pictured having to ask some of my diver friends to help me find and lift the vehicle from the bottom, as it would inevitably fall overboard. But it did not and the weekend visit went without a hitch.

For months, nothing else was talked about but the camp on Bere Island. The various officers planned and pestered me for their needs and equipment. I let them do as much as they could without my help but behind the scenes, I was making some essential administrative arrangements. One of the biggest problems for me was to send a convoy of trucks under armed escort ahead of the personnel of the regiment to carry all the weapons, beds, bedding, tables, chairs, cooking equipment and the many other items needed for a location that had little or nothing in that line to offer us. I had booked two carriages of an early Dublin-Cork train to carry the personnel and had arranged for a number of private buses to transport them from Ceannt Station in Cork all the way to the ferry landing for Bere Island. From there Patrick Murphy did a number of runs to ferry them all across to the island.

By a strange stroke of what could be regarded both as bad and good luck, I was not there for the big event – I did not stay on the island with the regiment for the duration of the camp. In June 1981, a week before D-Day, I was promoted to Lt-Col and appointed as the School Commandant of the Artillery School in Magee Barracks, Kildare. I was hugely disappointed by the move even if delighted with the promotion and especially with the appointment. Comdt Tony Wall was appointed as OC 7th

Regiment in my place, and the camp was a very difficult chore for him as he had not been involved at all in the long run up to what was quite a complicated project. He was thrown in at the deep end, but the camp passed off without major incidents of any sort.

I was told afterwards by some of the officers that the young Dublin gunners were simply delighted and astonished at the entire experience. For many of them it was their first time on a mainline train, their first time on a luxury coach, their first time on a ferry and their first time on a small offshore island. Apparently the entire venture was a great success. I did manage to visit the island during the middle weekend of the camp in the company of Comdt Ray Quinn, where I saw for myself just how well they were getting on.

Having been promoted School Commandant and posted to Magee Barracks, Kildare, I spent two happy years there, where my responsibilities covered all aspects of artillery training courses and firing practices in Glen Imaal. Then, on the retirement of Lt-Col Tom Ryan, I was posted as OC Depot and School, Magee Barracks.

In 1984, I was posted back to Dublin as OC 2nd Regiment, and felt as if I had come home. Comparisons have often been drawn between a military unit and a happy family. It comes from a mutual feeling of belonging where each individual is surrounded by trusted friends and is proud, happy and comfortable in his situation. From this contentment comes the desire to do his best for the unit – on parade, in sporting activities or when responding to demands such as those mentioned earlier. The analogy probably is more noticeable in stations outside the cities, as many of the soldiers come from the immediate area and are more connected with the community outside the barrack wall.

It rarely happens that an officer becomes a long term resident in any unit, subject as he is to the demands of his career development and the 'exigencies of the service', to use an oft-quoted military expression. Therefore, officers are the transients in the unit, especially the more senior officers, some of whom might spend as little as a few months with a unit before being moved again. My own career was a clear example of this. Because of this the NCOs have become the backbone of the Defence Forces and the reason is obvious. Apart from the occasional military course or a spell overseas with the UN, they spend by far the greatest part of their service life in the station to which they are first posted after recruit training. Consequently, they are the most stable element in the unit and know the soldiers far better than the officers ever could. They often marry and put down roots in the locality, thus creating a vested interest in the stability and success of their units.

In 1987, I was moved from the 2nd Regiment to Command HQ Eastern Command in Collins Barracks, Dublin, to become the Command Intelligence Officer. Because of the continuing troubles in Northern Ireland, this appointment was an important one at a critical time in the affairs of the State. I was dealing with both the capital city and the border region. While well aware of the cynical joke about military intelligence being a contradiction in terms, in my own case I felt that it had a ring of truth. I had never before experienced any time in this aspect of the military life nor had I ever received any formal training in the subject. However, I was very fortunate in my deputy, Comdt Jack Duggan, who was an acknowledged expert in this area. He had developed a great rapport with the senior members of An Garda Síochána and was able to introduce me to his many contacts.

On my appointment I protested to Brig.-Gen. Pat Monahan that I felt I was quite unqualified for the task but would do my best. As it happened, I was not too long in my task as Intelligence Officer when on 25 January 1989 I was promoted to colonel and appointed to the position that I had longed for for many years – Director of Artillery. I felt eminently qualified for my new role, having a very wide experience of all aspects of the corps, and having spent many hundreds of hours over the years in Glen Imaal. I had served in the 4th, 6th and 7th and 2nd Regiments. I had been an instructor in gunnery for a number of years in the Artillery School, had served as troop commander for the heavy mortar troop of the 41st Irish Battalion in Cyprus, had worked as the Senior Staff Officer in the Directorate and served as School Commandant of the Artillery School and later as OC Depot Artillery. Such a wide spread of experience within the corps did not occur by design or indeed by my own plotting, but simply seemed to happen of its own volition. I hugely enjoyed all forms of artillery training and practice, and wished to be part of no other corps. With such a background, I felt that I was really well equipped to give the maximum return to the corps that I loved and knew so well in my new position.

I did not know it then, but my connection with the Artillery Corps was about to come to a swift end after so many wonderful years. Only a few weeks later, in 1989, I was nominated to lead a team of officers to a UN Mission in South West Africa on a tour lasting a whole year.

Chapter 14

UNTAG ANGOLA

In 1989, rumours of a new UN mission to support the introduction of independence in Namibia were abounding but I took no notice of them. I had just recently been promoted to Colonel and had been given the appointment for which I had always longed – Director of Artillery. Thus, just as I was starting to settle into my new responsibilities, I was quite taken aback to be informed that I had been selected to travel to Namibia with UNTAG in March 1989 for a period of one year. An officer, for his own peace of mind, has to adopt a relatively relaxed and flexible attitude to prevent unnecessary distress at the thwarting of plans.

UNTAG was to provide a smooth and peaceful transition to independence for the new nation of Namibia. Known as German South West Africa since 1884, the territory had been ceded to the government of South Africa by the League of Nations when South African forces had invaded and defeated the German forces there in 1915. In 1956 the South West Africa People's Organisation (SWAPO) was formed and declared that it would achieve the liberation of Namibia, by force if necessary. The name Namibia was adopted by the UN General Assembly in 1968, and in 1976 SWAPO was recognised as the 'sole and authentic representative of the Namibian peoples'.

In 1971, the UN had stated that South Africa must withdraw its administration and end the occupation of the territory. In 1973, the first UN High Commissioner for Namibia was appointed – Mr Seán MacBride of Ireland – who established a base in Luanda, the capital of Angola. Mr Martii Ahtisaari of Finland succeeded him, an appointment he held until the Security Council passed a new motion, Resolution 435, on 29 September 1978. In that same year, Mr Ahtisaari was appointed SRSG. He then conducted a fact-finding tour of Namibia with Austrian General Hannes Philipp, then the FC of UNDOF in Damascus, accompanied by Irish Capt. Ray Twomey (then an UNMO in Tiberias) where they were briefed by South African officials and members of SADF (South African Defence Forces). They did not visit Angola, an area still under the colonial control of Portugal.

The UNTAG mission, as subsequently planned, became the framework of a new and experimental type of project for the United Nations. It was essentially a political operation with what was considered to be minimal military and police assistance. The intention was to 'sponsor' a new constitution and to provide stable conditions across the country to ensure that the first elections, using a version of PR voting, could be seen and accepted as 'Free and Fair' – a term that has today become regular international currency.

The mission was highly successful and finished on time and within budget. I was in Angola for the entire period, apart from a few brief visits to Windhoek, the capital of Namibia, where the HQ of UNTAG was located. While the mission was for the peaceful transition of Namibia to independence, my story is about the activities of what became known as UNTAG (A), a separate but vital mini-mission in Angola.

In Dublin, on 13 February 1989, I was informed that I was to be the senior of a group of officers to travel to Namibia as observers

for the new UN mission. There would be nineteen other officers and when I saw the list, I found that I knew them all, had served with some and, to my delight, they had all experienced UN service.

I was immediately launched into the medical examinations, vaccinations and the other administrative measures in preparation for departure in just about four weeks. Apart from the standard vaccinations, briefings and so on, we were issued with an unusually elaborate set of kit and equipment for the mission. This included the usual lightweight uniforms and sand boots, underwear, UN blue berets, Ireland shoulder patches, black leather military boots, steel helmets, body armour (flak jackets) and respirators (gas masks). For the first time in my UN experience, we were also issued with a comprehensive individual medical kit. This kit included the usual anti-malaria pills, treatments for headaches and bowel problems, a tourniquet, ready-to-use morphine syringes and morphine ampoules, as well as bandages, splints and triangular bandages. On reflecting on the extensive medical kits we were given, it would suggest that the health situation in Namibia was such that we were obviously expected to treat ourselves. It was not a pleasant thought.

Then, in yet another surprise, in early March I was informed of a change of plan. I was not going to Namibia with the others after all, I was now going to Angola as LO to the United Nations Angola Verification Mission, another UN mission already established and functioning there since January. This mission was established in January 1989 to oversee the withdrawal of all Cuban forces from Angola. Angola was a country about which I knew very little, so I had to start all over again, visiting the library and talking to some members of the missionary orders who had been working there for years. In addition, while I had a little French, I could not speak Portuguese.

Just before 15 March I was given new orders, yet again. Now I was to fly to Paris on 17 March to meet the Under Secretary General for Special Affairs, Marrack Goulding and his party, and to travel on to Angola with them. While on the ground at Charles de Gaulle waiting to meet the USGS, I got caught up in a bomb alert. Some unfortunate person had left a plastic bag of personal belongings unattended and the police were not going to take any chances. The explosion sprayed the corridor of Charles de Gaulle departure area with flour! I could only hope that this was not an omen of things to come.

In the departure lounge, I was trying to phone home when I saw the familiar face of Comdt Dermot Early approaching me with a large grin on his face. He introduced me to his companion,

Marrack Goulding, the USGS whose responsibility dealt mainly with peacekeeping matters. Also in the party was a Portuguese official from HQ in New York, Sr Jose Campino.

Mr Goulding spent the available time before take-off briefing me about my task in Angola. He left me in no doubt whatsoever that the success of the mission depended very much on how well I and my team performed. One of the most critical stipulations from the USGS was that under no circumstances was I, or any of our group, to get involved in any dealings or discussions with SWAPO about their political problems in Angola or elsewhere. So I had plenty to distract me from the champagne and the in-flight film on the long flight to Luanda via Cotonou. I forced myself to stay awake so that I could get a morning view of the city as we approached. I saw an attractive modern city with high-rise buildings wrapped around a large inlet and port, where many ships could be seen at the quays or at anchor offshore. It appeared to be a well-laid-out city with heavy traffic.

The reality on the ground was very different. It was very humid and the airport was quite shabby in appearance. I was surprised at the sight of so many Soviet military transport aircraft in evidence and also by the sight of the Angolan State airline, TAAG, (Transportes Aéreos Angolanos). The second surprise was that, despite the left-wing political leanings of the government, while most of the military aircraft were of Soviet design, the principal passenger aircraft of TAAG were Boeing 737s.

As if I had not enough to occupy me, I quickly discovered having gone through Arrivals that my two boxes had not kept up with me. Horror of horrors, this was not the way to make a good first impression. Fortunately, I was wearing a reasonable suit and had taken an overnight case with me in the cabin, containing toiletries, pyjamas and some changes of shirts, underwear and socks. It was enough to keep me going but it meant that each evening I had to do some washing in my hotel room. This was not an easy task as the water and the electricity supplies were frequently cut off without warning.

We were accommodated in the Hotel Presidente, a modern twenty-four-storey building overlooking the busy port. The lagoon was formed by a very large sand-spit, dominated by an old and picturesque Portuguese fort at the southern end. There were many fine high-rise buildings, broad avenues and small parks, but only at close quarters could it be seen that the buildings, the roads and the parks were in an appalling state and seriously in need of repair, painting and proper maintenance.

UNAVEM, the small UN mission established to verify the departure of Cuban forces from Angola, had its HQ in a camp owned by ESPA, a Brazilian mining company, on the southern outskirts of the city. The camp was long established with secure perimeter fencing, tennis courts, a swimming pool and good chalet accommodation for the seventy or so military and civilian staff. The mission was commanded by Brig.-Gen. Pericles Feirreira Gomes of Brazil, who could not have been more helpful and co-operative to me.

The following days in Luanda passed in a blur of meetings between Marrack Goulding and government ministers, personages from other UN agencies and the members of UNAVEM. Marrack Goulding brought me to all these meetings, and while I did not realise it then, my contacts with members of the government, FAPLA and SWAPO were to prove invaluable in Luanda in the months to come. I was even brought to the airport to witness the departure, under the close supervision of UNAVEM Observers, of a planeload of Cuban soldiers.

Over these early days, I was introduced to the Minister for Justice, Senior Van Dunen and Sr Vicenza da Moura, the Deputy Minister for Foreign Affairs, both excellent English speakers. Others contacts were Lt-Gen. Pedale, the Minister for Defence, Colonel Peyama, Chief of State Security, Lt-Gen. Francisco dos

Santos Ndalu Franca, Chief-of-Staff of FAPLA and General 'Gato' de Conceicão, LO to UNAVEM, all of them members of the Angolan Politburo. Lt-Col Paulo Lara, our senior LO, spoke no English, but had excellent French. We had many meetings with him in the following days. I also was introduced to General Rodrigues, OC Cuban Forces in Angola and Jorge Risquez, the Cuban Political Advisor.

From SWAPO, I met Hidipo Hamutenya, the Secretary for Information and Publicity, Nahas Angula, the Education Secretary and Peter Mueshehange, Secretary for Defence. Meeting with those individuals gave me a huge advantage in performing my duties later on. No amount of briefings in Dublin, no amount of reading of UN tracts or UNTAG notes could have given me the vital knowledge and confidence to deal with members of a revolutionary organisation (SWAPO) or a Marxist Government noted for their distrust of outsiders, particularly Westerners.

I was very lucky in one other important area also. Brig.-Gen. Gomes quickly instructed his staff, both military and civilian, to facilitate me in every way. His Chief Administrative Officer, Tom White, who previously had served as an officer in the Canadian Armed Forces, was particularly helpful and we struck up a close friendship. What little free time I had was spent in drawing up an Administrative Order for the establishment of UNTAG (A) at Lubango. I requested and was given a number of sets of maps of Angola and of the region in the south where I would be operating. I was permitted the use of the communications facilities in the offices of UNDP in the city and at UNAVEM in ESPA Camp, through which I could maintain some contact with UNTAG HQ in Windhoek.

On Monday 22 March, myself, Dermot Early and other officials accompanied Marrack Goulding on a one-day flight down to the south in a small aircraft belonging to the Brazilian mining company. Firstly, we visited the small port of Namibe, formerly known as Moçamedes, where an official reception and a fine seafood banquet was provided by the local officials for the USGS. Marrack Goulding told me that the airport was heavily defended by the best of Soviet guns, a radar system and air defence missiles. This visit gave me a good appreciation of the airport, the port town and its environments, a location with which I became very familiar as the mission developed.

From Namibe, we then flew inland to Lubango, getting a wonderful view of the impressive escarpment on the way in to yet another well-equipped and well-defended modern airport. Here we were given a second elaborate reception with many speeches in Portuguese. I was seeing for the first time the place in which I was to spend the next eleven months. While there, I was introduced to Colonel Vietnam, second-in-command of FAPLA in the Lubango area and Theo-Ben Gurirab, SWAPO's Foreign Minister. This man was unusual in that he was not a member of the Ovambo tribe like all the other leaders in SWAPO.

Lubango is a small and very attractive city of about 60,000 people, set about 1,600m above sea level, giving it a very pleasant climate. Many new arrivals from coastal areas such as Luanda found that it took a day or so to become acclimatised to the elevation. The city had a range of low hills to the west and south. The southern ridge ended in a small escarpment on which was placed a statue of O Christo Rei (Christ the King), a replica of the statue overlooking the Tagus at Lisbon. The small square in the centre of the old city was overlooked by some attractive public buildings, built in the Portuguese style. One of these buildings was The Palace, where VIPs were accommodated. The streets were broad and straight, well-surfaced and lined with trees and colourful shrubs.

There were three fine churches, one built in the traditional Portuguese architectural style, the Sé (cathedral), while the others were modern and would not be out of place in Ireland, although they were not as well fitted out or decorated. The city was well served with shops, laundries, garages, barber shops, a bank and a post office. All the services functioned, however badly, although I was told that fresh water was in short supply. The shops were virtually empty of goods and I discovered that most people survived by bartering. The official currency, the kwanza, was almost useless, at 2,500 kwanza to the dollar. Like all other Angolan cities, very large numbers of refugees had moved into Lubango, driven in by the activities of UNITA, and they were living in very poor conditions.

In the days of Portuguese rule, Lubango was a popular holiday centre for large numbers of tourists who drove up from Namibia to see the sights and to gamble in the well-situated casino. The principal sights were at Leba and at Tundevala where it was possible to have magnificent views of the dramatic escarpment, a feature that ran north-south for perhaps fifty kilometres. I was told that Tundevala was also used as a place of execution in the past – prisoners were thrown over at a spot where there was a sheer drop of 1,000 metres.

Lopes di Nascimento had been the first Prime Minister of Angola under President Neto and when the post of PM was abolished by the new President, Eduardo Dos Santos, he was appointed Commissario of Lubango, capital of Huile Province, where he reputedly ran 'a very tight ship'. He was widely accepted as one of the most able senior officials in MPLA. He had three assistants, only one of whom dealt with us – Sr Batista.

I went with Marrack Goulding and party from Luanda to Harare to meet the President of SWAPO, Sam Nujoma, who was attending an Organisation of African Unity meeting there. We flew in the executive Lear Jet of the Angolan President, which was beautifully fitted out. Later the next day, we met Sam Nujoma at his room in the Sheraton Hotel where he made a long political speech, during which he warned me of the likelihood of attacks on UNTAG personnel by UNITA. I also met Malaysian Colonel Shariff, the Chief-of-Staff of UNTAG, who had flown in from Windhoek to attend the meeting.

The following day, Marrack Goulding and Dermot Early returned to Luanda while Colonel Shariff and I flew to Windhoek via Johannesburg to meet the FC of UNTAG. When I was checking in at Jo'burg for my onward flight, I stated that I was a member of UNTAG and that I was travelling to Namibia. The large and rather dour policewoman promptly corrected me: 'You are not, Sir, you are travelling to South West Africa.' Strictly, she was right – SWA had another eleven months of life remaining.

While flying to Windhoek over the fascinating washboard terrain of southern Namibia in a Boeing 737 of SWA Airlines, our pilot announced, 'We are now flying over South West Africa.' Then he laughingly apologised and said, 'I'm sorry, I meant Namibia, I will get into trouble for saying South West Africa.' The confusion was working in both directions.

We were met at the airport in Windhoek by two Malaysian officers and brought to the Safari Hotel for the night. Many of the civilian and military staffs were staying in hotels around the city. In the morning I was collected and Col Shariff brought me to meet the FC, Lt-Gen. Dewan Prem Chand, at Suiderhof Barracks, a former SADF Barracks. On being ushered into his presence, I came to attention and said, 'Sir, I must firstly apologise for appearing in civilian clothes as my boxes went astray on the journey from Dublin to Luanda.' He looked up at me and laughed, 'Will you look at me, Mike, how do you think I am dressed? Can't you see that I too am in civilian clothes. Some of my boxes have not yet arrived from India.'

I immediately felt at ease and we had a good laugh over our predicaments. We had a brief discussion then about the ONUC mission in Katanga nearly thirty years before where, by coincidence, we both had served at roughly the same time. Later on, we both served at different times in Cyprus with UNFICYP.

We then talked at length about my mission in Angola and he told me how important it was and how difficult it was likely to be. He had some experience of the conditions in Angola as he had been there a number of times in 1988 and again in recent weeks. I briefed him on who I had met in Luanda and also my visits to the south. I also said that I was very relieved and impressed with the invaluable support I was getting from the USGS and General Gomes of UNAVEM. He told me that he would be sending some observers up to me as soon as possible, and that Comdt John Ryan was coming up from Keetmanshoop to set up a liaison office in Luanda. He also informed me that my title in Angola was to be CLO UNTAG (A) (Chief Liaison Officer, UNTAG, Angola) and that I would be based in Lubango.

The next two days passed in a blur as I had to check in with all the UN civilian offices. This task was made more difficult as 229 monitors had just arrived from India, Pakistan, Malaysia and elsewhere and were also being processed. The civilian offices were mainly in the Troskie Building in the centre of the city. I was much too busy to have a look around me in Windhoek, but the overall impression was that by comparison with Luanda, it was spotlessly clean, there were no potholes in the roads, the buildings were attractive, the shops were crammed with goods, cafés and restaurants abounded, and all the services worked perfectly. What a contrast to the tragic city I had just left.

Two officers, Major Otto Jakobe from Czechoslovakia and Major Eric Kimani from Kenya, were assigned to me on the second day, some days before John Ryan arrived. I promptly gave them responsibilities: Otto was to be in charge of logistics and Eric was to be operations and personnel officer. I handed them my shopping lists and told them to do whatever they could. This gave them something to worry about until we departed for Luanda.

At least they had the advantage over me as they knew their way around the HQ and the city.

I requested an aircraft to get us back to Angola and a ten-seater Lockheed Jetstar, piloted by South Africans, was hired. We four (John Ryan had arrived) flew to Luanda on 11 March, with Col Shariff, the COO and Jim Baldie, the UNTAG Chief of General Services. We were accommodated with some difficulty in the Presidente and later on that evening, I treated them to a nice meal at a restaurant called ESTA, patronised only by foreigners and senior government officials, where one could only pay in dollars.

As we needed to get to Lubango urgently, I put in a request to the government that we should be allowed to use our hired aircraft to continue our journey to the south, but it was not granted and the aircraft returned to Windhoek the next morning, much to my disappointment. As if to compensate for this, I was informed that my missing boxes had arrived – this indeed was a bit of good news. I was able to arrange for John Ryan to get accommodation with UNAVEM, again courtesy of Gen. Gomes. In a short time, he was set up in an office cleverly made from a shipping container. The use of containers as offices was a common practice in Angola and at UNAVEM. The container was small but well fitted out and it had arrived ready for occupation. It had windows, floor covering, a phone and all the usual office furniture, and more important, it had air conditioning, essential in such a clammy climate.

In pondering the situation I found myself in during those first days in Luanda, I found it very hard to believe that the UNTAG operation in Angola was nothing but a shambles. I had been thrown into a situation where I found myself having to beg, borrow or scrounge from UNAVEM and the other civilian UN agencies already in the country, and later from the various Field Service sections in Namibia. The mission had already started before my monitoring officer group was even in Angola, while the UN administrative support, in the person of the Field Service

Assistant, the man charged with looking after the finances, was the last man to arrive in Lubango. I had no UN civil or legal advisors to assist me, while the UNTAG Representative to Angola, Ambassador Clark, did not arrive until July.

Some years after the mission had ended I found out from Marrack Goulding that this situation had arisen because the Angolan government was wary of foreigners and were most anxious to preserve their independence. They were fighting a prolonged and costly civil war and the last thing they needed was to be saddled with further problems not directly relevant to Angola. They were very wary of the possible complications arising from a mixture of SWAPO and the UN military observers, all of whom were concerned with another country, Namibia. It apparently took a lot of persuading before they altered their stance and permitted a limited number of military observers to be based in their country.

On the more pleasant side of life, John and I were invited to meet the British Ambassador to Angola, James Glase, who was interested in the mission and what we hoped to do there. We were also introduced to his First Secretary, Tim Clifton. Both were very pleasant individuals and I felt that we could have turned to them if we found ourselves in serious difficulty.

We spent much of our time at the ESPA Camp, a few kilometres south of the city, where UNAVEM was based. Gen. Gomes provided us with access to his communications room, our only means of contact with Windhoek. John Ryan had arranged the hire of a car for our use, driven by a young man from São Tome who spoke some French. On my first visit to the office of the High Commissioner, I was pleasantly surprised to see a large framed photograph of Seán MacBride hanging on the wall behind his desk.

It was going to be another eleven days before we could finally travel to Lubango, mainly because of the shocking events about to unfold on the border with Namibia.

01 April 1989 – the commencement date for the UNTAG Mission

Nobody in their wildest dreams could have imagined that the UNTAG mission to Namibia would begin quite like it did. Following a period of more than ten years of debate, all the parties concerned had agreed to every clause of the agreement and there was an assumption that the mission would roll along peacefully from the starting date of 1 April. But nobody appeared to have explained to the PLAN fighters in Southern Angola exactly what was expected of them. Or if it had been explained, it had not been made sufficiently clear. Large numbers of armed and excited PLAN soldiers, isolated for years from their own homeland and families, simply swarmed across the border into Namibia on the assumption that the country was free and independent, and that they would be welcomed with open arms. The soldiers from Namibia, living for so long in the bush in remote areas and knowing very little of the international scene or the nuances of the complicated agreement, simply assumed that they were free to return home when the mission commenced. Many really believed that all they had to do was to cross the border on 1 April, hand over their weapons to the nearest UNTAG soldiers and go off to see their families.

This precipitous action almost wrecked the mission before it started. The date had been selected ten years earlier in Brazzaville at a meeting between the Governments of Angola, Cuba and South Africa. An inappropriate date to select for the implementation of such an important mission, it very nearly turned out to be an April Fool's Day for all concerned. On a practical level, the date had been chosen so that the elections could be held before the wet season commenced.

It would have been understandable if the South African government had walked away from the agreement there and then, as the SWAPO leadership had given them a guarantee that all hostile action would cease before 1 April. Instead, when the soldiers of PLAN crossed the border, fierce fighting immediately broke out between SADF, its militias and PLAN. But after the initial shock and understandable rage had abated, the South Africans honoured their commitments, and so the process righted itself and got under way again.

I have no doubt that the UN, the United States, the other Western powers and probably even the Soviet Union put enormous pressure on the South African government and SWAPO during those tense days. The US, for their own reasons, needed to see the end of Soviet activities in central Africa, taking advantage of the new policy of glasnost as advocated by President Gorbachev. Failure to implement the agreement as planned could have meant that the Cuban withdrawal from Angola, already underway, would cease. Even worse, those forces already withdrawn, some 3,000, could conceivably have been sent back to Angola again.

The problems on the ground were compounded by the fact that some UNTAG forces were not in place on time, a direct result of the severe budgetary problems in New York where some member states had failed to support the UN by paying their 'dues' over the preceding years. In addition, there was a certain unhappiness over some aspects of the plan. The Secretary General could not get the General Assembly to approve the proposed mission until 1 March, just four weeks before the deadline set for implementation of what was a complex agreement. The result was that, while most of the civilian administrative staffs were in place, few of the observers and none of the battalions so vital for control of the border were even in the country by the 1 April, while my monitoring group for Angola had not yet been assembled.

This was not the way to start a new and important mission to oversee the independence of a country. It was a dreadful mess from the word go and caused the avoidable deaths of a significant number of people.

This was the reason for the delay in our getting south to Lubango, the unexpected PLAN 'invasion' of northern Namibia. It was a very embarrassing time to be in Luanda in uniform as the foreign journalists and others were constantly making snide remarks such as: 'What are you doing about the incursion by PLAN and SWAPO?' 'Why are you not down on the border trying to clear up the mess?' I could have replied to such remarks by saying that it was not my duty to round up PLAN, it was the task of the Angolan government, but instead I simply tried to avoid the questions and the reporters as best I could.

Not surprisingly, Marrack Goulding and party made a hurried return to Luanda on 4 April while the DFC, Brigadier-General Daniel Opande, Mr Omayad and Mr Omotoso, senior advisors, arrived later on a flight from Windhoek to brief the USGS on the situation in Namibia. The usual round of meetings resumed with the Minister for Defence, Sr Pedale and later with the Chief-of-Staff, Lieutenant-General Ndalu. Four days later, the Goulding group made a hastily arranged flight to overnight in Lubango, where I met with Comrade Lopes de Nascimento, one of his three assistants, Comrade Batista, and other officials to make arrangements for accommodation for the UNTAG monitors.

Because nobody in Windhoek had anticipated the crisis that had struck the UNTAG mission, the DFC had come to Luanda in his civilian clothes. It appeared to be an affliction that was spreading. First the Force Commander, then myself, now the DFC. John Ryan quickly dived into his kit box and fitted the General out with a set of his green fatigues – they were about the same build – and gave him a spare UN beret. So the DFC, for a number of days, travelled around southern Angola dressed as a private in the Irish Army. There was a lot of joking over this, but he was very good-humoured about it, seeming to enjoy the unusual situation. In Namibia, I was told later on that he was known (behind his back) as Danny O'Pande, the Kenyan Irishman.

Chapter 15

'COMRADE COLONEL'

After what seemed like an eternity, the permission to move to Lubango arrived and on 11 April, we finally left Luanda for Lubango in an Antonov 26 of the Angolan Air Force. After a terrible start to what was proving to be a most difficult mission, we were finally under way, but well behind schedule.

In Lubango we were accommodated in 'O Compleixo PNUD', the UN Development Programme Complex. That evening in my new residence in Lubango, I met the FAPLA senior LO. He arrived at the chalet and introduced himself as Major 'Discipline' – pronounced in the Portuguese manner as 'Dishipleeneh'. He was taller than most Angolans, with powerful, hunched shoulders and a serious expression. He spoke little or no English, although he had a little French. In the main I had to depend on the Spanish-speaking monitor for communications between us. His name was Major Ejeddio de Sousa Santos and he came from northern Angola.

One evening after a long, hot and frustrating day, we ended up in the sitting-room of my chalet. The Major told me that as a small boy he had seen his father killed by Portuguese soldiers who had come to search his village in the north of the country. Some time later, he had been rounded up for service in the army and, as was

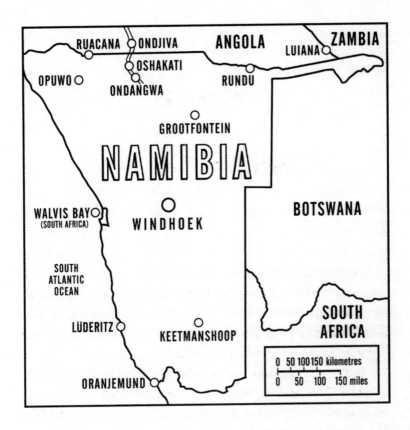

the custom, he was shipped to the opposite end of the country. (Not too long after this discussion, I saw for myself a group of about ten frightened young boys being marched along the street in Lubango roped together and under armed escort.)

One of my earliest concerns in this mission was the level of medical assistance available to us in the area. In Angola the standard of medical care was disturbingly low and I felt glad for the first time that I was in possession of such a well thought-out medical kit. Very quickly though, I discovered that the Medical Missionaries of Mary ran an excellent hospital and a small leprosarium at Tchiulo, some 300kms south of Lubango that catered for about 450 patients. Five of the surgeons and doctors were Irish and they had an excellent staff of Angolans, trained by them, at the adjoining nursing school. My chalet became a regular stopping point for the various members of the Medical Missionary community on their way to or from Tchuilo.

I was delighted to discover that a small medical and social welfare clinic in Lubango was operated at this point by Sister Veronica Tarpey from Mayo and Sister Aileen O'Kane from Dungannon, as well as Sister Brigit Egbuna from Nigeria. At an early stage I also met an Irish Holy Ghost Father, Barney Keane, whose brother, Bill, had been OC of the Air Corps. 'O Padre Bernardo' as he was known to the locals, had served thirty-eight years in Angola with the cattle-herding peoples of the Cunene and Huile provinces.

On 12 April, the first UN Field Service radio operator arrived unexpectedly from Windhoek via Luanda. His name was André, a cheerful and efficient radio operator, whom I had previously met at UNIFIL HQ in Lebanon in 1985. More importantly, he brought with him our first radio. This was indeed great news as up to now direct communication with Windhoek was impossible.

The following day, I saw my first PLAN camp at Chibemba. My duties, and those of my monitors, required us to remain in as close contact as possible with the many well-scattered and concealed camps of PLAN. The large group of visitors to the camp consisted of General Pedale, Sr da Mouro, General Ndalu, Marrack Goulding, Dermot Early, the DFC, myself and a group of SWAPO officials. We travelled in a large Soviet helicopter, complete with rocket pods, to a site in the bush where we saw and spoke to some PLAN fighters. Later that day, we flew south for further meetings with other officials of SWAPO at Cahama, a truly impressive Cuban-built twin-runway military air base.

On 18 April, General Daniel Opande, Jose Campino and I, accompanied by Angolan LOs, flew south in two Angolan Air

Force Dauphin helicopters to the border crossing with Namibia at Ruacana, refuelling on the way at Cahama. We flew at treetop height, as was the custom, to make it more difficult for UNITA, who might consider UN troops to be legitimate targets, to shoot us down using guided missiles or machine guns. We had travelled to meet the first of the two convoys carrying the monitors for UNTAG (A) that was due to cross the border on their journey to Lubango.

To my great relief, eight officers in four Landrovers arrived at the crossing by evening. The UNTAG monitors were carrying three very uneasy captive PLAN fighters with them, one of whom had been wounded in the foot. The captives were nervous of the South African soldiers at the border, who were their former enemies, but no problems arose as they crossed over into Angola.

We put the PLAN fighters in our helicopters and flew northward to the airfield at Cahama where their arrival created a great fuss. There was much filming and interviewing of the prisoners and officials. Marrack Goulding and party, together with President Sam Nujoma and a big following were there to receive them. Early the next morning we returned to Cahama to greet a convoy of approximately 300 PLAN fighters who had been rounded up by FAPLA. The Angolan Army had collected them at the border and was transporting them northward in accordance with their treaty obligations. They arrived into the village in a great flurry of excitement, and many speeches were made in front of a large group of journalists.

Returning with the DFC from Cahama, where we had spent the night, I was delighted to see, as we circled the complex before landing, the small convoy of white painted Landrovers driving into the UN compound, heralding the safe arrival of the monitors. At last our work was about to get underway properly. I gathered them together and spoke to them about our situation. I introduced myself and the two Majors, Kimani and Jakobe, and gave them an outline of our mission in Angola.

The second convoy was very late – there had been no contact with them all day. To my relief, they finally arrived in Lubango well after dark. There were twenty officers in four Landrovers as well as four Polish technicians in two 4x4 trucks. It was quite a struggle to get them fed and bedded down by early morning.

The following day, I paraded them and briefed them on their duties, the need for care in dealing with the local population and the prohibition on photography of public buildings and police and military installations. An unpleasant thought struck me as I looked at my new charges. Apart from John Ryan in Luanda, I was the only officer in the group with previous UN experience and I felt that this might create problems for me. The monitors were drawn from Panama, Peru, Kenya, Bangladesh, India, Pakistan, Poland, Togo, Malaysia and Czechoslovakia. The two civilian UN radiomen (I had two by now), fortunately for me, were seasoned UN operators.

I had not received any direction from Windhoek on the matter of carrying weapons so I took it upon myself to decide that we would be unarmed at all times. From my previous UN experiences, UNTSO in particular, I had seen for myself the value of being unarmed. In any case, a pistol was an inadequate weapon in the circumstances of South Angola, a region that was heavily militarised. I stressed to the group that the UN operated as far as possible in an open and fair-minded manner, and that we were not here to spy on Angola or SWAPO, but simply to ensure that Angola carried out its part of the agreement by rounding up all the PLAN fighters and disarming them.

I divided the group of officers into two monitoring teams and two mobile teams, six officers per team, and appointed team leaders for each. They would operate three-day shifts and would also take turns on the mobile teams, the more popular of the duties. The teams resting at Lubango would provide me with a reserve if required.

Selecting team leaders was a tricky task and I had to make my selections 'on the trot' even as I addressed them. First I had to achieve a racial balance between the different nationalities. I also had to ensure that at least one Spanish speaker was in each team to act as interpreter, as no Portuguese interpreters had been provided. Moreover, Major Ayassou from Togo, and his compatriot, Capt. Bignan, had to be together at all times, as the Major had no English and relied on the Captain's excellent command of the language to communicate with us.

I appointed Major Aslam Abu Mohammed, from Bangladesh, as my second-in-command, Major Razak Tumin from Malaysia as the Operations Officer while confirming Otokar Jakoube as Logistics and Transport Officer and Eric Kimani as the Information Officer. That they worked so well from the start was shown by the fact that I did not need to make any changes in this arrangement until the Mission was nearing its end.

One of my first instructions was that the officers were to go scrounging for a suitable pole within the complex on which to raise the UN flag and to my surprise they came back quickly with a large piece of scaffolding. So I organised a parade and invited Marrack Goulding and party to attend. The UN flag was raised and left flying day and night until the Monitoring Base closed in January the following year. After the ceremony, Marrack Goulding and Dermot Early departed for Namibe by road to fly back to Windhoek. At last we were alone and ready to go.

Later that first evening, Friday 21 April, the DFC, who had remained on for a few days, had requested a meeting with SWAPO and PLAN leaders at Chibemba, so I took four vehicles and eight monitors with me. There I met with the Chief-of-Staff of PLAN, Comrade Ho Chi Minh – Charles Phillips.

I noticed that many of the FAPLA and PLAN leaders were in the habit of taking pseudonyms, either to conceal their identities or perhaps because it made them feel better. I met leaders with names such as Comrade Danger, Vietnam, and so on. They always addressed me as 'Comrade Colonel'. Another surprise for me was the special handshake. I first met with this when out with General Opande in the camps. To shake hands, one firstly did the normal handshake as we know it, followed promptly by each seizing the other's thumb and shaking that, then finishing up by a conventional shake once more. I was embarrassed initially and fumbled regularly until I became accustomed to it.

A couple of pieces of good news arrived on Friday 21 April. Firstly General Ndalu announced that I would be allowed a weekly supply flight from Windhoek to Namibe airport on the coast, west of Lubango. I had to send a small convoy to Namibe each Friday to meet the supply flight from Namibia, for many weeks a C130 aircraft. The 180km, three-hour drive from Lubango west to the coast was spectacular and always fascinating. It involved the negotiation of a dramatic descent of the 1,000m escarpment with its ninety-two hairpin bends at Leba.

Secondly, it was with complete disbelief that I received the good news that our present vehicles would all be replaced as soon as possible by new Toyota Land Cruisers. We were having a lot of trouble with our elderly vehicles, the Polish mechanics were not familiar with them and we did not have spare parts nor could such be found in Lubango. The replacements would arrive two at a time via the Friday supply flights and the Landrovers were to be returned to Windhoek on the same aircraft.

The new vehicles had air-conditioning but unfortunately they also arrived fitted with road tyres. As a result, we had a whole series of punctures, as much of our driving was off-road across very rough ground. This was so bad that for a while we had to ensure that all patrols before departure from Lubango borrowed the spare wheels from the vehicles remaining in base. Eventually off-road tyres were sent to us.

We quickly settled into a routine now that the full group was assembled. The officers, who used ration packs initially, soon resorted to buying their own food at the markets in Lubango before going on duty, while I continued to use the restaurant in the complex for my meals. I had a 'force' of thirty-two officers, four Polish NCOs (all mechanics), two civilian radio operators and one Field Service assistant (effectively the account holder), Sr Gabriel Campos of Chile. He was the last of our group to arrive – on 28 April.

I lived in one of the chalets on base, which I shared with Majors Aslam and Jakoube. Our sitting-room came to be used as my office, doubling as both conference room and a reception room for visitors. It even became a house of prayer on one occasion when Major Aslam received my permission to use the room to celebrate the feast of Eide-Al-Azer with his fellow Muslim officers on 13 July.

Now that we had settled in, other aspects of daily life came into focus. The FC had sent us some sports equipment, of which the most popular were the volleyball nets, posts and balls. This became the principal activity both at the base and on the monitoring posts, and it was only a matter of time before we began to play the Soviets, alternating every two weeks in our compound and theirs. Theirs was a heavily fortified and well-guarded compound around a multi-storey building in central Lubango. I became quite friendly with a surgeon, Lt-Col Ivan Maximenko from Moscow, who had been in Angola for three years. He was thoroughly fed up with his situation and wished only to go home. As it happened, his desire was granted more quickly than he expected after the fall of the Berlin Wall in the November of that year.

In the early weeks in Lubango I made a point of going to mass in uniform. I felt that it would indicate that I had something in common with the inhabitants, who were overwhelmingly Catholic, while establishing my 'credentials' in dealing with the Marxist rulers of the country. It was a strange feeling to be the only white face among some 500 black faces in a crowded church.

From the very beginning, I was keenly aware of the ludicrous nature of our task of 'declaring that all PLAN fighters were under control within Angola and north of the 16th Parallel', in an area greater in extent than that of my own country. It was actually up to the Angolans to do this, not UNTAG, but I was expected to certify this fact to my satisfaction and that of the UN. Not only did I have to be satisfied that all the fighters were corralled, it was also my job to certify that FAPLA had collected all the PLAN weapons and had placed them in secure storage.

I had spent a lot of time worrying about this before I reached Lubango, but once we were in contact with the Angolan LOs and the PLAN leaders, I began to relax. It became clear to me quite quickly that the willingness of all the parties to uphold their own sides of the agreement would enable us to muddle through, but it was a desperately slow and frustrating process.

On 4 April, the South African government complained bitterly that major mechanised infantry and tank units of PLAN were being deployed just inside the border with Namibia and that another invasion of Namibia was being prepared. I responded using all the means available to me and was able to report to Windhoek that there was no foundation whatsoever for the allegation. PLAN simply did not have the capacity.

Some time later, in a follow up to this event, I finally succeeded in getting permission to inspect the PLAN armour. We were taken out to a camp we had never seen or heard of before, Palanka, outside Lubango, where we were shown a miserable collection of old and rusting T34s and BTR 10s (armoured personnel carriers). Major Aslam managed to get inside some of them and he assured me that they were unserviceable, had not been moved for some time and could only be used for defence of the camp.

On 27 April I was summoned urgently to a meeting at the comisariado to hear complaints over a statement attributed to the DFC in Windhoek. The comments had appeared in a Namibian paper, giving rise to allegations that UNTAG had changed their policies and this had made SWAPO very angry. The meeting was chaired by Col Peyama, the Chief of State Security. He was accompanied by Comrade Mweshehange, the Defence Minister of SWAPO and the Cuban Political Advisor, Jorge Risquez. I was handed a copy of the SWAPO statement that was being sent to the press in Luanda even as we were meeting. I immediately asked if it could be held over until UNTAG was given the chance to respond, but was told that it was too late for that.

I began by affirming that I had no intention of departing from the plans and policies under which I had been operating since my arrival. The Cuban advisor then made a long speech and when he had finished, I took the opportunity to state that I had spent a very happy three weeks in Cuba in 1967. I had been the captain of the Irish team participating in the World Spearfishing Championships. I said that we had expected to meet President Castro at the prize-giving ceremony at the end of the competition, but due to problems then being experienced in Bolivia by his close friend, Che Guevara, he did not show up. He and I then began to discuss Cuba, spearfishing and my experiences of his country and as a result, all the tension went out of the meeting. Jorge Risquez even hinted that I might get another chance to meet President Castro, but this time in Angola. I went home, happy to send a long cable to Windhoek about the meeting. The SWAPO press statement was never released and President Castro never came to Angola!

From my earliest days in Lubango, I was pressed by the FC to arrange for a formal counting of the PLAN fighters and for a list of their weapons. I used every opportunity to make these demands of Peter

Mweshehange, the PLAN Defence Minister, and anyone else who might have influence on the matter, but all I ever got were promises. Completely by accident, I found out in late April that there was to be a meeting of the JMMC shortly at the Angolan/Cuban air base in Cahama. I decided that my opportunity was at hand.

I wrote a letter directly to President Sam Nujoma of SWAPO in which I said that this meeting in Cahama was a great opportunity for him to demonstrate to the world that he would abide by his undertakings and to allow a formal count of his fighters by UNTAG. There was a prolonged and ominous silence and I began to worry that I might have committed some sort of diplomatic gaffe. It was not the correct channel for me to have taken of course, but time was short. However, just when I was beginning to give up, the news came through that there would be a parade on Saturday 13 May. Brig.-Gen. Opande was detailed to come up from Windhoek for the occasion. I prepared a double monitor team to accompany myself and the DFC to Chibemba, from where the count would begin.

We left Lubango very early and arrived at the monitoring post at 07.20hrs. There we had to wait and wait without explanation until about 13.00hrs. I had learned by now that the only way of doing things in Angola was the Angolan way. Finally, we were invited to move to the first of the five parades we were to see on that day. About 500 men and women armed and in uniform, were drawn up on three sides of a square with a smaller group of the leaders to one side. The fighters were all armed and well dressed in camouflage uniforms and they displayed their heavier weapons, HMGs, 82mm mortars, RPGs, etc., on the ground behind them. Over the course of a long and tiring day, we were brought to four other camps to count the assembled fighters.

The PLAN fighters in all cases were in good humour, sensing perhaps that their time in exile was coming to an end at last. They were singing and dancing to music, still in line, stamping their feet and raising huge clouds of dust. I had arranged that four groups of two officers each would walk along the front and the rear of each company of fighters, counting as they walked. After each parade I called the monitors together and we combined our figures and agreed on a total. In all, we reached a count of just over 5,000 fighters.

Afterwards, I was given to understand that the reason for the long delay that morning before the counting could begin was that the SWAPO leaders were waiting for a large party of journalists to arrive from Luanda. It seems that the press group flew into Lubango airport and were then ordered to transfer to another smaller aircraft to take them south to Xangongo, the nearest small airstrip to the parades. But instead of taking them on to the south, the second aircraft took off and flew them straight back to Luanda. This may have been the result of some disagreement between the government and SWAPO, apparently not an infrequent occurrence.

Saturday 13 May was the most important day of our entire period in Angola, although there was plenty more to do as the job was far from finished. But it raised the morale of our little group and there was a noticeable increase in co-operation and even friendship from FAPLA and PLAN afterwards. I never received an acknowledgement of my letter from Sam Nujoma though, but it did not matter, it seemed to have done the trick. We were walking on air for a while but, as always in Angola, we were quickly brought down to earth with a bump.

On 18 May, two West German journalists were arrested on the border at Ruacana Falls and taken to Lubango for detention and interrogation. The LOs Discipline and Luxase came to the chalet after midnight and woke me up looking for advice. They were under the impression that the two were South African spies. I emphasised to the LOs the importance of not doing anything rash, the agreement was much too important, and that the two

Germans should be properly treated. The two prisoners were moved to Luanda on 22 May on a TAAG flight, and I understand were sent back to Namibia later. About a month earlier, I had had a similar situation when an Australian journalist, Jill Jolliffe, who had written occasionally for *The Irish Times* on our activities, arrived from Luanda and was promptly arrested and detained in a hotel room. Apparently, she did not get prior permission to travel to Lubango. She had been in Lubango on more than one occasion before but had suffered no problems. Still under arrest, she was put on board a flight to Luanda, under orders not to return.

A few of days after this incident I was visited by Herman Toiva ya Toiva, Secretary-General of SWAPO, who wandered into my chalet without warning and without any staff, as both FAPLA and SWAPO officials were inclined to do. He told me that I would be asked to verify the release of a number of Namibians the following morning who had been prisoners of SWAPO. The following morning, Wednesday 24 May, in the company of a mobile team, I travelled out of Lubango on the Huambo road to a spot in the bush where none of us had been before. There we found a large group of men standing together to one side in a clearing, guarded by armed PLAN fighters. Herman Toiva ya Toiva told me that these men had been prisoners of SWAPO and were being released today under the terms of the agreement.

The men looked very uneasy and when I talked to some of them they told me that they were afraid of being killed by their captors as soon as I left. I did my best to console them, saying that SWAPO would not dare do such a thing, they had too much to lose. This situation was well outside my jurisdiction but I went over to where Toiva ya Toiva was standing with a stony expression on his face. I asked him to assure me once more that they would not be harmed, which he did. Then I said that we must take the names of all the men and he did not object. So we listed the names of 109 men – this took quite a while as it was important to get the correct spellings.

When the list of names was recorded, Toiva ya Toiva told me that I would have to go to another camp to witness the release of another group of prisoners. Before we left, the former prisoners made quite a fuss, demanding that I take them away with me. They really believed that they were going to be killed as soon as we left. One of them even dropped to his knees and threw his arms around my legs pleading to be taken away with us. I was quite taken aback and found it very difficult to turn my back and to walk away from those frightened men. As it transpired, SWAPO abided by their undertakings to release the prisoners.

We drove to another location not too far away and this time we witnessed the release of ninety-six women and several children, making a list of their names also. However, the tension there was much less than in the other location. The women appeared to have served longer spells of detention though and one woman said that she had been in custody for eleven years. That evening I sent full details of these events to Windhoek.

On 1 June, John Ryan came down for a week, just in time for the Kenyan National Day party. I discovered the significance of the date by accident at the morning parade and ordained that in future we were going to celebrate this and every national day from now on. The parties were very basic, consisting always of a barbecue and a sing-song after dark within the compound. Later, a new radioman, Chaluay Ungkuldgee from Thailand, arrived and introduced us to the pop song, 'Don't worry, be happy' – it seemed very appropriate to our circumstances and promptly became the 'anthem' of UNTAG (A).

On 12 June, Lt-Gen. Prem Chand, the FC, arrived for an overnight visit to Lubango and to see off from the airport the first of the repatriation flights from Angola to Namibia. There were two passenger flights and one cargo flight and the Namibians left amid scenes of great jubilation. The FC dined with us at the complex that night before retiring to The Palace where he was accommodated.

Later on that month, I was summoned to an urgent meeting at The Palace where I met Colonel Peyama, Head of State Security, Colonel Vietnam, the local military commander and Colonel Cafuchi, the State's Chief Legal Officer. As always, I brought two Spanish-speakers with me but to my surprise, they had no complaints, in fact they said that they wanted to say that their Government was very happy with UNTAG and appreciated what we were doing. I saw my opportunity and was able to get agreement for all my requests, such as a new headcount of PLAN fighters, a new monitoring post location as well as an agreement to the proposal of holding joint patrols to the border to investigate complaints from SADF. I reported all this to Windhoek that evening with great satisfaction.

At this time in June, the Cuban withdrawal to the north was in progress, and we were entertained almost on a nightly basis to the sight of large convoys of vehicles passing through Lubango. The Cuban soldiers seemed to be very happy and waved to all on the road. I had the opportunity of talking to some of them, many of whom were clearly of African origin, and was interested to hear that they had volunteered to serve in Angola as they had wanted to do something to help the land of their ancestors.

In July I was ordered to attend the next meeting of the JMMC, to be held in Luanda. The meeting, held over two days at the Presidente Hotel, included Mr Martii Ahtisaari, the FC and others from HQ in Windhoek. The meeting was disappointing from my point of view, but it was interesting to watch the different interests being pushed and to meet some of the personalities involved. What I found amusing was the number of individuals who said to me, 'So you are the Colonel Moriarty we've been hearing about?' At the end of the meeting, many of them wished me good luck, including the Russian Ambassador Ustinov and the SADF General Van Standen. The next JMMC meeting was scheduled to take place in Cuba in September, but unfortunately I was not invited to that one!

In Luanda that weekend I met Blessing Akporode Clark, a former Nigerian ambassador. He had arrived to take up the recently established post of UNTAG Political Representative to Angola. From my point of view his arrival was far too late, as many of the problems had already been solved. I briefed him on the operation in Lubango and invited him down to visit us as soon as he could arrange it. He proved to be a thorough gentleman, and although he was retired from the Nigerian diplomatic service, we addressed him as 'Ambassador'.

Some time after I returned to Lubango an incident relating to preparations for a send-off party for one of the radio operators created great hilarity. A young pig had been purchased by the organisers and was being kept and fed in a large plastic box at the rear of the accommodation block until the day before the party, when it would be killed and prepared. As I was shaving one morning I heard a great commotion within the complex. When I went to the back door I saw a group of officers shouting and whooping as they rushed around and behind the cafeteria building and the containers.

It appeared that the young pig had escaped from custody. The subsequent chase by under-exercised officers failed to catch him as he raced across the compound and around the buildings. He finally fled across the main road through heavy traffic and disappeared into a housing estate. It fell to the young Angolan sentry at the entrance to chase the escapee and he quickly returned, grinning from ear to ear with the pig securely held under his arm. He was well rewarded for his efforts by the panting and relieved officers.

Things were easing up a little in Lubango by this time so, with John Ryan, I was able to go down to Windhoek on 31

July for some business in HQ. While there, John Ryan and I received our UNTAG medals from the FC. After this I travelled to Keetmanshoop in the south to spend two days with the other Irish officers. It was a great treat to travel on the roads of Namibia – no potholes, the signs and the road markings were present and correct, and the roads were arrow-straight for up to 20kms at a time. During the four-hour journey south, we passed a very prominent mountain on our right: an extinct volcano called Brukkaros. The Nama peoples of southern Namibia, the original inhabitants of the region, firmly believe that the first man and woman on earth landed on this mountain from the stars. In view of the present-day opinions of anthropologists about the African origins of *homo erectus*, this belief of the Nama people has a curious ring to it.

The return flight to Angola a few days later became very complicated. Firstly, I flew from Eros (in Windhoek) to Grootfontein (northern Namibia) in a Beechcraft KingAir, a rented aircraft crewed by South Africans, to collect new officers for UNTAG (A), as well as a lot of essential stores. It soon became clear there was not room for all. I asked the captain if it was possible to bring us to Namibe and then return to Grootfontein to collect the remaining officers for a second trip. He said he had the fuel, so I told him to arrange the additional flight with traffic control at both airports. The aircraft returned for the remaining officers and brought them to Namibe without any difficulty.

The repatriation of refugees back to Namibia from Angola that had started in June was now in full flow, and by August, we noticed that the occupants of the PLAN camps were being fitted out with civilian clothes – a new development. This meant that most, if not all, of the civilians had returned to Namibia and now it was the turn of the soldiers of PLAN. The camps quickly became littered with cast-off clothing as the Namibians were simply dumping their uniforms where they changed.

By now too, the vast bulk of the weapons had been collected by FAPLA and stored in containers under the watch of our one remaining monitoring post at Mtundu, north-east of Lubango.

The flights carrying returnee Namibians from Lubango were frequent, but previously all flights had been under the auspices of UNHCR. Now it was the turn of UNTAG. I was present when the first UNTAG aircraft arrived in Lubango on 29 November. The C130 took a huge amount of luggage and 115 personnel and their few belongings. The next day three smaller Spanish aircraft arrived. The twin-engined planes swept in low over the airport and landed, one behind the other, so close together that the first was still taxiing on the main runway as the third was touching down. They 'sashayed' up to the terminal building in close formation, in a fine show of Spanish bravura, and came to a halt on the parking ramp, still in formation. It was a heart-warming sight for the Namibians and an inspiring one for us UNTAG monitors too.

It had been intended that these aircraft would return each day until all available Namibians were brought to Grootfontein. But SWAPO officials failed to abide by their own plans and did not produce the promised numbers, so I cancelled all subsequent flights. It emerged later that SWAPO had decided to resume road convoys to ensure the safe return of the considerable quantities of property still in Angola, but they had neglected to tell me. There was some protest from Windhoek at this, but I had no option but to stand by my decision – the alternative would have been an expensive waste of aircraft.

When the last aircraft was being loaded, I was standing beside a PLAN official, a small, smiling, officious leader who had been very busy all day in checking his lists and helping everybody to get on board the aircraft. Suddenly, to his horror, he found that he was the only one left on the tarmac – he had been too busy to notice. The aircraft was full and the Spanish sergeant in charge of loading was closing the tail doors when he saw this man standing there with a look of utter panic on his face. The sergeant told everybody to push towards the front and Haufiko scrambled in over the lower half of the door. He found his footing and turned to look back at me with a triumphant look on his face. I wished him luck and waved as the doors were closed.

That incident has remained vividly in my mind. I imagined the emotions of this man as he finally set out for home, having sent so many others before him that he nearly missed out himself. It was for me and for the countless officials in UNTAG full justification for so much hard work and belief in the rightness of what had to be done. I felt grateful for the opportunity, and very proud to have been able to make my own small contribution to the success of UNTAG.

After this last flight from Lubango, the repatriations continued by road and our little group, which was shrinking as monitors were withdrawn and not replaced, spent long hours travelling to and from the border, escorting large convoys of civilian trucks and cars, without any greater problems than punctures or the unexpected births of babies beside the road.

As the number of refugees returning from Angola and other countries began to mount up, the increasingly bitter political preparations for an election got under way in Namibia. Despite the release of the prisoners witnessed by us in Angola, the other parties accused SWAPO of not telling the complete truth. In particular, it was alleged that SWAPO still had many detainees in prison camps in Angola and Zambia. A list of 1,100 names of missing persons was handed in to the office of Mr Ahtisaari in Windhoek with a demand that it be investigated. A huge debate raged in Namibia and was a possible threat to the election, so the SRSG decided to establish a commission to investigate the allegations.

The highly respected Nigerian, Ambassador Blessing Clark, was nominated as head of the commission with a team of eight members of UNTAG. It included two advisers from the office of the SRSG, Edward Omotoso and Joachim Bilger, Andrew Grotrian, a jurist from the UK, Comdt John Ryan from Luanda and two policemen, Chief Inspector John Thurston from New Zealand and Inspector P.J. McGowan from Ireland.

The commission arrived into Lubango on Saturday 2 September and when greeting them at the airport, I was informed to my surprise that I had also been appointed to it. Thus began a very interesting task lasting twenty-seven days that took us all over Angola and Zambia and back to Windhoek.

I provided the transport for the commission and arranged for the Angolan and SWAPO LOs who brought us over the month to all the camps already known to us, as well as to some new ones we had not seen before. We were shown the remains of buildings that could have been used as prisons and we saw some pits that would certainly have been used to confine prisoners. But in all cases they were empty and the buildings were roofless and clearly had not been used for some time.

The commission started off in the Lubango area, where it stayed for six days, after which we moved to Luanda. It was the same story there. We saw one camp at Viana outside Luanda in which was stored a large collection of shipping containers containing the personal possessions of SWAPO and PLAN personnel.

On 14 September, we took a four-and-a-half hour flight from Luanda to Lusaka, Zambia, in a small, hot, very full plane with an unserviceable toilet. The dash to the nearest toilet on landing was less than decorous! In Zambia, our group was given full co-operation for our seven-day visit. We visited many SWAPO camps, initially around Lusaka, and later we travelled by air to Ndola, Kitwe and Broken Hill (now Kabwe), places I had visited in 1961. One of the camps, Nyonga, contained many women and children, said to be families of those PLAN and SWAPO members who had died for the cause.

By coincidence, when travelling near Lusaka on 18 September, we came across the memorial to Dag Hammarskjold who died in a UN plane crash on the night of 17–18 September 1961. He had been involved in negotiations to end the fighting in Katanga. We signed the visitor's book and took photographs. On 21 September, before leaving for Windhoek at the end of our work, we were invited to a reception at the presidential palace. There President Kenneth Kaunda insisted on pouring tea for us all, despite having injured his left hand playing golf.

From Zambia, we returned to Windhoek to prepare our final report. We were able to reduce the list of 1,100 names of the missing to a little over 200, principally because of duplication or incorrect spelling of names in the original preparation of the list. The report helped greatly in reducing the turmoil and tension before the elections, which went ahead on 1 November without major controversy.

Back in Lubango, after living the high life as a member of the Clark Commission, it was business as usual, although our numbers had fallen and the activities were reduced considerably. I availed of the opportunity to take three weeks home leave from 4 October. My departure from Luanda was a little stressful because three days before, the flight to Paris had been blown up in mid-air.

Shortly after my return from Ireland, Gen. Gomes and most of his UNAVEM group arrived in Lubango to spend some days with us to verify that the Cubans had left their many locations to the south of our location. We provided them with vehicles, guides, radios, accommodation and entertainment, greatly enjoying their company. It was an ideal opportunity to repay Gen. Gomes and his staff for the kind assistance they gave to me when I found myself stranded in Luanda earlier in the mission.

For very many weeks we had been reporting to Windhoek on the collection by the Angolans of PLAN weapons, which they were storing in shipping containers beside our monitoring post at Mtundu, about thirty minutes to the north of Lubango. The DFC had come up from Windhoek to be present for the final PLAN parade, along with Ambassador Clark and Col John Crocker, an Australian engineer officer. A total of 291 unarmed smiling individuals paraded at Mtundu on Friday 24 November 1989, all dressed in civilian clothing. They entertained us to some very happy singing.

Later that evening, Lieut Pedro Barboso, a young Angolan ordnance officer, produced a list for me in which he certified that all the PLAN weapons were now under Angolan control, a list that I promptly sent on to the FC. However, it took another few weeks before the containers were actually recovered and brought into FAPLA storage in Lubango. Yet another very crucial hurdle had been cleared in the long road to peace. Events were now moving very rapidly and all our efforts were devoted to getting the remaining ex-PLAN fighters repatriated to Namibia.

Shortly afterwards, I was ordered to attend a meeting at Ondangwa in northern Namibia about the reduction of numbers and the repatriation of officers. I went down by road with one of our repatriation escorts. We crossed over into Namibia at Oshikango and changed our watches to Namibian time, finding ourselves among cheering locals. However, they were not cheering for us, but for the results of the election on 1 November, just announced. SWAPO won forty-one seats while the opposition, DTA, managed twenty-one seats.

Shortly afterwards, we began to plan for our medal parade, which was to be held on 19 December at the complex. The recipients were those officers and NCOs who had not already received their medals in Namibia. The ceremony was attended by the Chief-of-Staff of FAPLA, Gen. Francisco Ndalu, and the Commander of Cuban Forces, Gen. Polo Cintra, as well as many Irish and Angolan friends from Lubango.

Having survived the festive season, it was time to do the

inevitable, as ordained by the FC. On Sunday 31 December, I brought practically all available officers and NCOs out to dismantle the last remaining monitoring post at Mtundu, where we held a little ceremony before getting to work. We were back in Lubango by 11.00hrs and I invited all into my chalet to celebrate our going out of business in Angola. It had been a long hard slog of forty weeks of sometimes intense frustration, fortunately crowned with success.

I received instructions from the FC to prepare for closure of the base at Lubango and then to move to Luanda to remain there for an unspecified period. I had been expecting this for some time and swiftly put into place the winding up of our operations, under the title 'Operation Obrigado' – 'thank you' in Portuguese. The tents, the radio room and the antennae had to be dismantled and prepared for loading for the last convoy down into Namibia, while other items had to be sent back to UNAVEM in Luanda. By now our numbers were very small and Maj. Darshi Chowdhary, an excellent Indian officer, had become my second-in-command. On 3 January I finished the final Weekly Report – No. 37 – and gave it to Maj. Chowdhary, instructing him to deliver it to the FC in Windhoek. He was to make any alterations that he considered necessary on his arrival in Namibia. He was now officer commanding the monitoring base for the remaining days and for the withdrawal from Angola. I departed for Luanda by a TAAG flight on Friday 5 January.

In Luanda, I checked in with Gen. Gomes and his operations officer, Col Arvid Geirulf. I was accommodated in the chalet of the CAO, Tom White. We closed down the office of Ambassador Clark (he had left earlier) and brought all the files to the UNTAG office in ESPA. I was now into serious recreation time, being able to relax for the first time since I arrived in the country. With tennis and a swimming pool, I was not lost for exercise.

When John Ryan returned from home leave he brought

a package containing peacekeeper medals for both of us. We organised a small party to be held in John Ryan's house and invited a number of friends. After a suitable warming up period, and to applause from the group, John solemnly pinned on my medal, after which I did the same for him. I believe that I may have been the first Irish colonel to be presented with his UN service medal by an Irish commandant!

On the evening of 17 January, I delivered a lecture on our UNTAG activities to a group of about twenty diplomats in the home of the Swedish First Secretary. A few days later, John Ryan and I went to the airport for departure to Windhoek, via Harare and Johannesburg.

In the best traditions of the mission and of Angola, I found myself in trouble when my passport was being checked at the airport. The official said I could not depart as my passport did not carry an admission stamp to show that I had entered Angola. I could not depart because I had not arrived! No amount of gesticulation, no amount of my (basic) Portuguese, had any effect on him. I was simply an illegal immigrant. Fortunately, the High Commissioner for Namibia, Sr Chola Omariega, arrived to say goodbye to us. He took the official to one side and cleared up the problem just in time for us to catch the TAP (Air Portugal) flight to Harare.

In the days leading up to the ceremony for Independence Day in Windhoek, I was invited, along with many others, to a cocktail reception hosted by the FC at his residence. During the evening somebody caught my elbow and said, 'Come over here, I want you to meet someone.' The someone was a SADF general. So I put on my best smile and shook his hand warmly. I was completely unprepared and utterly taken aback when his very first words were, 'So you are the one that was sending us all those lies for the past twelve months.' I was shocked – I had expected anything but this attack and I just could not think of a suitable reply. Now I am renowned at home for my inability to tell a joke properly, generally giving the punch line too early in the story. So I looked hard at him to see if he might be having the same problem. However, there was no evidence of this. So the best I could manage was to glare back at him, turn my back and walk away without saying a word. We never met again. I have no doubt that he probably wrote me off as a thick Irishman while I certainly felt that he was everything I had been warned about in relation to dense and stubborn South Africans.

To this day I regret my actions as I truly and desperately wanted to discuss and possibly clear up for him some of the many misconceptions that arose between us. However, to be fair, the mission was over, we both would be going back to our own countries, probably to retirement, so there was no great imperative to make amends. In compensation for that incident, I later met Gen. Timothy Dibuama of UNNY who congratulated me on my efforts in Angola.

Independence Day was 21 March 1990 and many VIPs came for the big day, including the Irish Foreign Minister, Gerry Collins, who arrived in an aircraft of the Air Corps. I saw many of the world's leaders passing through the airport, but was particularly pleased to meet once more the Angolan Chief-of-Staff Francesco Ndalu. I did not attend the Independence Ceremony, preferring to watch it on TV, as in a curious way I felt quite detached from the event, having spent all my time and energies elsewhere.

An unexpected aspect of what was to be my last mission with the United Nations was that I learned to appreciate the beautiful country that is Angola and the many friends that I made there. It is careless of politicians and journalists in Ireland to perpetuate the idea that this very attractive country is dangerous for outsiders, since despite its international reputation, for one entire year, neither I nor any of my colleagues ever felt threatened there.

On 24 March 1990, along with the remaining Irish officers, we departed Windhoek for Harare and onward passage to Dublin via Frankfurt.

EPILOGUE

Coming back to Ireland after the challenges and the pressures of my time in Angola was not easy. Having been on a knife-edge for nearly twelve months in a strange country, listening to so many strange languages and having to meet so many deadlines, I found it very difficult to settle down to my new appointment. Life at home did not create quite the same feeling of doing an important job under the pressure of deadlines and unexpected emergencies.

I did not get back to my former job as Director of Artillery. I found myself in Collins Barracks as the second-in-command and Executive Officer Eastern Command, working first for Brig.-Gen. Pat Monahan and then for Brig.-Gen. J.J. Flynn, DSM. It was a pleasant job and I met many interesting foreign military and civilian dignitaries on their visits to Ireland. I also had to take over and stand in for the General when he was on leave or not available. It was not too demanding, I was out of the limelight, so I was able to spend my time practising my languages.

I also managed to achieve some of my long-held wishes. In one I flew with the maritime squadron on a patrol along the east and south coasts of Ireland, a fascinating experience that lasted some four hours. On another occasion I flew in a Fouga of the Light Strike Squadron and enjoyed it immensely, even surviving the best aerobatics of the pilot. In November 1991, I drove down to Haulbowline, County Cork, and joined the crew of the LÉ *Aisling* for a four-day patrol along the south and east coasts. The professionalism that I witnessed in both the members of the Navy and the Air Corps, for whom all missions are operational ones, was very impressive. My respect and admiration for both arms of the Defence Forces – always very high – was reinforced by these experiences.

I retired on 23 January 1992 and while I would have liked, like any other soldier, to have had another promotion, I still felt a great sense of relief when it was over. I could now concentrate on my hobbies and interests. I was the president of the Ireland Portugal Society, which I ran for nearly fifteen years, I became more active with the Curragh Sub Aqua Club, the club I had founded in 1958, and I then turned my attention to travel and to writing. I visited Portugal frequently and managed to fulfil one of my long-held dreams – to live in the south of France for a prolonged period.

When yet another re-organisation of the Defence Forces was announced in 2005, a stand-down parade of the 7th Regiment was held in McKee Barracks on 18 September to mark the occasion. I attended and was cornered by some of the officers, typically Alan Maybury and Pete Murray, to lead the group of former members of the regiment in the march-past at the end of the ceremony. I resisted this suggestion strongly as I was now a civilian and felt that I had no business taking part in a military parade. However, they put a lot of pressure on me and I eventually gave in. The salute was taken by Col Paul Pakenham, the Director of Artillery. While initially I had been very reluctant to take part, I am immensely glad today that I did, hugely proud that I marched for the last time in the company of so many long-time friends and fellow gunners.

POSTSCRIPT

The military life is a strange one, where training is deliberately designed to ensure that when ordered to do so, a soldier will, however reluctantly, put his comfort or even his life in jeopardy. It is not the natural instinct of any human being to do this – nature has endowed us all with the instinct to run away or at least to attempt to avoid danger. What could ensure that hundreds of thousands of rational young men would obey their orders to climb over the parapet and advance into no man's land in the absolute certainty that a great number of them would die in the next few minutes? Is it a madness that only affects excitable young men once they put on a uniform and get a minimum of military training? Is it a weakness or failing in the human makeup that conflict can be appealing or glamorous and even worth dying for. Could it just be perhaps that a young person is so afraid of showing cowardice in front of his fellows that he would prefer to risk his life? Why would the New York firemen have continued to run upstairs when everybody else in the buildings was running downstairs? Was it stupidity? It was not, it was the personal realisation that each individual had prepared for this for a long time, had volunteered for such events, that people expect this of him and he felt that he would let himself or his comrades down if he did not do his duty.

Even today, in peacetime Ireland, in organisations such as the Red Cross, the Civil Defence, the Coastguard or the RNLI, individuals are prepared to place themselves in situations where their lives or limbs would be at risk. They will do what they have been trained for and will cheerfully put themselves at risk for something as simple as the satisfaction of a job well done or the thanks of those they have helped.

To obey an order that will put one's own or many other lives at risk is an aspect of military life that is seriously misunderstood or even mocked by those who have never experienced any form of military-style service. If young men and women believe in what they are asked to do and if they believe that it is a good and just cause, they will, however reluctantly, be prepared to pay for that belief with their lives. There would never be armies, police, firemen or lifeguards if members of these organisations were not prepared to place themselves in jeopardy. Civilians who cannot or who do not want to understand this approach should be glad that there are those who are prepared to make the ultimate sacrifice on their behalf.

Certainly, this trait of unquestioning obedience has also led in the past to unethical or disgraceful acts by soldiers who obey blindly without assessing their own actions or questioning the motives of their seniors. Obedience within the military life should and must be as a result of a belief in the ethical correctness of the mission and must be conducted at all times with due regard to the human element and the sanctity of human life.

Armies can attract brutal men for whom authority is an aphrodisiac. They get their rewards from their own certitudes, they are right and all others are weak, wrong or disloyal. They love rank, pomp, uniforms, power and ceremony. The armed forces of any country in the world will tend to be magnets for these undesirables. They should be spotted at an early stage and weeded out before they can do damage.

Society may well have been better off without armies or great masses willing to obey leaders with exaggerated ideas about their own greatness. But how would we manage without those who protect us, who enable our modern societies to function as we wish them to? Would you, a rational individual living a comfortable life, be willing to get up, walk outside your home and put your life in danger just because somebody said it was the thing to do? Would you willingly go into the streets at closing time in order to restrain those who are committing unlawful or anti-social acts? Would you go into a pub to sort out a fistfight? You would not. Yet the reality is that there have been many examples of just such apparently irrational acts.

If a secretive and ruthless group of misguided citizens are intent on taking over the State by all means, including force of arms, who is going to prevent them? The average citizen might be willing, but he is neither trained nor equipped to do so. He could ask for assistance from another State or from the United Nations, but this is unlikely to be the first course of action and the damage would already have been done. This State has been threatened by such a possibility more than once in its short history. The existence and the willingness of the armed forces of the State and An Garda Síochána, inadequately equipped as they were, provided that final insurmountable obstacle to those who would have taken over our State for their own misguided purposes.

War is an unpleasant business and the professional volunteer soldier understands this better than anybody else. He would prefer peace at any time. Only psychopaths or the 'deeply offended' politicians demand action to avenge an imagined or a contrived insult.

We will always need soldiers, sailors, airmen, policemen, firemen and rescue volunteers who will, in a well-ordered society at least, maintain the stability and the peace of the community. We will always have need of the security services to guard our comforts and to do the nastier work on our behalf. It is only the unthinking few, who, dreaming of Utopia, would wish to do away with those essential pillars of a free and democratic society.

Looking back over my career, I firmly believe that the isolation and inward-looking society that was Ireland began to change with the dispatch of the first soldiers to the Congo in 1960. The entire population was galvanised by the decision of the government of the day to dispatch not just one but two battalions of some 700 soldiers each to join the international community in a peacekeeping mission to assist a suffering people. The motives were pure, the justification unquestioned and the parades of those first battalions down O'Connell Street were received by a huge and enthusiastic population who clearly approved of the decision of the government. It was a decision that brought our little country onto the international stage in a manner that just could not have been predicted.

In my opinion, the dreary years of the Emergency were firmly left behind and the emotions of the Irish people, many of whom might have had mixed feelings about our stance of neutrality during the Second World War, were now being exorcised in a most unexpected way. It could be argued that Ireland began the long road from the isolation of the Emergency years into the society of the western world that led in turn to the present state of our nation. This journey brought the Irish people unimagined prosperity where our country reached the present valued and respected position on the European and world stages.

The level of support and enthusiasm for the concept and practical commitment to UN peacekeeping in 1960 united the country and brought on a national sense of euphoria that had not previously been experienced. It has to be said that our soldiers left Ireland to take part in a peace-keeping mission with the full approval of the population. It should also be remembered that in 1961 this noble mission, for reasons that are still being argued about to this day, unexpectedly changed to a peace-enforcing mission midway through the tour of the 35th Battalion. This alteration from a peace-keeping to a peace-enforcing role, with all the implications of that move, was made without any reference to the Dáil or to the Irish people. No voices were raised, no alarm bells were sounded. Fortunately it all worked out for the best and so far that change of direction has not been repeated. It should remain, however, as a warning to us all of the deceptive simplicity of some UN peacekeeping missions.

It is worth asking, if Ireland had been a member of the UN when the Korean War broke out in 1950 (Ireland became a member in 1955), what would have been the reaction of the government and the people if we had been asked to contribute troops to what was, on the face of it, a UN-endorsed war? Would the same sense of approval, enthusiasm and support have been evident across the country? The Korean War was not a well-intentioned attempt to bring peace and stability to a hard-pressed people, it was a modern war fought under the aegis of the UN but directed by the US as part of the Cold War process. I am not questioning the rights or wrongs of the war, I am merely posing the question: 'Would the Irish people have been so enthusiastic if asked to send troops to a real live shooting war in Korea in 1950?' If the government had agreed, we probably would have supplied a small token force, and most assuredly our soldiers would have been willing to go.

The lessons to be derived from the truly awful disaster that was the UN Assistance Mission for Rwanda from July 1993 to September 1994 should remain as a warning to us all. The possibility of becoming involved in 'Desert Shield', yet another UN sponsored – and US-led – battle to dislodge the Iraqi Army from Kuwait seems not to have been raised with our government at the time. The possibility of such a question arising, however, could easily be asked of us in some future situation. We all should be prepared and ready with our responses.

Sinn é mo scéal anois, táim críocnaithe. Tá súil agam go bhain tú suim as. Táim fíor-buíoch go raibh an neart agus an leighis agam ar fúd na bliana chun na h-eactraí seo a chuir ós bhur gcóir. Tá sé soléir in aigne agus im chroidhe agam freisin an slua mór de na cháirde mhileata a raibh agam, eadair gineráil agus gunadóir – go raibh míle maith agaibh go léir. Táim fíor bródúileach as uacht an tAirm Nua, an tSerbhís Cabhlaigh Nua agus muintear an tAer Cór freisin a bhí ar pharáid i mBaile Átha Cliath sa bhlian 2006. Cómhgárdacais agus go n-eirí an bothar libh go léir. Gan dabht, ba chóir go mbheadh muintear na hÉireann lán sásta bródúileach leo freisin.

APPENDIX A

No. 1 Platoon – A Company, 34th Battalion, 1961

Platoon Comdt:
Lieut M. Moriarty

NCOs:
Sgt J. Flanagan (replaced by Sgt J. O'Brien, Support Platoon)
Cpl G. Parkes
Cpl E. Prunty
Cpl F. Clarke
Cpl A. Flynn
Cpl T. Lewis
Cpl J. Mooney

Pte J. Denton	Gnr E. Donnelly	Pte O. Dunne
Pte T. Fennel	Pte K. Geraghty	Tpr N. Gough
Tpr M. Handebeaux	Pte P. Hughes	Pte W. Lawless
Pte J. L'Estrange	Tpr T. Livingstone	Pte P. Merrigan
Pte T. McCann	Pte J. O'Leary	Pte T. O'Neill
Pte P. Rogan	Pte W. Smailes	Tpr S. Tully
Pte P. Walsh	Pte F. Ward	Pte J. Murphy (on temp. attachment)

APPENDIX B

Extract taken from the September/October 2005 issue of *Echo Ireland*, the journal of the Irish Radio Transmitters Society, with the kind permission of the editor. The information for this article was originally related by Fr Stone to Jimmy Upton.

'In 1960, civil war broke out in the Congo, following independence from Belgium. A UN peacekeeping force was dispatched there including a contingent of Irish troops. Irish HQ was in Albertville (now Kalemie) and two other stations were located in Kamina 800kms to the south-west and Goma, 500kms to the north. The army radio equipment could not operate above 10MHz. This restriction meant that, while contact could be made between Albertville and the others, contact with DFHQ in Dublin was almost impossible.

'Terry Tierney, working as an engineer on a hydro-electrical project in Ginga, Uganda, was in regular radio contact with Fr Jim Stone, a priest in Killester, Dublin. One day, Terry overheard an Irish voice calling any station, using the Curragh Army Radio Club callsign E15C. The radio operator was Captain Brendan Deegan, of the Army Signal Corps, operating from Goma. Surprised to hear that the army could not contact Ireland directly by radio, Terry relayed messages from home to the captain for a number of days. Terry then offered to build a 28MHz transmitter for Captain Deegan, also giving him the use of a BC348 receiver.

He quickly built the transmitter and arranged to meet Captain Deegan at Kinsoro and to pass both equipments to him. Kinsoro was 500kms away, a difficult and dangerous twelve-hour drive.

'The following day, Terry contacted Goma to be told that the equipment was already installed and working. He then arranged with Fr Stone to look for the new station at Goma. Two-way contact was established and in Goma improvements were carried out to the antenna. Word quickly spread that contact had been established with Dublin, a morale boost for the soldiers. Fr Stone told an army friend about this, and the Chief-of-Staff, Lt-Gen. Seán MacEoin, when he heard of it, he went to Killester and asked to speak to Goma.

'The COS had a long discussion with Lt-Col Buckley, OC 32nd Battalion, and while they were on air, word broke of the Niemba ambush on 8 November 1960. The Chief-of-Staff was able to get the names of those who had lost their lives in the ambush, thanks to this fortunate radio link. Regular contact between Dublin and Goma continued for some time until the army managed to have a direct telex link established.

'Amateur radio had played its part in filling a telecommunications gap when it was most needed, thanks to the resourcefulness and enthusiasm of Terry Tierney, Fr Jim Stone and Captain Brendan Deegan.'

The transmitter of Fr Jim Stone can be seen on permanent display in the Radio Museum at the Martello Tower in Howth. The museum has made an appeal for the recovery of the Goma transmitter and receiver, they would be very anxious to have them for the exhibition. The museum website is www.qsl.net/ei5em/museum.html

APPENDIX C

The following awards were made by direction of the Minister for Defence to members of the 46th Irish Battalion, UNIFIL, on 14 April 1983:

THE MILITARY MEDAL FOR GALLANTRY WITH DISTINCTION:

0.8639 Captain Adrian Ainsworth
'For displaying exceptional bravery and compassion of a high order when at At Tiri, South Lebanon on 7 April 1980, at grave danger to his own life from direct and sustained fire, he, without hesitation, crawled a distance of 200 metres to aid a grievously wounded comrade, and still under fire on the return journey, brought him to a place of safety.'

0.8956 Lieutenant Anthony Bracken
'For displaying outstanding initiative and exceptional bravery, under heavy fire on 8 April 1980, at the village of At Tiri, South Lebanon, when he voluntarily left his position, regardless of the safety of his own life, went to the aid of two injured comrades, and whilst still under heavy fire, assisted them over a distance of 200 metres to safety.'

830092 Corporal Michael Jones
'For displaying outstanding initiative and exceptional bravery,

under heavy fire on 8 April 1980, at the village of At Tiri, South Lebanon, when he voluntarily left his position, regardless of the safety of his own life, went to the aid of two injured comrades, and whilst still under heavy, sustained fire, assisted them over a distance of 200 metres to safety.'

844653 Private Michael John Daly

'For displaying exceptional bravery and compassion of a high order when at At Tiri, South Lebanon on 7 April 1980, at grave danger to his own life from direct and sustained hostile fire, he, without hesitation, crawled a distance of 200 metres to aid a grievously injured comrade, and still under fire on the return journey, brought him to place of safety.'

The Distinguished Service Medal with Distinction:

820217 Sergeant John Power

'For his devotion to duty, for displaying outstanding qualities of courage and leadership, while under threat, provocation, harassment and frequent daily fire, in an isolated position with meagre supplies of food and water, he commanded his post at OP RAS, South Lebanon, from 6 April to 18 April 1980 with exceptional efficiency, steadfastly refusing to surrender until relief was arranged.'

ADDITIONAL READING

IRELAND

Courtney, David, *Nine Lives* (Mercier Press, Cork 2008)

Doyle, Rose, with Leo Quinlan, *Heroes of Jadotville – The Soldiers' Story* (New Island, 2006)

Duggan, John P., *Neutral Ireland and the Third Reich* (The Lilliput Press, 1989)

Duggan, John P., *A History of the Irish Army* (Gill and Macmillan, 1991)

Fanning, Ronan, *Independent Ireland* (Helicon Limited, 1983)

Fisk, Robert, *In Time of War – Ireland, Ulster and the Price of Neutrality, 1939–45* (Gill and Macmillan, 1983)

Girvin, Brian, *The Emergency, Neutral Ireland 1939–1945* (Macmillan, 2006)

Harman Murtagh (ed.), 'The Emergency 1939–45', *The Irish Sword*, Vol. XIX, Nos 75 & 76

Keatinge, Patrick, *A Singular Stance – Irish Neutrality in the 1980s* (The Institute of Public Administration, 1984)

Kennedy, Dr Michael, *Guarding Neutral Ireland* (Four Courts Press, 2008)

Lee, J.J., *Ireland 1912–1985: Politics and Society* (Cambridge University Press, 1989)

McCaughran, Tom, *The Peacemakers of Niemba* (Browne and Nolan, 1966)

McGinty, Tom, *The Irish Navy* (The Kerryman Ltd, 1995)

McIvor, Aidan, *A History of the Irish Naval Service* (Irish Academic Press, 1994)

Military Archives, *The Nation is Profoundly Grateful – The Irish Defence Forces 1939–1946* (The Defence Forces Printing Press, 1996)

O'Brien, Conor Cruise, *To Katanga and Back* (Four Square, 1965)

O'Donoghue, David, *The Irish Army in the Congo, 1960–1964* (Irish Academic Press, 2005)

Ó Drisceoil, Donal, *Censorship in Ireland 1939–1945 – Neutrality, Politics and Society* (Cork University Press, 1996)

O'Halpin, Eunan, *Defending Ireland: The Irish State and its Enemies since 1922* (Oxford University Press, 1999)

O'Neill, John Terence and Nicolas Rees, *United Nations Peacekeeping in the Cold War Era* (Frank Cass, 2005)

O'Shea, Comdt Brendan (ed.), *In the Service of Peace. Memories of Lebanon* (Mercier Press, 2001)

Power, Declan, *Siege at Jadotville – The Irish Army's Forgotten Battle* (Maverick Press, 2005)

Raeside, Archie, *The Congo – 1960: The First Irish United Nations Peacekeepers* (Anderin Publishing Company, 2004)

Smith, Raymond, *The Fighting Irish in the Congo* (Lilmac, 1962)

Smith, Raymond, *Under the Blue Flag* (Aherlow Printers, 1980)

Whelan, Michael, *The Battle of Jadotville – Irish Soldiers in Combat in the Congo* (South Dublin Libraries)

Wills, Clair, *That Neutral Island. A Cultural History of Ireland during the Second World War* (Faber and Faber, 2007)

United Nations

Childers, Erskine (ed.), *Challenges to the United Nations – Building a Safer World* (Catholic Institute for International Relations, 1994)

Dallaire, Lt-Gen. Romeo, *Shake Hands With the Devil – The Failure of Humanity in Rwanda* (Arrow Books, 2004)

Goulding, Marrack, *Peacemonger* (John Murray, 2002)

Parsons, Anthony, *From Cold War to Hot Peace. UN Interventions 1947–1994* (Michael Joseph, 1995)

Siilasvuo, Enzio, *In the Service of Peace in the Middle East 1967–1979* (Hurst and Company, 1992)

United Nations, *Basic Facts about the United Nations* (New York, 1987)

United Nations, *The Blue Helmets – A Review of United Nations Peacekeeping* (New York, 1985)

United Nations, *The Blue Helmets – A Review of United Nations Peacekeeping* (New York, 1948–1990)

THE MIDDLE EAST

Barker, A.J., *The Yom Kippur War* (Ballantine Books, 1974)

Chami, Joseph G., *Lebanon – Days of Tragedy* (n.d., Shonshar, Beirut)

Fisk, Robert, *Pity the Nation* (Andre Deutsch, 1990)

Forrest, A.C., *The Unholy Land* (McClellend and Stewart, 1972)

Gilbert, Martin, *The Arab-Israeli Conflict – Its History in Maps* (Weidenfield and Nicholson, 1974)

Gilmour, David, *Lebanon – The Fractured Country* (Sphere Books, 1983)

Hensen, G.H., *Militant Islam* (Pan Books, 1979)

Kiernan, Thomas, *The Arabs: their history, aims and challenge to the industrialised world* (Abacus/Sphere, 1978)

Kippur – Special Edition December 1973 (University Publishing Projects, Tel Aviv)

Laffin, John, *The Dagger of Islam* (Sphere Books, 1979)

Schiff, Zeev, *October Earthquake. Yom Kippur 1973* (English edition, University Publishing Projects Ltd, 1974)

Sunday Times, *Middle East War* (Andre Deutsch, 1974)

Taheri, Amir, *Holy Terror – The Inside Story of Islamic Terrorism* (Hutchison, 1987)

AFRICA

Heitman, Helmoed-Romer, *War in Angola. The Final South African Phase* (Ashanti Publishing Limited, 1990)

Pakenham, Thomas, *The Scramble for Africa 1876–1912* (Weidenfeld & Nicolson, 1991)

Steenkamp, Willem, *South Africa's Border War, 1966–1989* (Ashanti Publishing Limited, 1989)

Hodder-Williams, Richard, *An Introduction to the Politics of Tropical Africa* (Unwin Hyman, 1984)

Ya-Otto, John, *Battlefront Namibia* (Lawrence Hill and Company, 1981)

OTHERS

Ambrose, Stephen E., *Citizen Soldiers – The US Army from the Normandy beaches to the Bulge to the Surrender of Germany June 7, 1944 to May 7, 1945* (Simon and Schuster, 1997)

Hanson, Victor Davis, *Why the West has Won. Nine Landmark Battles in the Brutal History of Western Victory* (Faber and Faber, London 2001)

Schwartzkopf, General H. Norman, *It Doesn't Take a Hero* (Bantam Press, 1992)

Taylor, Irene and Alan (eds), *The Secret Annexe. An Anthology of*

War Diaries (Canongate Books, 2004)

Zakaria, Fareed, *The Future of Freedom. Illiberal Democracy at Home and Abroad* (W.W. Norton, 2004)

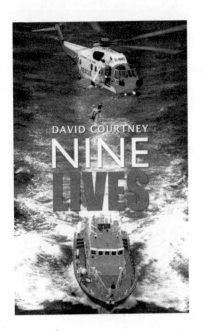

Nine Lives

David Courtney

978 1 85635 602 2

Nine Lives is an account of becoming a rescue pilot, from learning to fly to the thrills and terrors of dangerous and complicated night rescues. As the story unfolds David Courtney introduces the reader to the people who work with rescue crews, and how the entire system works.

Courtney recounts his experiences, good and bad, in a way that is open and honest about fear, danger, disappointment, elation and happiness. Contrasting the extraordinary with the everyday, Courtney delves into day-to-day family life, showing how it can empower each of us to confront the dramatic.

www.mercierpress.ie

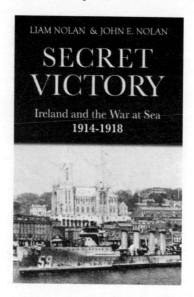

Also available from Mercier Press

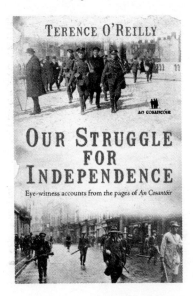

OUR STRUGGLE FOR INDEPENDENCE
Terence O'Reilly

978 1 85635 614 5

From the first shots of the War of Independence, through the many ambushes, raids and actions, to the disastrous raid on the Customs House, *Our Struggle for Independence* provides a fascinating selection of the views and analyses of the men who fought for Irish freedom.

Some of the men who fought in the War of Independence went on to form the core of the Irish Army. Using articles taken from *An Cosantóir*, the magazine of the Irish armed forces, this book provides a real insight into their experiences of combat. Some of the accounts remain controversial even now, while others offer fresh perspective on Irish tactics in the struggle for independence.

www.mercierpress.ie